DATA PROCESSING IN JAPAN

INFORMATION RESEARCH AND RESOURCE REPORTS

VOLUME I

Editors-in-Chief:

F. WINKELHAGE

and

N. SZYPERSKI

Gesellschaft für Mathematik
und Datenverarbeitung mbH Bonn

NORTH-HOLLAND PUBLISHING COMPANY – AMSTERDAM • NEW YORK • OXFORD

DATA PROCESSING IN JAPAN

GMD

H. J. WELKE

Gesellschaft für Mathematik
und Datenverarbeitung mbH Bonn

1982

NORTH-HOLLAND PUBLISHING COMPANY – AMSTERDAM • NEW YORK • OXFORD

ISBN: 0 444 86379 6

Published by:
NORTH-HOLLAND PUBLISHING COMPANY – AMSTERDAM • NEW YORK • OXFORD

in cooperation with:
Gesellschaft für Mathematik und Datenverarbeitung mbH Bonn
Postfach 1240
Schloss Birlinghoven
5205 St. Augustin 1

Sole distributors for the U.S.A. and Canada:
ELSEVIER SCIENCE PUBLISHING COMPANY, INC.
52 Vanderbilt Avenue
New York, N.Y. 10017

Library of Congress Cataloging in Publication Data
Main entry under title:

Data processing in Japan.

    (Information research and resource reports ;
v. 1)
    Bibliography: p.
    1. Electronic data processing--Japan. I. Welke,
H. J. (Herbert-Jürgen), 1940-   . II. Title.
III. Series.
QA76.D327   001.64'0952   82-2271
ISBN 0-444-86379-6   AACR2

PRINTED IN THE NETHERLANDS

日本における

情報処理

The Japanese title of this report, i.e. "NIHON NI OKERU JOHO SHORI", was written in the Japanese script by Prof. Yuko Sato.

PREFACE

In 1973 the Japanese and the German governments made an agreement to exchange data processing experts. In connection with this agreement the author of this report stayed in Japan from January 1979 until June 1980. His desk was in the Data Processing Administration Division of the Ministry of International Trade and Industry (MITI) which has, in the field of data processing, similar tasks as the Bundesministerium für Forschung und Technologie (BMFT, Federal Ministry for Research and Technology) in Germany. He also worked in the Japan Information Processing Development Centre (JIPDEC), which is a sister company of the Gesellschaft für Mathematik und Datenverarbeitung (GMD, research institution for mathematics and data processing).

This report describes the situation of information processing in Japan, which the author studied during his stay. The sources of information were mainly

- discussions with his Japanese hosts in MITI and JIPDEC

- visits to various Japanese institutions which are concerned with data processing. Reports have been written in manuscript form about most of these visits (see [REPORTS])

- various Japanese periodicals, written in English, which are concerned with dp, mainly periodicals of JIPDEC (JIPDEC-Report (JR) and Computer White Paper (CWP)); EDP Japan Report (EJR) of IDC Japan; JECC News; Japan Economic Journal and others

- discussions with foreigners, mainly Germans, who had earlier, like the author, been learning about the Japanese situation of data processing.

vii

All subjects have not been treated in the same depth, but they have been described as far as the author could research them. Some aspects have not even been mentioned, e.g. there is no chapter about the education of information processing, or about CAD or CAM.

The author expresses his thanks to all those who helped him to get an overview of the Japanese situation, in particular to Mr. Watanabe of MITI, and Mr. Yamadori of JIPDEC, as well as the members of their divisions who discussed with the author any problem about dp without restriction; to Mr. Ogino of IDC Japan, who gave the author a good introduction to the Japanese situation; to the representatives of the institutions visited, who warmly welcomed the author and gave him freely any information he required; to Dr. v. Krosigk, scientific attache of the German Embassy; to Dr. Wattenberg of the Tokyo branch of GID (Association of Information and Documentation); and to Mr. Reible of Siemens Tokyo office.

This report, printed with the help of a text processor, was typed by Mrs. Annette Calkin of the GMD, who checked and corrected the author's English and suggested improvements in style.

CONTENTS

1. INTRODUCTION

Japan was very successful in developing its information industry, so that Japanese companies are now capable of competing with the giant US computer manufacturers. Japan is the only country in the world where the market share of IBM is less than 50%.

The situation of the Japanese information industry can be characterised by the following aspects:

- a strong leadership by the government (GYOSEI SHIDO), mainly by the Ministry of International Trade and Industry (MITI) and the Ministry of Posts and Telecommunications (MPT)

- a good co-operation between government and industry in formulating the economic policy and in its application

- a strong and self-confident domestic computer industry

- strong foreign computer manufacturers which are highly competitive with the domestic companies

- strong and experienced users of data processing which have large data processing divisions and which take advantage of the competition between the numerous computer manufacturers

- a weak and under-capitalised computer service industry which is dependent on the assignments of the computer manufacturers and general companies

- a software market which is still "underdeveloped".

These enumerated aspects are discussed in the following chapters.

1

2. THE POLICY OF THE JAPANESE GOVERNMENT CONCERNING INFORMATION PROCESSING

2.1 Ministries and Agencies concerned with Information Processing

2.1.1 Organisation of the Japanese Government

Figure 1 is the organisation chart of the Japanese government. The ministries which are concerned with the information processing policy are mainly

* Ministry of International Trade and Industry (MITI)

* Ministry of Posts and Telecommunications (MPT)

* Prime Minister's Office

* Ministry of Finance (MoF)

Concerning the information processing policy MITI is the most important ministry. It issues the laws for the promotion of information processing and defines the promotion measures. Its Agency of Industrial Science and Technology (AIST) is responsible for the promotion of R & D in industrial science and technology.

MPT is concerned with the data communication policy and issues the data communication laws. Because data communication and data processing are related MPT also plays an important role concerning the information processing policy, and there is even in some way a competitive relationship between MPT and MITI. The Nippon Telegraph and Telephone Public Corporation (NTT), which is supervised by MPT, conducts a considerable amount of research in the field of data communication and data processing, and because of its great technical know-how and also because of its immense purchase of dc and dp equipment it has much influence on the computer industry.

The Ministry of Finance (MoF) must approve all subsidies, loans and other promotion measures in favour of information processing, as well as the information processing budgets of the government.

The Economic Planning Agency (EPA) of the Prime Minister's Office is responsible for the formulation of the basic economic policy, and the Science and Technology Agency (STA) of the Prime Minister's Office is responsible for planning and promoting the fundamental policy on science and technology. In the field of data processing they are not concerned with concrete measures, but in the field of information and documentation, however, STA is responsible for the Japan Information Centre for Science and Technology (JICST). The Administrative Management Agency co-ordinates and assists the data processing activities of the government. These three agencies are headed by a Minister of State.

3

```
                    ┌─────────────────────────────┐
                    │   GOVERNMENT OF JAPAN       │
                    └─────────────────────────────┘
```

[Legislative Branch]　　　　[Executive Branch]　　　　[Judicial Branch]

DIET	CABINET	COURTS
House of Representatives	Board of Audit	Supreme Court
House of Councillors	Prime Minister's Office	High Courts (8)
Judge Impeachment Court	Ministry of Justice	District Courts (50)
Judge Indictment Committee	Ministry of Foreign Affairs	Family Courts (50)
National Diet Library	Ministry of Finance	Summary Courts (575)
	Ministry of Education	Committees for the Inquest of Prosecution (207)
	Ministry of Health and Welfare	
	Ministry of Agriculture and Forestry	
	Ministry of International Trade and Industry	
	Ministry of Transport	
	Ministry of Posts and Telecommunications	
	Ministry of Labour	
	Ministry of Construction	
	Ministry of Home Affairs	

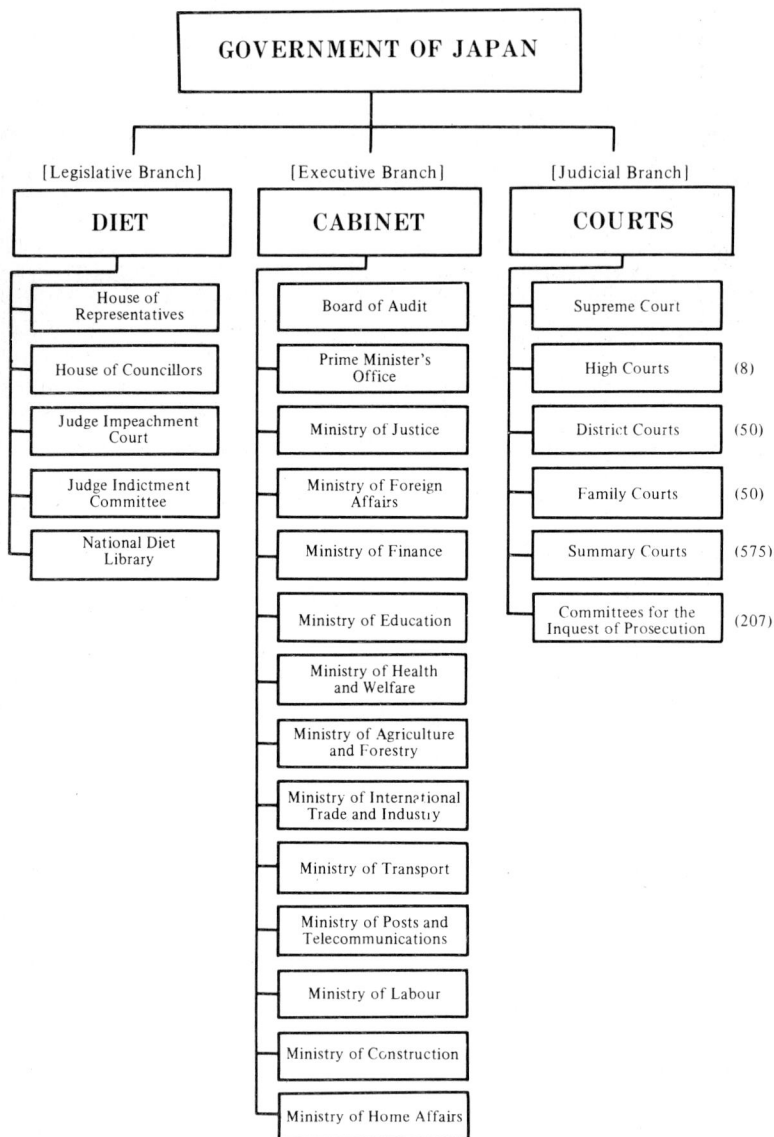

Figure 1 Government of Japan
       (from "Organisation of the Japanese Government", published by the
       Administrative Management Agency, 1978, see [AMA16])

2.1.2   Important Ministries and Agencies concerning Information Processing

2.1.2.1 Ministry of International Trade and Industry (MITI)

Figure 2 shows the organisation chart of the Ministry of International Trade and Industry (MITI, in Japanese: TSUSHO SANGYO SHO – ministry of trade and industry – abbreviated TSU SAN SHO). Concerning the information processing policy the Machinery and Information Industries Bureau is most important. Its Electronics Policy Division (DENSEIKA) is responsible for defining the information processing policy, its Electronics and Electrical Machinery Division (DENDENKA) is responsible for the promotion of hardware, and its Data-Processing Promotion Division (JOSHINKA) for the promotion of software. The parts of the Machinery and Information Industry Law (KIJOHO) concerning the information industry were worked out by these three divisions; and subsidies, loans and tax measures in favour of the information industry are being adjusted and controlled by them. But the law was issued by the General Affairs Division, because some parts of the law were adjusted by other divisions, e.g. the Industrial Machinery Division.

The Industrial Policy Bureau decides on the economic policy of MITI. In the beginning of 1980 they prepared the "Vision of MITI Policies in 1980s" (see [AIST2] and Appendix 1). The data concerning the information industry will be delivered by the three above-mentioned divisions.

When defining the economic policy the General Co-ordination Department of the Agency of Industrial Science and Technology (AIST) will prepare the first version. Then the paper will be revised and actualised by the Industrial Policy Bureau ·and authorised by the Industrial Structure Council (SANKOSHIN). Those parts concerning the information industry will be proposed by the three above-mentioned divisions and authorised by the Information Industry Sub-Committee (JOHO SANGYO BUKA) of the Industrial Structure Council. The council and its sub-committees are the minister's advisory boards organised within MITI. The Information Industry Sub-Committee is an ad hoc committee. Its members, who were selected in the beginning of 1980 for preparing the report on the problems of the information industry in the 1980s (see [AIST11] and Appendix 1), are professors, presidents of large computer manufacturers, and representatives of industrial organisations (see also [REPORTS], report of MITI's Electronics Policy Division).

2.1.2.2 Ministry of Posts and Telecommunications (MPT)

Figure 3 is the organisation chart of MPT. The Communications Policy Division, the General Management Planning Division, and the Office of the Director General of Telecommunications (recently upgraded to the Bureau of Telecommunication Policy) of the Minister's Secretariat are concerned with defining MPT's data communication policy. They issue the laws concerning dc, supervise NTT, grant the permission for use of data communication circuits, and co-operate with MITI in defining the policy relating both to data processing and data communication. Since there are some areas in which data processing and data communication are important, there arise problems whether this is the jurisdiction of MPT or MITI (see also [REPORTS], report about MPT).

MINISTRY OF INTERNATIONAL TRADE AND INDUSTRY
(Minister and Vice-Ministers)

MINISTER'S SECRETARIAT	Personnel Division / General Coordination Division / Budget & Accounts Division / Regional Bureau Administration Division / Public Relations Division / Data-Processing Administration Division / Welfare Administrator RESEARCH AND STATISTICS DEPARTMENT Administration Division / Commercial Statistics Division / Industrial Statistics Division / Statistics Analysis Division / Senior Officer for Statistics Planning / Statistics Administrators
INTERNATIONAL TRADE POLICY BUREAU	General Affairs Division / MITI Information Office / The Americas-Oceania Division / West Europe-Africa-Middle East Division / South Asia-East Europe Division / North Asia Division / International Trade Research Division INTERNATIONAL ECONOMIC AFFAIRS DEPARTMENT International Economic Affairs Division / Tariff Division ECONOMIC COOPERATION DEPARTMENT Economic Cooperation Division / Technical Cooperation Division
INTERNATIONAL TRADE ADMINISTRATION BUREAU	General Affairs Division / Export Division / Import Division / Agricultural & Marine Products Division / Foreign Exchange & Trade Finance Division / Export Insurance Division (Planning) / Export Insurance Division (Long-term) / Export Insurance Division (Short-term) / Export Inspection & Design Division
INDUSTRIAL POLICY BUREAU	General Affairs Division / Research Division / Industrial Structure Division / Industrial Finance Division / Business Behavior Division / International Business Affairs Division / Commerce Policy Division / Commercial Affairs Division / Consumer Protection Division / Price Policy Division / Okinawa Int l Ocean Exposition Administrator
INDUSTRIAL LOCATION & ENVIRONMENTAL PROTECTION BUREAU	General Affairs Division / Industrial Relocation Division / Industrial Location Guidance Division / Industrial Water Division / Environmental Protection Policy Division / Environmental Protection Guidance Division / Safety Division / Mine Safety Division / Coal Mine Safety Division
BASIC INDUSTRIES BUREAU	General Affairs Division / Iron & Steel Administration Division / Iron & Steel Production Division / Nonferrous Metals Division / Chemical Products Safety Division / Basic Chemical Products Division / Chemical Products Division / Chemical Fertilizer Division ALCOHOL BUSINESS DEPARTMENT Administration Division / Personnel Division / Business Division
MACHINERY & INFORMATION INDUSTRIES BUREAU	General Affairs Division / International Trade Division / Industrial Machinery Division / Cast & Wrought Products Division / Electronics Policy Division / Data-Processing Promotion Division / Electronics & Electrical Machinery Division / Automobile Division / Weights & Measures Division / Aircraft & Ordnance Division / Vehicle Division / Machinery Credit Insurance Division
CONSUMER GOODS INDUSTRIES BUREAU	General Affairs Division / International Trade Division / Fiber & Spinning Division / Textile Products Division / Paper & Pulp Industry Division / Household & Miscellaneous Goods Division / Recreation & Miscellaneous Goods Division / Ceramics & Construction Materials Division / Housing Industry Division / Textile Inspection Administrator

Figure 2   Organisation of the Ministry of International Trade and Industry (MITI), from MITI-Handbook, 1977/8, (see [MITIO])

Attached Organizations and External Bureaus

AGENCY OF NATURAL RESOURCES & ENERGY	Director-General's Secretariat / Petroleum Department / Coal Mining Department / Public Utilities Department
PATENT OFFICE	General Administration Department / First Examination Department / Second Examination Department / Third Examination Department / Fourth Examination Department / Fifth Examination Department / Department of Appeal
SMALL & MEDIUM ENTERPRISE AGENCY	Director-General's Secretariat / Planning Department / Guidance Department / Small Enterprise Department
AGENCY OF INDUSTRIAL SCIENCE & TECHNOLOGY	General Coordination Department / Standards Department / Laboratories & Research Institutes

Regional Bureaus of International Trade & Industry

Regional Mine Safety & Inspection Bureaus

Industrial Manufactures Inspection Institute

Textile Products Inspection Institutes

Training Institute of MITI

Weights & Measures Training Institute

Mine Inspector Training Institutes

Safety Technology Training Institutes

Industrial Property Library

Industrial Property Institute

Figure 2 (continued)

Secretarial Division
Documents Division
Examination Division
Communications Policy Division
General Management Planning Division
International Cooperation Division

Minister's Secretariat

Postal Bureau

Postal Savings Bureau

Office of Chief Inspector
Office of Director General of Telecommunications
Supplies Department
Building Department

Parliamentary Vice-Minister

Minister

Administrative Vice-Minister

Post Office Life Insurance Bureau

Radio Regulatory Bureau

Personnel Bureau

Accounts and Finance Bureau

Regional Postal Inspection Bureau (11)
Regional Postal Services Bureau (11)
Regional Radio Regulatory Bureau (10)
Okinawa Office of Posts and Telecommunications
Local Postal Savings Office (28)
Local Post Office Life Insurance Office (7)

Museum (1)
Hospital (16)
Clinic (72)
Personnel Training Institute (12)
Radio Research Laboratory (1)

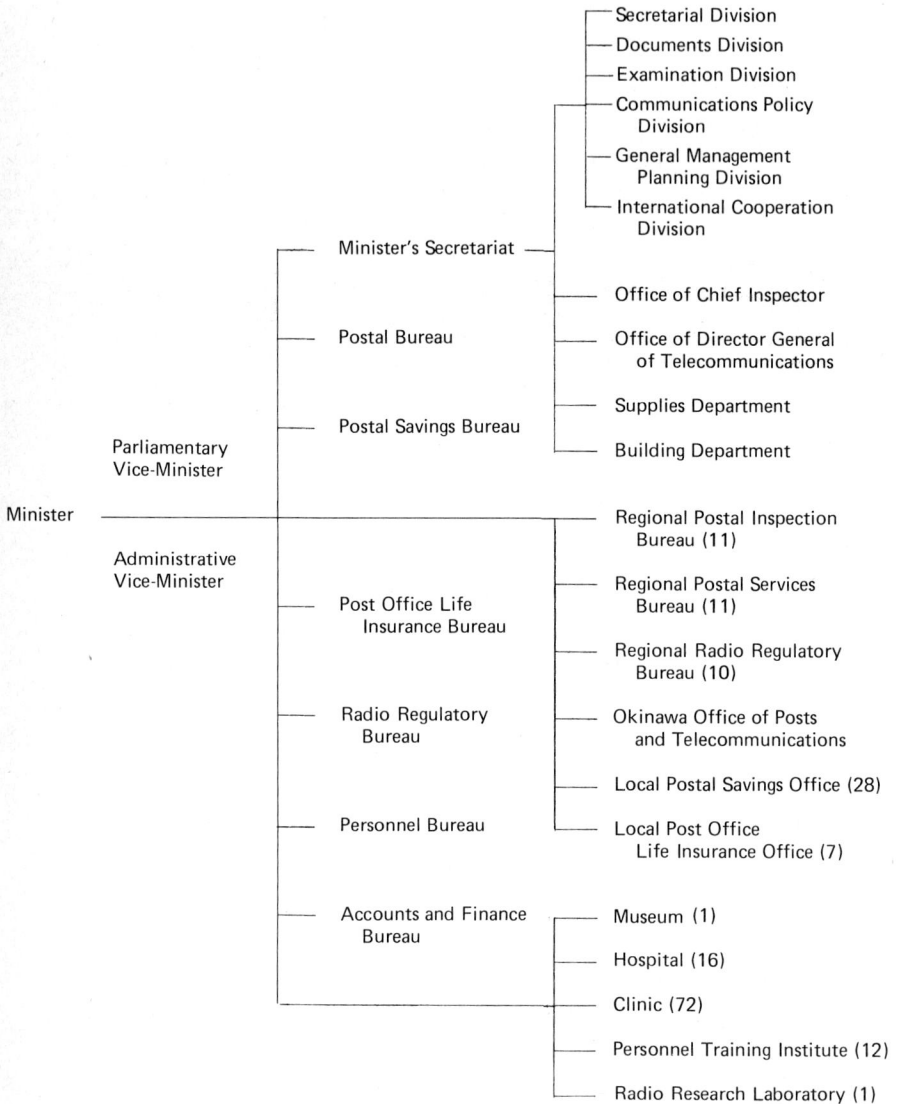

(As of March 31, 1979)

Note: The figures in parenthesis show the number of facilities

Figure 3   Organisation of the Ministry of Posts and Telecommunications (MPT)

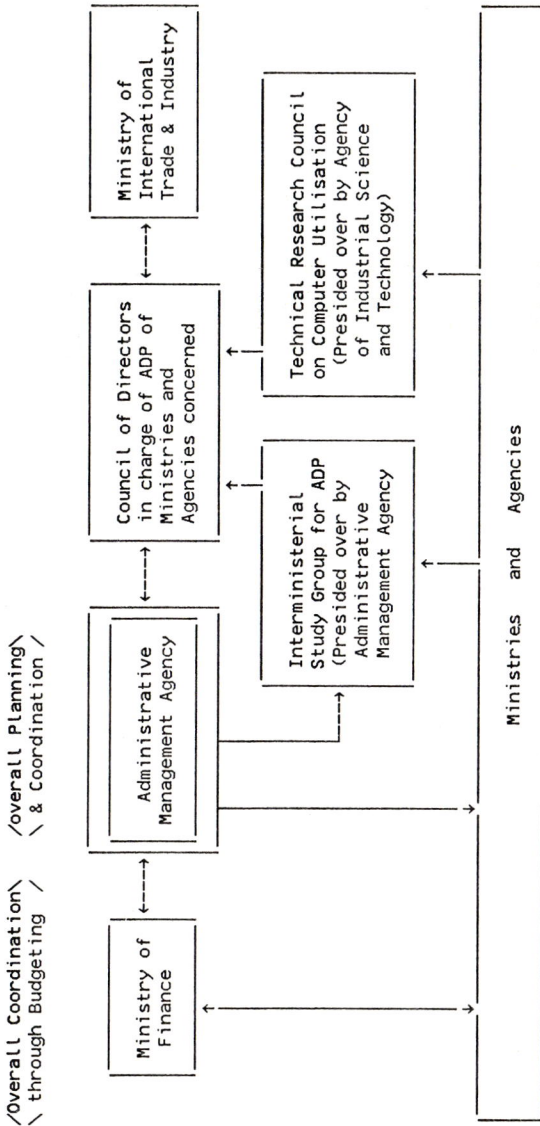

Figure 4 Promotion and organisation of information processing in the national government, from "The Status of Computer Utilisation in the Japanese Government", published by the Administrative Management Agency, February 1979

2.1.2.3   Co-ordinative Bodies within the Government

The Administrative Management Agency is an independant organisation of the Prime Minister's Office headed by the Director-General who is a Minister of State. In the field of data processing it is responsible for overall planning and co-ordination of computer utilisation within the government. Figure 4 shows the position of the agency in relation to other co-ordinating governmental bodies. The Technical Research Council on Computer Utilisation (RIYOKEN) was organised in 1968 under AIST in order to give advice and guidance to ministries and agencies. It is open to all technical experts from ministries and government agencies. Several Inter-Ministerial Study Groups of ADP, established since 1977 under the initiative of the Administrative Management Agency, carry out activities with respect to the improvement of efficient use of computers, data security and privacy protection.

Problems, which have been discussed and prepared by the Administrative Management Agency, the Technical Research Council or the Inter-Ministerial Study Groups, will be approved by the Council of Directors in Charge of ADP of Ministries and Agencies concerned (established in 1969), by the vice ministers or by the cabinet. Examples for such decisions concerning information processing within the government are: the "Request for Proposals" for the acquisition of computers, the decision for the "unbundling" of software, or the decision not to handicap foreign computer manufacturers when purchasing computers for the government (see also chapter 5.2.1).

The above mentioned bodies, especially the Technical Research Council on Computer Utilisation, are responsible for data processing projects within the central government. But the promotion of information processing in industry is the concern of MITI's Electronics Policy Division (see also [REPORTS], report about the Administrative Management Agency).

2.1.2.4 Other Ministries

The other ministries do not play an important role in defining the information processing policy. They are merely carrying out data processing in their own field of business. Some of them have big computers and large networks.

2.1.3   Public and partly Public Organisations promoting Information Processing

2.1.3.1 Information-technology Promotion Agency (IPA)

IPA was founded in 1970 .according to the Law concerning the Information-technology Promotion Agency in order to promote and aid program development and utilisation, as well as the information processing service industry itself. The Agency is a special juridical body under the jurisdiction of the Ministry of International Trade and Industry (MITI). The basic fund of 2.08 billion Yen was paid by the government and 286 commercial companies:

—	Government (MITI)	1,050 Mill. Yen
—	six main hardware manufacturers — 75 Mill. Yen each (Fujitsu, Hitachi, NEC, Toshiba, Mitsubishi, Oki)	450 Mill. Yen
—	the three long-term credit banks — 80 Mill. Yen each (Industrial Bank of Japan, Long Term Credit Bank of Japan, Nippon Credit Bank)	240 Mill. Yen
—	Software Industry Association (SIA)	25 Mill. Yen
—	Japan Information Processing Centre Association (JIPCA)	23 Mill. Yen
—	companies from all branches of industry	292 Mill. Yen

The main activities of IPA are (see also Chapter 2.2.1.2):

1) development on commission and buying up of advanced, general use programs

2) sales and leasing of programs

3) guaranteeing of loans borrowed by information processing companies, software houses or general enterprises

4) conducting of surveys in the field of information processing, especially preparing the "Program Registration Book"

5) recently, the issuing of certificates for programs in order to achieve a tax reduction in connection with the "General Purpose Software Package Registration System".

(a) development on commission of software

IPA receives subsidies from MITI and distributes them to software houses and information processing centres for the development of software systems. At present one part of the subsidies (in FY (fiscal year) 1979: 1.522 bill. Yen) is assigned to the Joint System Development Corporation (JSD) for the Project of Software Production Technology Development (JSD-Project) and is distributed to the participating software houses by JSD. Details about this project and the task of JSD, see Chapter 2.1.3.2 .

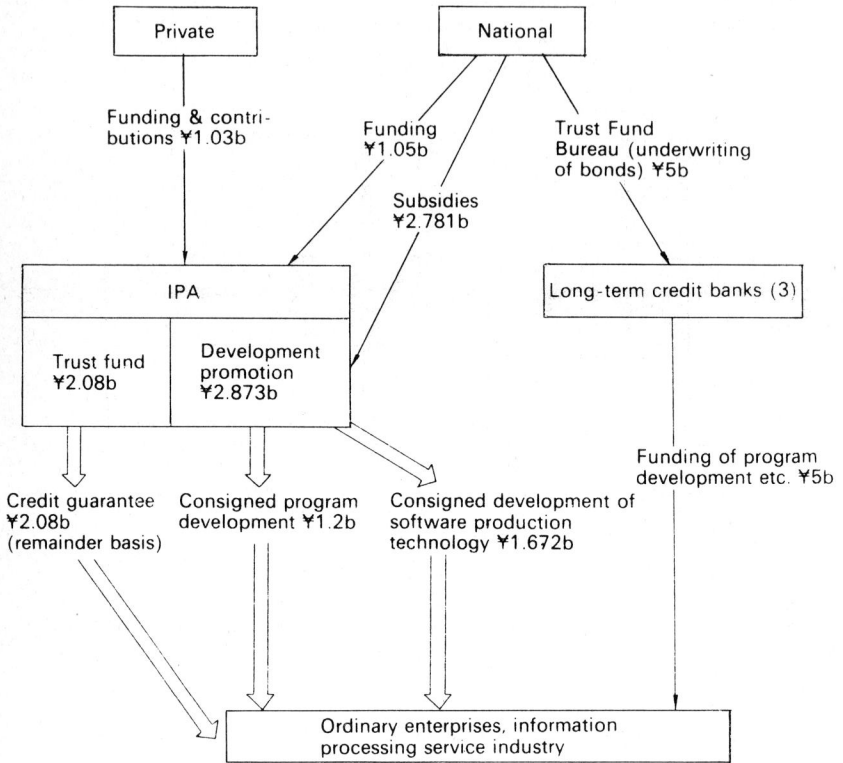

Figure 5   IPA operational organisation (FY 1980) (from CWP 1980, page 36)

The other part of the subsidies is distributed by IPA directly to the developing software houses and information processing centres (in FY 1979: 1.058 bill. Yen).

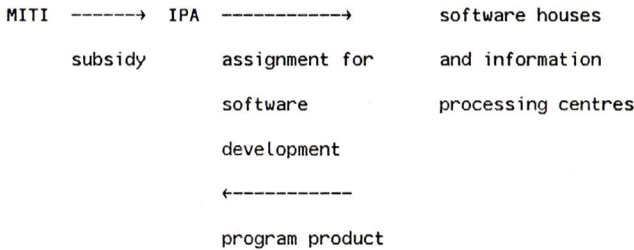


```
MITI  ------→  IPA  ------------→        software houses

      subsidy        assignment for     and information

                     software           processing centres

                     development

                     ←-----------

                     program product
```

Subjects to be promoted are selected by MITI and MPT in co-operation with other ministries and defined in the "Plan for Improvement in Electronic Computer Usage". This plan is to be reviewed every 5 years. The second plan was valid from 1976-1980 and covers about 20 areas, and out of each area about one project would be subsidised. According to this plan all projects are concerned with generalisation and standardisation. In 1979, 21 programs were subsidised (see [IPA3]).

The applicants are mostly software houses and dp service centres. DP sections of computer users would very seldom be selected, because the budget for program development is limited, and IPA cannot afford all proposals but concentrates on the proposals from software firms.

Software development is subsidised 100% and the program product is a property of IPA. The marketing expenditures are financed by sales services and the remaining profit is shared by IPA and the software house which developed it. In March 1978 IPA had about 250 contracts for 76 out of 83 developed programs. The number of users varies widely, a FORTRAN H Compiler for the office computer NEAC System 100 being the most popular. The total income from leased systems is small, e.g. in FY 1979 only a little more than 10% of the income was revenue from leased software systems. Since 1976, however, repayment conditions have been tightened up, and the target of the pay-back percentage was raised to 70% of the development expenditures.

Furthermore IPA may use the subsidies in order to buy software systems on the market, but has not done so as yet.

(b) loans for the promotion of information processing

In order to enhance the level of information processing in Japan, IPA guarantees loans for software houses, information processing companies and general companies (see Chapter 2.2.2.8 part 5.6). According to Article 28, Sentence 5 of the IPA-Law, loans to general companies are limited to the expenditures for program development, whereas according to Article 28, Sentence 4, software houses and information processing companies may get loans for their total in-house business.

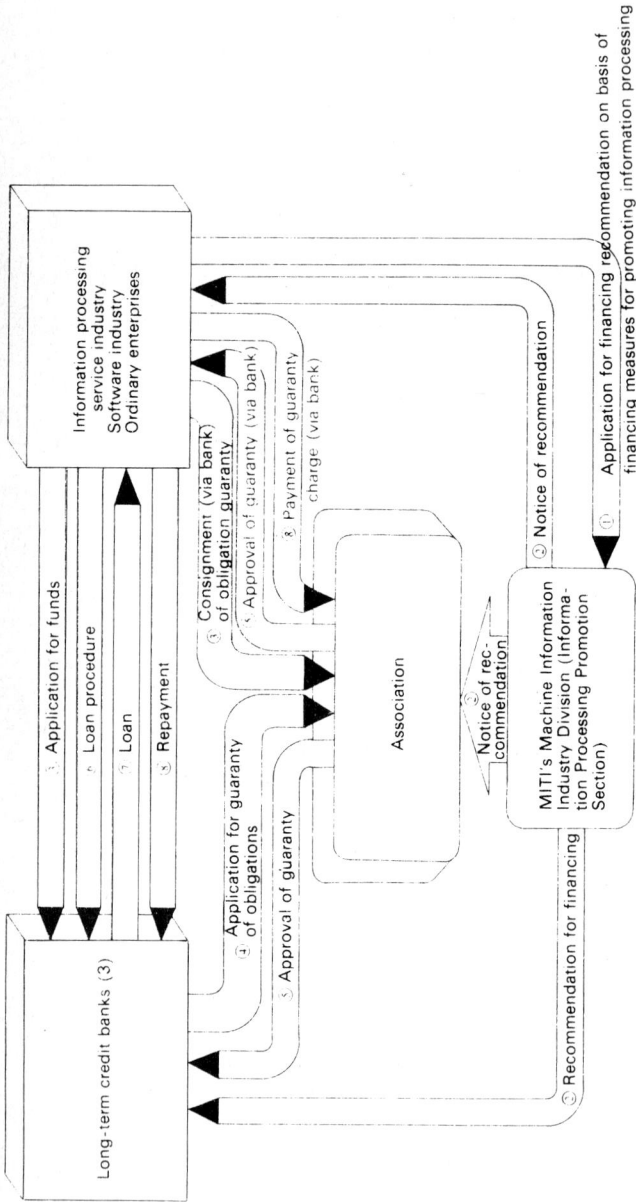

Obligation guaranty: conditions
Period of guarantee.   In principle, not more than 3 years   Financing limit: 80 % of required funds
Guaranty charges: 0.7 % per year of balance of amount of guaranty   Annual interest: 8.5 %
Guaranty amount: 95 % of amount of financing   As of March 1, 1980

Period for accepting applications for recommendation: In April, July, October & January of each
fiscal year

Figure 6   IPA credit guarantees (from CWP 1980, page 45)

As the information supply industry is not included in Sentence 4, data base
service companies can receive loans only in the same way as general companies;
but so far IPA has never received an application from a data base service company. At present there is a discussion about the inclusion of the information
supply service industry into the measures according to Article 28, Sentence 4.

If data processing service companies, software houses or general enterprises
want to borrow money from the three long-term credit banks, they must apply to
MITI and one of the long-term credit banks, who then together with IPA will consider whether the applicant is creditworthy. The final decision rests with MITI.
IPA guarantees 95% of the loan, the residual 5% is the risk of the bank concerned. The period of the loan is, in principle, up to 3 years, the interest
rate in Summer 1979 was 7.7% plus 0.7% guarantee fee, in March 1980 the interest
rate was 8.5% (see also CWP 1980, page 45).

From FY 1970 until FY 1979 (10 financial years) the following loans have been
granted:

beneficiary	number of loans	average amount in mill. Yen
software houses and data processing comp.	859	38
general users	68	72
manufacturers	41	147

(c) program registration book

According to Article 5 of the IPA-Law, MITI is to prepare a program registration
book (similar to the ICP Directory of the USA), in which details about programs
being offered on the market by Japanese companies are described including the
conditions of sale and leasing. IPA began the investigations for this book in
1977 and every year sends inquiries to approximately 1800 computer users, software houses and data processing companies. By the end of 1979 the registration
book contained over 2000 programs. Every two years an up-to-date version will be
published.

(d) General Purpose Software Package Registration System

This is a new activity which has not been mentioned in the IPA-Law. In 1979 special tax measures for the promotion of general purpose software were issued in
connection with the Information Industry Law (KIJOHO) (compare [MITI14], page
9). According to these measures 50% of the sales revenues of general use software which has been developed in Japan can be reserved in a tax free fund for 4
years (see also Chapter 2.2.2.7 (1)).

Those who desire this tax reduction benefit, must apply for a certificate from
IPA confirming that the applied program is for general use and was developed in
Japan. This certificate must be submitted to the tax office. Application forms
from the domestic main-frame makers would be submitted to IPA through JECC, and
from others (i.e. software houses, data processing companies, general users of
data processing, and Japanese juridical persons partly capitalised by foreign

main-frame manufacturers, e.g. Nippon IBM, Nippon Univac, NCR) through the Software Product Centre (SPC) of SIA (compare Chapter 4.2.2).

In the period of FY 1979 a total number of 562 programs were registered (410 system programs and 152 application programs), and 85 separately certified subprograms, totalling in all 647 certificates:

<u>System Programs</u>

* 51 control programs

* 58 communication control programs

* 189 language processors

* 112 program development aids and operation management programs

<u>Application programs</u>

* 10 public system programs

*   7 special application programs

* 66 business management programs

* 10 circulation service programs

* 15 production control programs

* 44 scientific application programs.

The system programs were normally developed by the main-frame makers. The registration of so many system programs means that the manufacturers are paying attention to the unbundling of software. Unfortunately the number of application programs is low at this stage. IPA is endeavouring to promote in particular the circulation of application systems through this registration system.

2.1.3.2 Joint System Development Corporation (JSD)

The Joint System Development Corporation (JSD) was founded in 1976 under the guidance of MITI by 17 leading software firms representing about 123 software firms categorised into 17 groups according to their specialised fields. It is remarkable that among the 17 selected software companies there are 5 daughter companies of hardware manufacturers and 4 daughter companies of larger users. If a software firm wishes to become a member of JSD, it needs the agreement of JSD and the representative software company of the group to which it wants to belong. The condition of membership is to have some experience on software development.

JSD was established with the aim of strengthening the power of the software firms enabling them to compete with the makers in the software market. The means by which JSD achieves this are:

- to solicit contracts for the development of large scale software projects and to organise, manage and promote them;

- to co-ordinate the selling activities of the members.

There are two types among the large-scale projects: one is a project whereby JSD is only soliciting, promoting and organising the project; the other is a project in which a large part of the research activity is done by JSD itself, by personnel who are on loan from the member software houses and who return to their companies after the project is finished. At present these number about 25 persons, but the administrative personnel are JSD employees.

Hitherto JSD carried out three large-scale projects:

- the Project of Software Production Technology Development (IPA-Project)

- the Software Engineering Project

- the Health and Welfare Engineering Project.

The IPA-project is financed out of MITI's budget, the money being distributed by IPA, e.g. in 1978 this was 1.1 billion Yen, (compare Chapters 2.1.3.2 (a) and 2.2.2.2). The Software Engineering Project and the Health and Welfare Project are financed by a small amount of the surplus of the Professional Bicycle Racing Association which is distributed by SIA (1.2 mill. Dollars in 1978) and by the Japan Society for the Promotion of Machine Industry (JSMI) (20 mill. Yen in 1978). The last two projects have a 4-year plan for surveying, modelling, programming and evaluation, the money, however, being granted only for periods of one year.

Whithin these projects the member software houses have the possibility for research and development which one software house alone cannot undertake because of lack of money. Normally software houses have no R & D division.

2.1.3.3 Japan Information Processing Development Centre (JIPDEC)

The Japan Information Processing Development Centre (JIPDEC) was established in 1967 with the support of MITI, MPT, computer manufacturers and a large number of users of information processing systems. It is a foundation (ZAIDAN HOJIN) with the aim of promoting the welfare of the people as well as the profit of industry.

JIPDEC is being financed by:

- the interest from the basic fund (invested at the start);

- fees from the current 215 members;

- subsidies out of the data processing promotion fund of the Professional Bicycle Racing Association (KEIRINREN); and

- project contracts from industry, government and public organisations.

In 1980 the annual budget was 2,287 million Yen.

JIPDEC produces a project plan every year and submits it to MITI who, in turn, checks whether the activities of JIPDEC are in accord with the aims of JIPDEC defined at its outset, and directs KEIRINREN to provide JIPDEC with the funds.

The main activities of JIPDEC are:

- Surveys, studies and publications

   JIPDEC carries out studies and surveys in various interesting fields of information processing, e.g. micro-computers, office automation, Kanji processing. Besides these surveys on special subjects it observes the trends in information processing in Japan and around the world and makes this information available in its publications, . among others in the English periodicals: 1. JIPDEC-Report (JR, published quarterly) and 2. Computer White Paper (CWP, published annually). This broad knowledge about the trends in information processing enables JIPDEC to participate in numerous bodies and committees on information processing.

- research and development

   In 1980 the main scientific projects were

   * Resource Sharing System (RSS, successor of the JIPDEC network system (JIPNET))

   * Distributed Data-base System (DDB)

   * 5th generation computer

   MITI, MPT and the Administrative Management Agency are the main customers of the R & D projects. Besides the above-mentioned projects JIPDEC carries out numerous small software projects, mostly for ministries and agencies, sometimes in connection with the supply of consultation and data processing services by its computer centre.

- education and training

   The Institute of Information Technology, an annex organisation of JIPDEC, conducts courses for educating and training information processing technicians.

2.1.3.4 Research Institute of Telecommunications and Economics (RITE)

The Research Institute of Telecommunications and Economics (RITE) is a non-profit making, independent organisation established under the sponsorship of MPT, NTT, KDD, the Japan Broadcasting Corporation (NHK), communication equipment manufacturers, other telecommunication-related organisations and industries, and the main banks. The subjects of research are communications and telecommunications as well as their roles in human society. In 1981 the research and study projects covered the following areas:

   - basic researches into information, communication and telecomunication;

   - applied researches into laws and regulations, tariffs, accounting, financing, services, marketing, and other relevant matters;

- researches into the trends of telecommunication industries abroad.

Most of the research projects are entrusted to RITE by its members. In 1981 approx. 20 projects were carried out under the sponsership of MPT, NTT, KDD, NHK, the Communication Equipment Manufacturing Association, the Communications Wire and Cable Manufacturing Association, and others (see [RITE1]). On the basis of these research activities RITE contributes to the forecasting of the trends of telecommunication and information technologies, and their roles in a future society.

RITE's budget is financed out of the revenue from its research and study projects and from members fees. In 1981 the budget was about 520 million Yen.

2.2   Policy of MITI

2.2.1   Laws concerning Information Processing

2.2.1.1 The Information Processing Promotion Laws

The following laws were the legal base for the promotion measures in favour of the information industry and information processing:

    1956   Law concerning Temporary Measures for the Promotion of the Machinery Industry (Machinery Promotion Law, KISHINHO)

    1957   Law concerning Temporary Measures for the Promotion of the Electronic Industry (Electronics Promotion Law, DENSHINHO)

    1971   Law concerning Temporary Measures for the Promotion of Specified Electronic Industries and Specified Machinery Industries (Electronics and Machinery Promotion Law, KIDENHO)

    1978   Law concerning Temporary Measures for the Promotion of Specified Machinery and Information Industries (Machinery and Information Industry Law, KIJOHO).

Until 1970 the government promotion of the electronics industry and the machinery industry were carried out under separate laws, but in 1971 the two laws were consolidated under a single law in order to combine the promotion policies for these two industries. The 1971 law emphasised the promotion of hardware development, whereas the 1978 law places stress on the development of software, and it deals with the machinery, electronics and software industries as a whole.

In the 1978 law the conditions for the promotion of hardware are more strict than for software. Electronic apparatus manufacturing companies can be promoted

-       if their production techniques are not yet fully established in Japan and the acceleration of R & D is of a particular necessity,

-     if their production techniques are non-existing or extremely low in terms
      of volume and their increase or commencement are of a particular
      necessity,

-     if the acceleration of the improvement of performance and/or quality, or
      the reduction of production costs or rationalisation is of particular
      necessity,

and if the promotion measures are designated by a government order (see Article
3, Sentence 1). There are similar conditions for the manufacturing of machinery.
Regarding software, the only condition is that it must be general purpose software, (see e.g. EJR Vol. 5 Nos. 12 & 13; and JR No.34, page 16-19).

But the new Machinery and Information Industry Law did not cause an abrupt
change because of the long-sightedness of MITI's promotion measures (compare
[AIST11] and Appendix 1). Although the new law emphasises the software industry,
the largest amount of financial aid is still being granted to the computer industry (compare Chapter 2.2.2.8).

Another feature which distinguishes the new promotion law from the former law is
that, instead of providing special tax concessions for the computer
manufacturers, it provides such measures for the computer users (Article 14).

2.2.1.2 Law concerning IPA

In 1970 the Law concerning the Information-technology Promotion Agency (IPA-Law)
was issued in order to promote program development and usage. The law includes
the measures of IPA in order to promote information processing.

-   According to Article 28, Sentences 1, 2 and 3, IPA distributes subsidies,
    which have been granted by MITI, to software houses for the development of
    software systems.

-   According to Article 28, Sentence 4, IPA guarantees loans for data processing
    companies and software houses for their total in-house business.

-   According to Article 28, Sentence 5, IPA guarantees loans for general com-
    panies for the development of programs.

-   According to Article 5, IPA prepares a program registration book with details
    about programs being offered by Japanese companies.

-   The Plan for Improvement in Electronic Computer Usage, which defines the sub-
    jects to be promoted, is based on Article 3.

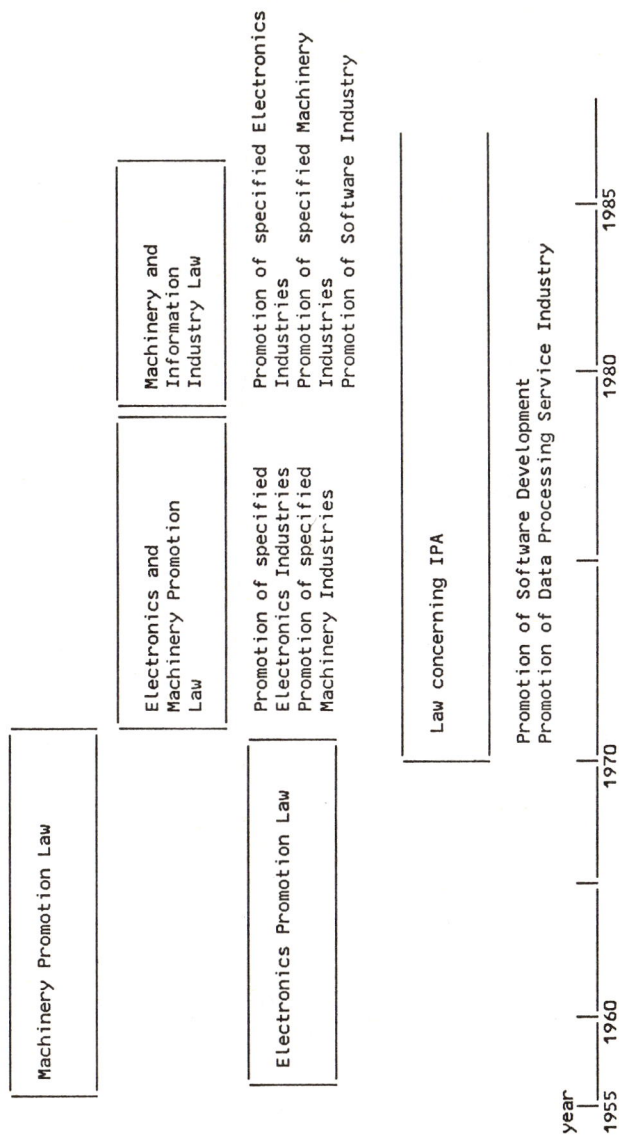

Figure 7: Outline of the legal system for promoting the information industry
(from CWP 1980, Japanese edition, page 68)

2.2.2   Promotion Measures of MITI

The annual data processing budget of MITI contains the promotion measures for
the information industry and for information processing. The beneficiaries are
mainly

- the information industry

    * computer industry (manufacturers)

    * information processing industry

        ₀ data processing service industry (computer centres etc.)

        ₀ software industry

        ₀ information supply industry (data base services etc.)

- users of data processing

- other institutions concerned with projects, studies or surveys which are
  promoted by the government.

The promotion measures are

- direct subsidies (11.2 billion Yen in 1979)

- loans from the Japan Development Bank (JDB) and the three long term credit
  banks (60 billion Yen in 1979)

- tax reduction (6 items in 1979)

- expenditures for special purposes, e.g. national projects, basic expansions
  on data processing (3.5 billion Yen in 1979).

These figures do not include MITI's expenditures for its own data processing and
the data processing of the research institutes which are being supervised by
MITI, neither the subsidies out of the Machine Industry Promotion Funds of the
Professional Bicycle Racing Association (KEIRINREN) and others.

2.2.2.1 Subsidies for the Computer Industry

There were three major programs in favour of the computer industry. The computer
industry formed associations in order to accept the subsidies:

- 1972 → 76 Technology Research Association of Advanced Computer Series, sub-
          sidies totalling 62.1 billion Yen

- 1976 → 79 VLSI Technology Research Association, subsidies totalling 30.54
          billion Yen

- 1979 → 83 Basic Computer Technology Research Association, subsidies
          totalling 23.5 billion Yen

The sequence of programs shows that the programs are based on each other, and that there are long term plans for the development of computer technology. The first program promoted the development of Japanese computers which should be equal to the comparable models of IBM and other American computer manufacturers. Indeed by this aid the foundation was laid for the present computer models which are successful against their American competitors. In the second program the development of VLSI was promoted because the technology of integrated circuits was expected to become very important for computer technology. Through this promotion program the basis was laid for Japan's leading role in VLSI technology. The present plan promotes the development of basic software and peripheral equipment, but no longer main-frame equipment, because software has become the most critical part of the computer. It is interesting that, although the promotion subject is software, the beneficiaries are only hardware manufacturers.

Subsidies were part of MITI's economic policy. Through these measures MITI enforced its information industry policy because subsidies were only granted under certain conditions:

- Financial share of the companies.
  MITI granted only 50% of the research and development costs. Including the administration costs the percentage of promotion was less than 50%.

- The duration of the subsidies was strictly determined, there was no opportunity for the industry to receive subsidies after the predetermined period.

- The results of the research, especially the patents, became the property of the Japanese government.

- The promoted companies were forced to co-operate with each other in joint research laboratories.

The last of these conditions was the most important. In the first research association 1972-76 the six major Japanese computer manufacturers were re-organised into three groups,

- Fujitsu Ltd.; Hitachi Ltd.

- Nippon Electric Company (NEC); Tokyo Shibaura Electric Co. Ltd. (Toshiba)

- Mitsubishi Electric Corp.; Oki Electric Industry Co.

Within the Technology Research Association of Advanced Computer Series (see also Chapter 3.2.1) the three groups developed new computer series capable of competing with the IBM/370 System (the so-called 3.5 generation machines). During the 5 years from 1972 until 1976 the development of new computer types was subsidised by 57.5 billion Yen, and the development of peripheral equipment by 4.6 billion Yen (see e.g. CWP 1976, page 30, or JR No.34, page 14). The result of the efforts were the three computer series announced in 1974:

* Fujitsu – Hitachi : M-series

* NEC – Toshiba :   ACOS-series

* Mitsubishi – Oki : COSMO-series.

Under the Financial Assistance Program for the Promotion of VLSI for a Next Generation Computer (see also Chapter 3.2.2) the computer industry was consolidated into two groups:

- Fujitsu, Hitachi and Mitsubishi

- NEC and Toshiba.

In co-operation with the Electro-Technical Laboratory (ETL) of MITI and the Electrical Communications Laboratory (ECL) of NTT, the VLSI Technology Research Association developed ultra large scale integrated circuits to be used in new computer series capable of competing with IBM's future systems (FS) (see JR No.34, page 14, and EJR Vol 3, No.2 & 3, page 7). The promotion program enabled Japan to reach the level of American LSI technology and to get even more advanced in some fields. E.g. NTT and NEC were the first companies in the world to develop 256 k RAM chips (in different technologies).

The Computer Basic Technology Research Association (see also Chapter 3.2.3) will exist from 1979 until 1983. Within the association 10 companies have been organised, in two groups, in order to elevate the level of Japanese software technology as follows:

- one group for the development of new operating systems; members are Fujitsu, Hitachi, Mitsubishi Electric, NEC, Toshiba, NEC-Toshiba-Information Systems (NTIS) and the Computer Development Laboratory (CDL).

- a second group for the development of new peripheral equipment; members are Fujitsu, Hitachi, Mitsubishi Electric, NEC, Toshiba, Oki, Matsushita-Tsushin-Kogyo and Sharp.

The total R & D budget for these four years is 40 billion Yen for operating systems (subsidised 50% by MITI) and 7 billion Yen for peripheral equipment (subsidised 50% by MITI). The administration expenses are 9.4 billion Yen (not subsidised by MITI).

2.2.2.2 Subsidies for Software Development

Subsidies for software development are being distributed by IPA. About one half is assigned to JSD for the Project of Software Production Technology Development (1.5 bill. Yen in 1979, see Chapter 2.1.3.3), and the other half is assigned to software houses for program development according to the current Plan for Improvement in Electronic Computer Usage (1.1 bill. Yen in 1979, see Chapter 2.1.3.2 (a) and also e.g. JR No.34, pages 6 and 7).

2.2.2.3 National Research and Development Projects and Other Large Projects

MITI promotes national projects which have the aim of enhancing the national welfare. Some of these are projects of the National Research and Development Program (popularly known as the Large-scale Project System, see [AIST1] page 7). The projects are supervised and managed by a public institution, and Japanese companies carry out the research and receive the subsidies. The administrative expenses are financed by other sources.

1. Pattern Information Processing System

The Pattern Information Processing System (PIPS), a national R & D project, is being supervised by AIST (see [AIST4]; JR No.32, page 2; EJR Vol.4, No.22). The basic and in-house studies are conducted by the Electro-Technical Laboratory (ETL) of AIST, and the development work by private companies as contractors. From 1971 until 1980 subsidies amounting to about 22 billion Yen were allocated. ETL received about 35% of this amount and the contractors about 65%.

The R & D activities are divided into four areas:

- devices and materials

- information processing systems

- pattern recognition systems

- integrated system prototype.

In the area of pattern recognition systems, Toshiba and Fujitsu are concerned with character recognition, Toshiba and Mitsubishi with picture recognition, Hitachi with 3-D object recognition, and NEC with speech recognition. Further contractors are Sanyo, Konishiroku, Matsushita, Hoya Glass and Tohoku Metal.

2. Comprehensive Automobile Control Technology Project

The Comprehensive Automobile Control Technology Project, one of the national R & D projects, is also being supervised by AIST , the subsidies totalling 7.7 billion Yen during the period 1973-1979. The aim of the project is to develop a route guidance system in which the vehicle can be informed about the quickest available route, traffic conditions, etc. The system includes two-way communication between vehicles and intersections, roadside units capable of information processing and software for the prediction and control of complicated traffic streams (see [AIST1] page 10, and [NEC10]). Contractors are Toyota Motor Co., Nippon Denso Co., Sumitomo Electric Industries, NEC, Hitachi, and others.

3. Optical Measurement and Control System

The Optical Measurement and Control System, another national R & D project, is being supervised by AIST, and 20 billion Yen will be spent between 1976-86 (see [AIST1] page 14). The system will apply light transmission paths and light sensors instead of electrical signals, and will be more precise and reliable than current systems. Furthermore picture processing will be easier by using the new optical technology.

The project consists of a control sub-system, a measurement sub-system concerning data for supervisory control, and a communication sub-system for the information flow between the terminals and the control equipment.

4. Health Care Network System

The Health Care Network System (1978-1983) is being supervised by the Medical Information System Development Centre (MEDIS-DC) which has been founded by MITI and the Ministry of Health and Welfare (MHW). MITI and MHW each pay 50% of the project costs, and some part of the administration costs is being financed out

of the Machine Industry Promotion Funds of the Professional Bicycle Racing Association and the Professional Auto Racing Association. MEDIS-DC consists of about
30 persons, but it has about 300 outside researchers and experts who work part-
time for the project. If a new sub-project is to be started, a committee will be
formed out of the external research staff. This committee will do the research
itself or give contracts to research companies, think tanks, big software companies or hardware manufacturers. After the concept has been finished the system
will be realised by hardware manufacturers only, because they have the knowledge
of hard- and software. If the hardware manufacturers sell the products they must
pay back some part of the revenue to MEDIS-DC. The Medical Information System
consists of the following 7 main sub-systems (see [MEDIS1]):

- Regional Medical Information System

- Shared Hospital Information System

- Instruments and Systems of Medical Information

- Health Care Network System

- Medical Information Service System

- Medical Computer Assisted Instruction System

- Public Relations, Public Education and Survey.

5. Hi-Ovis

The Highly Interactive Optical Visual Information System (Hi-Ovis) has been under development since 1972. The project developed a two-way communication system
between a centre and houses in its area. The purpose is both to accelerate computerisation in individual life and to promote the formation of a regional community. Fiscal Year 1979 was the last year of system development. Technical and
sociological evaluations were continued after the experimental broadcasts began,
in July 1978 in the Higashi-Ikoma New Town in Nara Prefecture. (See e.g. JR
No.34, pages 8 and 9; or JR No.35, pages 3 ff.)

6. Energy-Saving Urban Machinery System

The Energy-Saving Urban Machinery System is composed of a regional energy
centre, a central computer system, and home terminal devices. It will help to
save energy in cities and solve various types of urban problems. During 1978/79
a feasability study and a fundamental design were performed (see e.g. JR No.38,
page 19).

7. International Trade Information System

The International Trade Information System, co-ordinated by JIPDEC, has been
carried out since 1975. Many other ministries and agencies are participating,
among which are MITI, MoF and MPT. The project aims to computerise international
trade transactions and to standardise the used codes and forms (see e.g. JR
No.34, page 9).

2.2.2.4 Preparation of the Information Processing Infrastructure

1. Model system for small and medium enterprises

Since 1978 MITI is promoting a survey about the state of computer usage in small and medium enterprises. The results will be used to compile a collection of case studies on exemplary computer utilisation in small and medium enterprises (see e.g. CWP 1978, page 26).

2. Assistance for computer installations at Chambers of Commerce and Industry

If Chambers of Commerce and Industry purchase used computers of JECC at about 60% of the original price, 50% of the costs will be paid by the government, 25% by the manufacturers and only 25% (equivalent to 15% of the price when the computer was new) by the Chamber of Commerce and Industry and the municipal commercial or industrial association. These computers are used for accounting services of small and medium enterprises (see e.g. JR No.34, page 12).

3. System auditor system

R & D activities are carried out for a system to train system auditors who will be capable of checking and verifying the reliability of computerised accounting systems (see CWP 1978, page 25).

4. Examination of data processing specialists

MITI promotes the qualification tests of data processing specialists which are conducted under the Law concerning the Information-technology Promotion Agency (IPA-Law) (see e.g. CWP 1977, page 41).

5. Measures for the security of the information processing industry

As from 1980 MITI is granting subsidies for the preparation of a list which contains the security measures of all information processing service companies. Thus a client can obtain information about the measures which the information processing service company is carrying out in order to protect his data (see also Chapter 2.5).

2.2.2.5 Surveys, Studies and Small Projects

MITI also promotes several surveys, studies and small projects which totalled 35 million Yen in 1979 and 1980:

- survey on the state of information processing

- survey on information systems used by industry

- monthly survey on computer deliveries

- survey on dp personnel problems

- register of dp service companies

- information week

- study on safety of software

- survey on legal protection of software

- program register.

2.2.2.6 Loans

Loans which are granted for the promotion of information processing are lent by
the Japan Development Bank (JDB), the three long-term credit banks, or the Small
Enterprise Public Bank. The loans from JDB are based on the Machinery and Information Industry Law. In 1978, 1979 and 1980 the total amount of JDB-loans was 56
billion, 50 billion and 48 billion Yen, respectively.

1. JDB-loans for JECC

JDB grants loans for JECC in order to secure its rental business (compare chapter 2.1.3.1). The JDB-loans for JECC are the largest part of the JDB-loans for
information processing (see e.g. CWP77, page 36; JR No.34, page 4).

2. JDB-loans for the structural improvement of the computer industry

The establishment of co-operative ties between the six Japanese computer
manufacturers is being financially supported by JDB-loans. This measure was introduced in 1972 when the Japanese computer manufacturers began the production
and marketing of new computer series (see e.g. JR No.34, page 5).

3. JDB-loans for software development

JDB-loans are granted for computer manufacturers and software firms to provide
them with funds for software development and for facilities to train information
processing personnel (see e.g JR No.34, page 5).

4. JDB-loans for the promotion of data processing systems

These loans are granted for data processing systems used by

- data processing service companies (not including on-line services companies)

- on-line systems of multi-companies

- systems which are contributing highly to the social welfare.

5. Loans for safety measures of computer systems

For the implementation of security measures, based on the "Guidelines of Security Measure Standards for Electronic Computer Systems", issued by MITI in April
1977, JDB grants loans for general companies and the Small Business Finance Corporation for small and medium enterprises (see Chapter 2.5 and e.g. JR No.34,
page 12).

6. Loans for the Promotion of Data Processing

These are loans granted by the three long-term credit banks for data processing service companies, software houses and general companies guaranteed by IPA according to Article 28, Sentences 4 and 5 of the IPA-Law (see chapter 2.1.3.2 (b), and e.g. JR No.34, pages 6 and 7).

2.2.2.7 Tax Concessions

1. General Purpose Software Package Registration System

This measure promotes the development of general purpose software and supports the introduction of the separate payment for software systems ("unbundling"). Companies which register their developed software packages in the General Purpose Software Package Registration System of IPA (see chapter 2.1.3.2 (d)) can reserve 50% of their sales revenues in a tax free fund for 4 years. This measure is based on the Machinery and Information Industry Law of 1978.

2. Special depreciation for on-line computer systems

According to the taxation law there is a list of important machine complexes which can be written off more quickly. Based on the Machinery and Information Industry Law on-line computer systems, which have a huge performance, have been included in this list in 1979, so that an additional depreciation of 25% was granted for the first year of its acquisition. This was reduced to 13% in 1980.

3. Reserve fund for computer re-buy losses

When a user returns a rented computer to JECC, the manufacturer must repurchase it from JECC at the residual value at the time of return. To prepare for such losses the computer manufacturers can set aside a fixed percentage of income in a tax free reserve fund (set at 10% in 1968 and raised to 15% in 1970 and again to 20% in 1972). This measure was limited until 1978, but in 1979 it was prolonged for a further 2 years (see JR No.34, page 5).

4. Program guarantee reserve fund system

This system was established in 1972 in order to make the management of software companies more sound and stable by permitting the build-up of tax-free reserves for program maintenance services. Until 1977 the limit was 2% of the sales of application programs, but in 1979 it was reduced to 0.5%, and in 1980 to 0.25% (see JR No.34, page 8 and CWP 1980, page 34).

5. Tax deduction for the training of data processing personnel

According to this measure 20% of the yearly increase of expenditure for the training of information processing personnel can be put against tax in order to overcome the quantitative and qualitative deficiencies in such personnel.

2.2.2.8 Table of Promotion Measures

Remarks :

* "LAW" is the legal base of the measures:

  ₒ MIIL — Machinery and Information Industry Law

  ₒ IPAL — IPA Law

* "Period" is the time during which the measure was valid

* "Amount" is the amount of money spent in the quoted period in million Yen.
  If, in the case of loans, the amount has an asterisk (*) this is the total
  amount for all loans granted by JDB in the respective year. If the field is
  blank, the contents are unknown. A dash ("--") means that the field is
  meaningless or that the measure did not yet exist.

* The promotion figures for the financial years 1978 to 1980 have been taken
  from SHOWA 54 NENDO JOHOSHORI KANREN SHISAKU NO JUTEN and SHOWA 55 NENDO
  JOHOSHORI KANREN SHISAKU NO JUTEN (important points of the information
  processing policy for 1979 and 1980, respectively) published by MITI; also
  from JR Nos.34 and 38; and CWPs 1977, 1978 and 1980, published by JIPDEC. The
  budget proposals for 1980 have been taken from SHOWA 55 NENDO NO JOHOSHORI
  KANREN SHISAKU proposed by MITI, Machine and Information Industry Bureau, and
  published in TOHOKA KENKYU No. 24, Sept. 1979.

  For 1980 the budget proposals are listed, as well as the granted promotion
  figures, in order to demonstrate the discrepancies between planning and decisions. Basically, the granted amounts are approximately 5% lower than the
  budget proposals.

Measure	LAW	Period	Amount per period	Amount 1980 proposed	Amount 1980 realized	Amount 1979	Amount 1978
1. Subsidies for the information industry							
1.1 VLSI-Technology Research Association		76-79	30,540	—	—	6,906	10,052
1.2 Computer Basic Technology Research Association		79-83	23,500	6,080	5,785	1,700	—
1.3 Project of Software Production Technology Development (JSD-project)		76-80	—	1,812	1,672	1,522	1,112
1.4 Operation of IPA	IPAL	since 70	—	1,249	1,109	1,058	1,167
1.5 Pattern Information Processing System (PIPS)		71-80	about 22,000	1,965	1,846	2,803	2,514
1.7 Comprehensive Automobile Control Technology Project		73-79	7,300	—	—	150	580
1.8 Optical Measurement and Control System		79-86	20,000	951	927	51	—

Measure	LAW	Period	Amount per period	Amount 1980 proposed	Amount 1980 realized	Amount 1979	Amount 1978
2. Subsidies for information systems increasing the national welfare							
2.1 Health Care Network System		78-83		256	222	191	192
2.2 Hi-Ovis		72-79	about 2,800	--	--	34	39
2.3 Energy Saving Urban Machinery System		78-		83	42	9	9
2.4 International Trade Information System		75-		38	34	25	33

Measure	LAW	Period	Amount per period	Amount 1980 proposed	Amount 1980 realized	Amount 1979	Amount 1978
3. Subsidies in order to prepare the infrastructure of information processing							
3.1 Model system for small and medium enterprises		78–		5	4	5	5
3.2 Computer installations at Chambers of Commerce and Industry				190	190	127	104
3.3 System Auditor System				5	5	5	6
3.4 Examination of data processing specialists	IPAL			77	68	62	57
3.5 Measures for the security of the Information Service Industry		80–		10	2	–	–
4. Subsidies for small projects, surveys and studies (total amount)				–	35	35	37

Measure	LAW	Period	Amount per period	Amount 1980 proposed	Amount 1980 realized	Amount 1979	Amount 1978
5. Loans for the information industry							
5.1 JDB-loans for JECC	MIIL	since 61	--	45,000	48,000*	50,000*	56,000*
5.2 JDB-loans for the structural improvement of the computer industry	MIIL	72-80	--	2,100	48,000*	50,000*	56,000*
5.3 JDB-loans for software development	MIIL		--	2,000	48,000*	50,000*	56,000*
5.4 JDB-loans for the promotion of data processing systems	MIIL		--	3,000	48,000*	50,000*	56,000*
5.5 Loans for safty measures of computer systems:							
a) JDB-loans	MIIL	since 78	--	6,000	48,000*	50,000*	56,000*
b) loans from the Small and Medium Enterprises Fund		since 78		5,500	3,000	3,000	2,500
5.6 Loans for the promotion of data processing	IPAL	since 70	--	9,000	5,000	7,000	8,000

Measure	LAW	Period	Amount per period	Amount 1980 proposed	Amount 1980 realized	Amount 1979	Amount 1978
6. Tax measures							
6.1 General Purpose Software Package Registration System	MIIL	since 79	—		50% of sales revenues	50% of sales revenues	—
6.2 Special depreciation for on-line computer systems	MIIL	since 79	—		13% in first year	25% in first year	—
6.3 Computer re-buy losses	TAX	since 68	—		20%	20%	20%
6.4 Program Guarantee Reserve Fund		since 72	—		0.25% of sales	0.5% of sales	2% of sales of application programs
6.5 Tax deduction for training data processing personnel			—		20% of increase of training expenditure	20% of increase of training expenditure	20% of increase of training expenditure

**2.2.3   Promotion of Information Processing by the Agency of Industrial Science
          and Technology**

The Agency of Industrial Science and Technology (AIST, in japanese KOGYO GIJUTSU
IN) is one of MITI's agencies, headed by a Director General,   which is responsible for the promotion of R & D in industrial science and technology (see [AIST1]
page 6). Its main tasks are

— the planning of an industrial science and technology R & D strategy

— co-ordination of   R & D   activities of   the affiliated laboratories and institutes

— promotion of the National R & D Program (Large Scale Project System)

— the support and stimulation of R & D activities in the private sector

— the promotion of industrial standardisation.

Figure 8 is the organisation chart of AIST.

a)   Affiliated laboratories
AIST co-ordinates the activities of   its **16** affiliated laboratories and institutes,   nine of which are located in the Tsukuba Research Centre and the rest
elsewhere. The Electro-technical Laboratory (ETL) is researching in the field of
information processing.

b)   Industrial R & D strategy
AIST is also concerned with planning the industrial R & D strategy.   Until   1980
nine research categories were being promoted: energy, resources, city, environment, information, production systems, medical applications, disaster, and food.
From every category several projects were being promoted.

In early 1980 the plan for the promotion of these categories was totally revised
and committees   were   established with   members   from   industry,   universities,
organisations,   and experts from AIST.   The committee members proposed R & D
projects which were evaluated according to certain criteria.   AIST gathered all
proposals from   the   committees and submitted them to the Industrial Technology
Council of MITI for approval.   (Final results were not   known when the author
wrote this report.)

Furthermore   AIST is concerned with planning MITI's industrial policy, e.g.   it
prepared the basic version of the "Vision of MITI Policies in the   1980's"   (see
Chapter 2.1.2.1, [AIST2],   EJR Vol.6,   page 111, and Appendix 1). In this field
AIST co-operates with MITI's Electronics Policy Division and with the Industrial
Structure Council.

c)   National R & D Program
The National R & D Program   (or Large Scale Project System,   see [AIST1] page 7)
promotes technical themes which are of particular importance from   the   national
point of view and which cannot be carried out by private companies alone because
of their high portion of R & D.

Ministry of International Trade and Industry (MITI)
Agency of Industrial Science and Technology (AIST)
Industrial Technology Council
Japanese Industrial Standards Committee
(Research Institutes and Laboratories)

(Headquarters)

General Coordination Department — National Research and Development Program Sunshine, Moonlight Projects (R & D on new energy, energy conservation technology)

Counsellor for Technological

General Coordination Divivision — Comprehensive coordination in Agency, Planning of industrial technology administration, Secretariat of Industrial Technology Council etc.
R & D Utilization Office
Computer Utilization Technology Office

Personnel Affairs Division — Personnel affairs, welfare

Budget and Accounts Division — Financial affairs

Research Administration Division — R & D Programs for affiliated Laboratories and Institutes, contact with other public research institutes, patent management
(Industrial Science and Technology Advice Office)

Planning Division — Preparation for Transfer to Tsukuba R & D Center of 9 Laboratories and Institutes
Office for Tsukuba Construction

Technology Promotion Division — Support for R & D in private industries by subsidies, tax exemptions, Government loans. Research Association for Promotion of Mining and Manufacturing Technology. R & D on medical and welfare equipment technology.

Technological Research and Information Division — Survey of technological affairs, public relations, library, planning of long-range Industrial R & D Strategy, Technology Assessment
AIST Library

Tsukuba Administration Office — Management and administration of joint facilities at Tsukuba Research Center, staff welfare

Research Coordinator for Prevention of Industrial Pollution — Planning of R & D on pollution prevention technology at affiliated laboratories and institutes. Contact with public and private testing and research organizations

Senior Officer for International Research and Development Cooperation (ITIT) — International cooperation in Industrial Science & Technology

Senior Officer for Development Program (General Coordination) (3) — Supervision for National Research and Development Program, Sunshine Project and Moonlight Project

Senior Officer for Development Program (14) — Promotion for National Research and Development Program, Sunshine Project and Moonlight Project

Standards Department

Standards Division — Comprehensive coordination in Standards Department, surveys, propagation of JIS and JIS Mark, Japan Industrial Standards Committee, International Standardization
International Standards Office

Material Standards Division — Industrial Standards for basic common items in metal, civil engineering, construction, mining etc.

Textile and Chemical Standard Division — Industrial Standard for chemicals, textiles, ceramics, daily necessities, packaging

Machinery Standards Division — Industrial Standards for machinery, aircraft, ships, railway carriers, automobiles, bicycles, industrial vehicles etc.
Transportation and Aeronautical Standards Office

Electricity Standards Division — Industrial Standards for information, electronics, electric communications, medical equipment, combustion equipment, atomic power; R & D on reliable electronic parts
Reliability Technology Development Office

National Research Laboratory of Metrology
Mechanical Engineering Laboratory
National Chemical Laboratory for Industry
Government Industrial Research Institute, Osaka
Government Industrial Research Institute, Nagoya
Fermentation Research Institute
Research Institute for Polymer and Textiles
Geological Survey of Japan
Electrotechnical Laboratory
Industrial Products Research Institute
National Research Institute for Pollution and Resources
Government Industrial Development Laboratory, Hokkaido
Government Industrial Research Institute, Kyushu
Government Industrial Research Institute, Skikoku
Government Industrial Research Institute, Tohoku
Government Industrial Research Institute, Chugoku

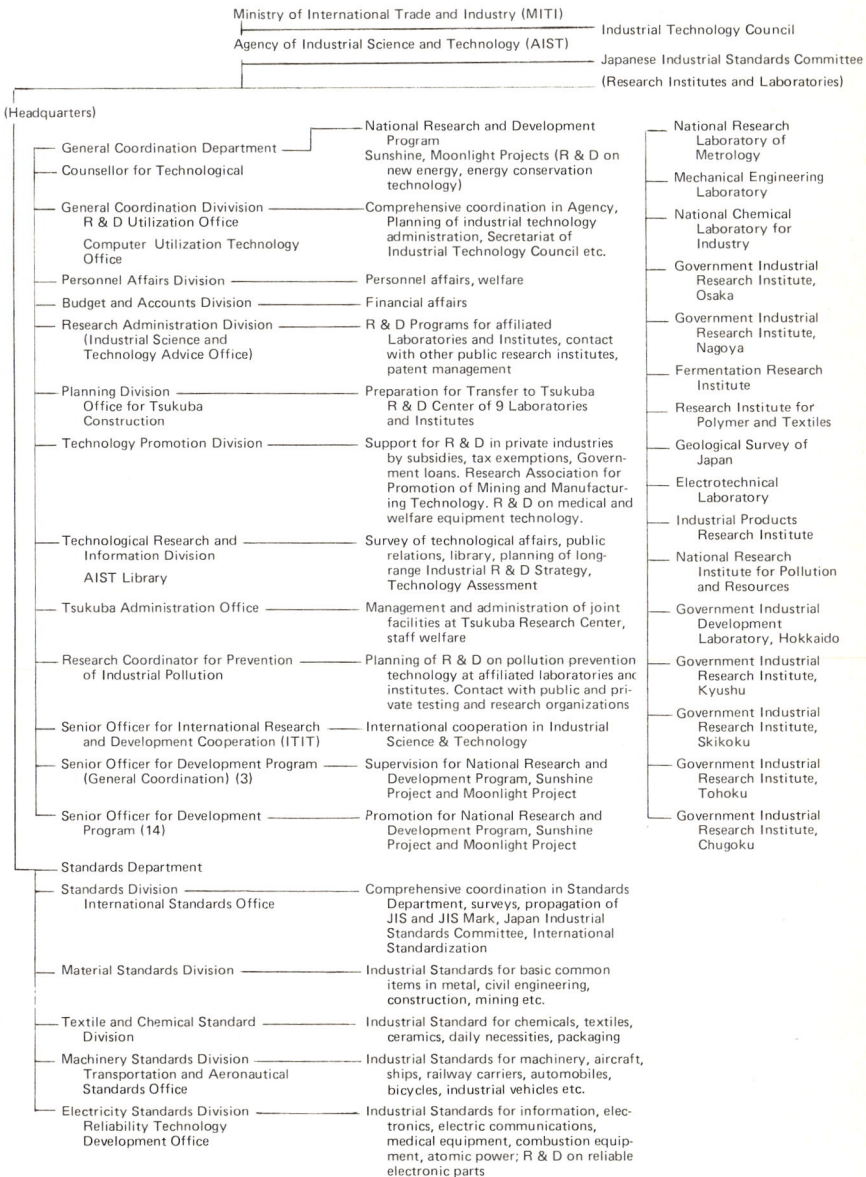

Figure 8   Organisation of AIST (from [AIST1], page 5)

The projects of this program are being supervised by the Industrial Technology Council of AIST, the laboratories of AIST carrying out the the fundamental research and giving contracts to private companies for applied research and development. In the field of information processing there were three National R & D Projects in 1980 carried out by ETL:

- Pattern Information Processing System (PIPS, see also Chapter 2.2.2.3 (1), and [AIST4])

- Optical Measurement and Control System (see Chapter 2.2.2.3 (3))

- High performance flexible manufacturing system complex provided with laser (see [AIST6] page 4).

National R & D Projects of ETL which have been completed are:

- Comprehensive Automobile Control Technology System 1973-79 (see Chapter 2.2.2.3 (2))

- Super-high Performance Electronic Computer Development 1966-71 (see Chapter 2.2.2.1).

The National R & D Program is fully financed by MITI, the funds for the research by AIST being granted from AIST's budget, and the funds for the contracted R & D from MITI's information industry promotion budget, (see [MITI14] and Chapter 2.2.2.3). The licences resulting from this research are the property of the Japan Industrial Technology Association (JITA) of AIST (but in the case of research which is not fully subsidised by MITI – e.g. in the VLSI Technology Research Association – the licences belong to the companies which researched them, or to the joint research association).

2.2.4   Import Restrictions and their Liberalisation

When the Japanese computer industry was still weak, the government decreed import restrictions in order to protect the domestic market against the American computer manufacturers, especially IBM. Computers were classified as an import quota (IQ) item in the Tariff Schedule, and if a Japanese company wanted to purchase a foreign computer it required MITI's approval on a case-by-case basis. The import authorisation could be obtained without difficulty in the following cases (although this is not stated in any official document):

(1) Computers that cannot be replaced by domestic products. MITI did not object if the user badly needed the foreign computer involved.

(2) Import of peripheral equipment related to foreign computers already imported and in operation.

(3) Switchover to improved computers of the same category. For instance, if the user wanted to replace his IBM 360-20 with an IBM 370-145, he had only to explain to MITI that there would be no need for a conversion of the programs, and that the adoption of a substitute domestic product would cost far more.

(4) Import of back-up machines for users of imported computers. The importer could obtain MITI's approval by explaining that, unless he obtained a back-up machine, he would be charged with a violation of his support con-

tract with his computer users. (Compare EJR Vol. 1, No. 2, page 8.)

The problem was that MITI compared the computers intended for import with corresponding domestic products in terms of paper specifications only. But the fact
that, before the liberalisation, the portion of foreign computers was even
higher than at present shows that MITI's approval was not too difficult to obtain.

There were also restrictions for capital imports. Normally MITI did not allow a
foreign company to establish a daughter company in Japan because MITI was afraid
that the Japanese market could be captured by strong foreign companies. But
there were exceptions, too. MITI allowed at least one foreign company in every
branch of industry under the condition that domestic industry could benefit from
the technological knowledge of the foreign company. The most famous example of
this kind is IBM Japan, a 100% daughter of IBM WTC, which started its operation
after World War 2 in 1950 (IBM had already established a daughter company before
the war in 1937, Nihon Watson Tokei Kaikei Kikai). Foreign capital investments
of less than 50% have been permitted, however, in a number of cases.

Table 10 shows the timetable of the liberalisation. Import liberalisation means
the shift of an IQ (Import Quota) item to the AIQ (Automatic Import Quota)
category. Once a commodity is specified as an AIQ item, MITI will give automatic
approval of its import in one to two weeks. As regards capital imports, MITI's
policy after the liberalisation is to permit any foreign capital investment in
the Japanese market, and at present the impediments for foreign investors are
not much harder than for domestic investors.

The Japanese computer manufacturers wanted the liberalisation to begin much later and proposed April 1977 for the start of import decontrol. But MITI, in
order to avoid American criticism about its economic policies, chose an earlier
date.

On the restricted markets for ministries, agencies, local governments, universities, etc., the market share of foreign computer manufacture is much less than
on the open market (only about 14% in comparison to over 50%), because public
users were urged to buy domestic products. But in January 1978 the Cabinet made
a decision to give foreign manufacturers the same chance as domestic
manufacturers in this market.

Furthermore the Japanese government plans to cut import tariffs on main frame
computers, peripherals and terminals from the present 10.5% and 17.0% to 4.9%
and 6.0% respectively by 1986. Reduction will be achieved each year on a step-
by-step basis to reach the final percentage goals.

	Mainframe	Peripherals / Terminals
1979	10.5%	17.0%
1980	9.1	14.25
1981	8.4	12.875
1982	7.7	11.5
1983	7.0	10.125
1984	6.3	8.75
1985	5.6	7.375
1986	4.9	6.0

Table 9 Schedule of tariff reduction (from EJR Vol. 6, page 85)

| | Capital Liberalization | | Liberalization | Liberalization of |
	50%	100%	of Import	Installation of Technology
Calculator	Aug.4,1974	Dec.1,1975	April 19th, 1973	July 1st, 1974
Computer — CPU	Aug.4,1974 (including IC for computers)	Dec.1,1975	Dec. 24th, 1975	July 1st, 1974
peripherals — memory + terminals			Dec. 24th, 1975	
others			Feb. 1st, 1972	
parts			Dec. 24th, 1975	
Software	Dec.1,1974	Dec.1,1976		July 1st, 1974
IC — Number of components below 100	Aug.4,1971 (except IC for Computers)		Sept. 1st, 1970	June 1st, 1968
below 200		Dec.1,1974	Apr. 19th, 1973	
over 200			Dec. 25th, 1974	

Table 10: Timetable of liberalization
(from NIHON NO DENSHI KOGYO (Japan's Electronic Industry)
published by Computer Age Co., page 21)

2.3   Policy of the Ministry of Posts and Telecommunications

2.3.1   Telecommunication Laws

There are three principal telecommunication laws:

- Public Telecommunication Law (KOSHU DENSHI TSUSHIN HO, see [MPT2])

- Wire Communications Law (YUSEN DENSHI TSUSHIN HO, see [MPT3])

- Radio Law (DEMPA HO).

Concerning data communication (dc) and data processing (dp) the Public Telecommunication Law is most important. This law enables NTT and KDD to provide telecommunication services to the general public (see Article 1). Among other things it is concerned with the telegraph, telephone and telex services. In 1971 Chapter III-4, regarding the data communication service, was added. The new Articles 55-(9) to 55-(22) regulate the dc circuit utilisation contract (Section 1) and the dc facility utilisation contract (Section 2). According to Section 1 NTT or KDD can offer dc circuits to users, and according to Section 2 they can offer dc services such as DRESS and DEMOS, or individual services such as the All Banking Exchange System (ZENGIN-System).

The dc regulations were liberalised three times:

- since 1971 leased lines could be used for data transmission, but not telephone lines.

- since 1972 telephone lines and optional telephone equipment could be used for data communication.

- in 1976 the rules concerning the third party use were changed, but not the law itself. Before 1976 only one computer centre could be used for third party traffic, but since 1976 two or more centres could be used on the condition that the transmitted data were to be processed at the centres. Message switching without processing is not allowed at present.

In spite of the three liberalisation steps, many dc users want all restrictions to be removed. E.g. the Japan Information Processing Centre Association (JIPCA) and the Telecommunications Users Association (TUA) issued catalogues of demands concerning the liberalisation of dc regulations (see [MPT9] and [MPT10]), the main points of which are

- all kinds of sharing must be free

- all restrictions on third party use must be removed.

The present restrictions are especially annoying for those Japanese companies which have subsidiaries or branch offices abroad and for those which belong to the same holding company although the companies are independent juridical bodies (see EJR Vol.6, pages 17,18). Furthermore many users criticise NTT's high rental charges and the long waiting time which is needed to get NTT's approval.

A special problem is MPT's policy towards foreign companies concerning

- the establishment of foreign information supply services in Japan

- the purchase of dc equipment for NTT from foreign companies

- the permission of foreign equipment to be used in dc networks.

After the last liberalisation step of the Japanese computer market (compare Chapter 2.2.4) capital imports are not restricted any more, and some sources say that, concerning the purchase of NTT's equipment, the liberalisation of NTT's market has already been decided by the government. Indeed, since Japanese companies proposing a motion to NTT or MPT have the same complaints as foreign companies, the restrictive policy of MPT does not seem to be a discrimination of foreign companies in particular (see also EJR Vol.7, page 106).

2.3.2   Data Communication Promotion Measures

A data communication promotion law does not exist yet. In 1979 MPT proposed to the Ministry of Finance (MoF) some promotion measures in favour of dc including the establishment of a dc council, but MoF did not grant budget for these measures.

In 1980 the promotion budget for pure dc was 348 mill. Yen. This sum included the subsidies from MPT for CAPTAINS and the Tama New Town Coaxial Cable Information System (TAMA CCIS). (See e.g. JR No.35, pages 12 and 29, and JR No.38, page 20). Nevertheless other MPT promotion measures, e.g. for broadcasting or space development, also include dc. There are no loans or tax concessions in favour of dc.

There is a problem about the area which covers dc and dp, and it is not clear whether this is the responsibility of MPT or MITI. For this reason the information supply industry (data base service industry) has not been included in the Machinery and Information Industry Law (KIJOHO).

2.3.3   Nippon Telegraph & Telephone Public Corporation

The Nippon Telegraph & Telephone Public Corporation (NTT) established in 1952 is one of Japan's three public corporations (KOSHA). It is being supervised by MPT, and most of its important activities are being regulated by law, mainly the NTT Public Corporation Law (see [MPT7]). NTT must report annually to MPT and government committees, especially the Posts and Telecommunications Committee (TEI SHIN IINKAI) which also supervises KDD. NTT must submit its annual budget plan to MPT who will discuss it with other ministries, especially MoF, and will submit it to the Cabinet and the Diet for authorisation. When NTT wishes to start a new service, MPT must authorise it and announce the tariff or, if necesary, a new law must be established.

According to Article 3 of the NTT Law, NTT's main task is to perform the public telecommunication business and conduct the business assigned by MPT.

NTT's role in the dc business is manifold:

- NTT has the monopoly to lease dc circuits.

- NTT offers four authorised public network systems

  * public telephone exchange network

  * TELEX network

  * telegraph exchange network

  * DDX, Digital Data Exchange Service
    Recently NTT established its Digital Data Exchange Service (DDX) in-
    cluding circuit and packet switching services. The circuit switching
    service which started in 1979 is charged according to speed (7 classes
    from 200 bps to 48 kbps), distance (8 classes), and connection time
    (minimum of 1 second). The packet switching service which started in July
    1980 depends on speed (6 classes), distance (3 classes) and number of
    packages.

- NTT is a communications service vendor, and is offering the broadest range of
  EDP services in Japan, e.g.

  * Dendenkosha Realtime Sales Management System (DRESS)

  * Character and Pattern Telephone Access Information System (CAPTAINS)

  * Dendenkosha Multi-access On-line System (DEMOS)

  * Facsimile Intelligent Communication Service (FICS),

  which are adaptive systems on the telephone network and later also on DDX.
  Thus NTT is competing with the private sector of dc service vendors. As a
  result private companies complain about NTT's duplicate role in offering dc
  services and being responsible (together with MPT) for granting communication
  circuit permits to dc vendors.

- NTT designs and develops custom-tailored dc systems for various users,
  particularly to banks and government agencies. The first system was the Exchange On-line System for Gumma Bank, and to date NTT has installed 36 systems. In this field NTT is a competitor of software houses and hardware
  makers.

- NTT developed the Data Communication Network Architecture (DCNA) in co-
  operation with the Japanese hardware manufacturers. In DCNA, NTT implemented
  the CCITT and ISO standards, e.g. X.21, X.25, HDLC. Since the standards of
  ISO and CCITT are not compatible with IBM standards as they have been implemented in IBM's SNA there arise some problems, especially because most of
  Japan's large-scale on-line systems have been developed by IBM users (see EJR
  Vol.6, page 91).

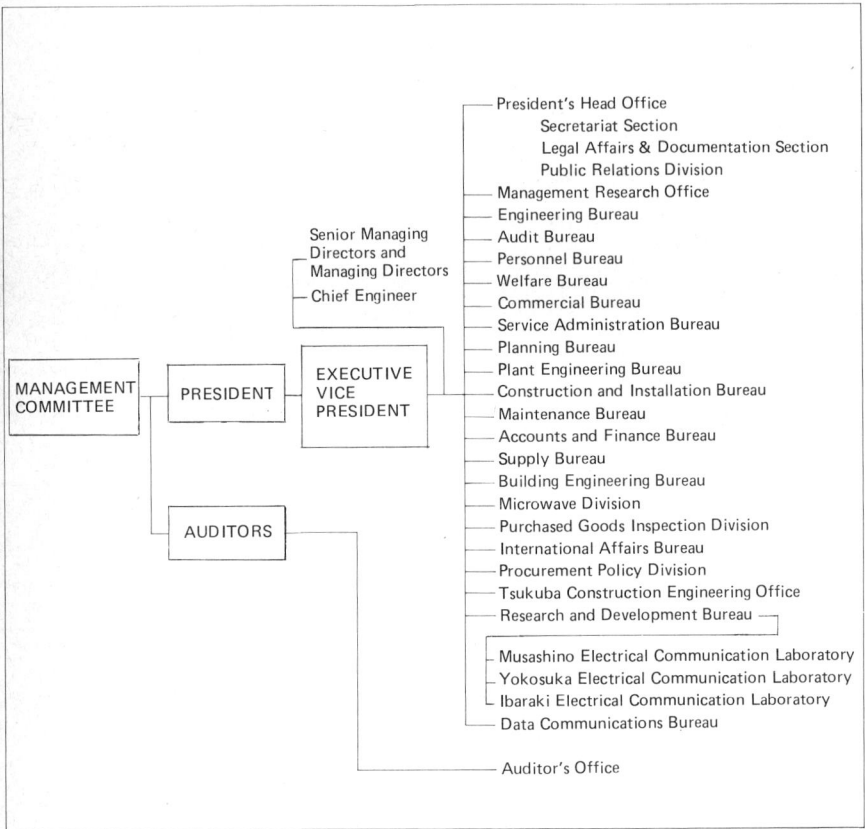

Figure 11 · Organisation of the Head Office of NTT
(from Annual Report 1978/79, page 24)

NTT has a huge R & D budget in order to develop the technologies for the above
mentioned services, the R & D being carried out by its own staff in co-operation
with hardware manufacturers. The three Electrical Communication Laboratories in
Musashino, Yokosuka and Ibaragi (see Figure 11) are developing the new technologies, but they do not produce equipment themselves. Once the development of
a new product has been finished NTT defines the specifications, and private companies produce and market the product. These companies often participate in the
development, too. NTT's main co-operators in the field of dc are NEC, Fujitsu,
Oki and Hitachi. Furthermore NTT co-operated with the research associations of
the hardware manufacturers, e.g. the VLSI Technology Research Association (see
Chapter 2.2.2.1). Figure 12 shows the above described mechanism of co-operation.

NTT   Manufacturer

```
┌─────────────────────────────────────────┐
│ Determination of a Development Theme     │
└─────────────────────────────────────────┘
                    │
                    ↓
┌─────────────────────────────────────────┐
│ Selection of Manufacturers              │
│ (In most cases, so-called "family member│
│ manufacturers" are selected as R & D and│
│ production contractors at the present    │
│ time)                                    │
└─────────────────────────────────────────┘
                    │
                    ↓
┌───────────────────────┐   ┌──────────────────────────────┐
│ Joint Development      │←──│ Dispatching Research Staff   │
│ (basic design stage)   │   │ at Manufacturer's Own Expense│
└───────────────────────┘   └──────────────────────────────┘

         └──────────────────→┌──────────────────────────────┐
                             │ Production of Prototype Model │
                             └──────────────────────────────┘
                                        │
                                        ↓
                             ┌──────────────────────────────┐
                             │ Mass Production              │
                             └──────────────────────────────┘
```

Figure 12: Relationship between NTT and its "family member"
           manufacturers in R & D and production
           (from EJR Vol.6, page 21)

The Data Communications Bureau (see figure 3) is developing complete systems containing communication computers, lines and programs; it plans, designs, implements, installs, operates and maintains the systems, mostly in co-operation with the hardware manufacturers.

Through the assignment of large orders for R & D and for equipment, NTT has a great influence over the computer and data communication industry. In 1979 NTT bought equipment amounting to 640 bill. Yen (about 3.2 billion US Dollars, see EJR Vol.5, Nos.23 and 24, and EJR Vol.6, pages 15-25). At present only Japanese dp and dc manufacturers which belong to the "NTT family" are delivering equipment to NTT, mainly NEC, Fujitsu, Oki and Hitachi. Therefore foreign companies (especially American) and Japanese dc manufacturers which are not members of the "NTT family", e.g. Toshiba, Mitsubishi and Matsushita, asked NTT to open its telecommunication equipment market. In the meantime NTT has opened the market to further Japanese and foreign suppliers (see EJR Vol.6, page 12, EJR Vol.7, page 79 and page 124).

Figure 13 shows the situation of NTT at a glance: It is supervised by MPT in a similar way as the International Telephone and Telegraph Company (KDD) which, however, is a different kind of juridical body. NTT offers numerous services, as described before. Besides its own research at its Electric Communication Laboratories it dispatches orders for the development of dp and dc equipment to the mainframe manufacturers. The Dendenkosha Information Processing System (DIPS) is a well known example of such an R & D project carried out in co-operation with the computer manufacturers. DIPS is a large-scale general-purpose computer which is being used in NTT's dc systems for communication control.

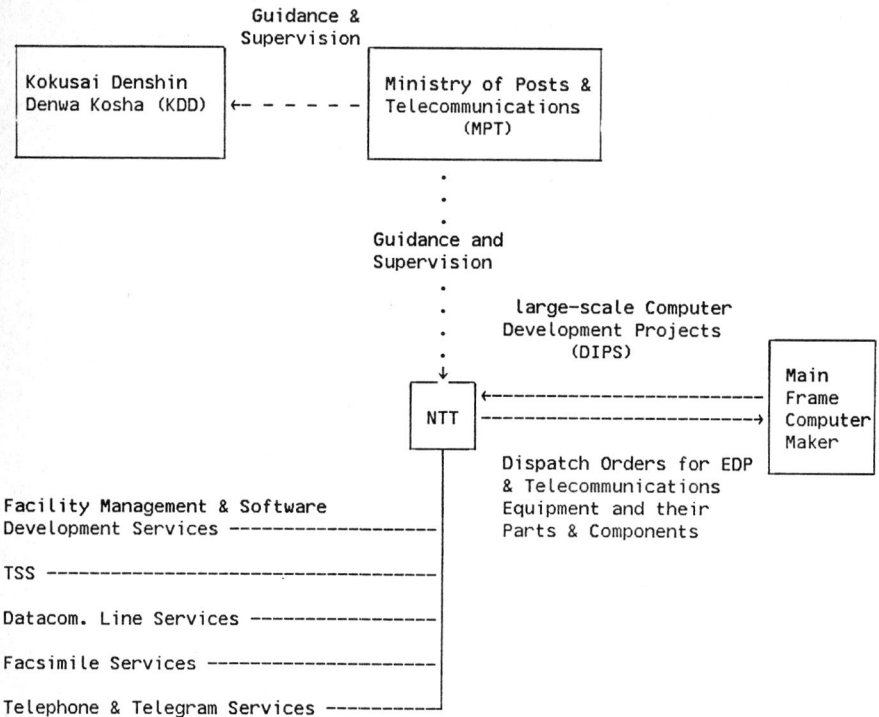

Figure 13 : NTT and related organisations
(from EJR Vol.4, No.2, page 6)

2.4   Evaluation of the Information Industry Policy

Japan is being critisised by the USA and European countries that, by over-
subsidising its information industry, it would be an unfair world competitor.
However, according to papers received from AIST the government funding of R & D
in Japan is less than that in USA and Europe. The 1977 total Japanese research
expenses in the field of natural sciences including universities were 3,234
billion Yen (about 14.4 billion US Dollars), out of which 27.4% was funded by
the government. The corresponding figures in USA and West-Germany were 11,519
billion Yen, 50.5% and 3,161 billion Yen, 48.5% respectively. The total R & D
expenditures of Japan, USA and West Germany in 1977 were 1.7%, 2.4% and 2.0% of
the GNP, respectively.

The effectiveness of the Japanese R & D promotion policy seems to result from
other reasons:

-   The average expenditure for one researcher in Japan is less than that in USA
    and Europe. This is mainly due to the fact that the infra-structure costs are
    low in Japan (e.g. large offices, small desks, small administrative depart-
    ments).

-   The governmental promotion policy concentrates on a few areas. Which fields
    of R & D should be promoted is being discussed on a large scale; and MITI
    assures that the decisive committees and bodies include members from all
    branches of industry, universities, government, organisations, etc. By the
    close co-operation of government and industry MITI also wants to assure that
    the R & D activities will correspond with the need of the market. Since the
    1950's information processing was one field to be particularly promoted,
    because it was and is a knowledge-intensive technology which will become im-
    portant in all branches of industry.

-   In the field of information processing the government promotion concentrated,
    in the past, on hardware and computer technology, but at present it con-
    centrates on software technology. Furthermore MITI supported mainly strong
    and experienced companies in order to assure a good result of the R & D
    activities, although it was conscious of the fact that a broad support of the
    industry was also important. E.g. only five companies were members of the
    VLSI Technology Research Association, although many more companies are
    developing and producing integrated circuits.

-   MITI granted the subsidies only on certain conditions, it especially urged
    the computer industry to co-operate with each other in order to assure an
    effective usage of the promotion funds. Through the research associations of
    1972-76, 1976-79 and 1979-83 MITI reorganised the computer industry into
    three, two and one group(s) respectively.

-   Further conditions of MITI were

    *   Financial share of the subsidised companies, e.g. in the research asso-
        ciations of the computer industry MITI granted less that 50% of the total
        costs (50% of the research expenditure, administration costs were not in-
        cluded).

    *   Predetermined period of promotion, and the industry is not to assume that
        the period will be extended.

-   Through the National R & D Program the information industry was also urged to
    co-operate, different parts of the projects being carried out by different
    companies. The same is true for the R & D projects organised by NTT, e.g.
    DCNA, DIPS, and CAPTAINS.
    The National R & D Program has a similar effect on the promotion of R & D as
    the space and military projects in the USA, but in a much smaller range.

-   MITI has a great authority in Japanese industry and it can also carry out its
    intentions without laws or regulations (GYOSEI SHIDO, administrative
    guidance). Because MITI employees are supposed to be very competent (e.g.
    partly because of the very difficult entrance examinations) the industry has
    confidence in the measures taken by MITI, even if these, in special cases,
    are not very convenient.

-   Private companies in Japan make long-term plans and might even accept a
    temporary deficit if a profit can be foreseen in the future. The long-term
    planning of Japanese companies is eased by the following characteristics:

    *   Because most large Japanese companies are multi-product companies they can
        afford losses in one area if the total result is positive.

    *   Japanese industry has the highest investment rate in the world.

    *   The willingness to take a risk is comparatively high, because all im-
        portant decisions are only made after a broad consultation process, so
        that a failure must not be suffered by a single person (compare "Ringi
        system" as explained, for example, in [VOGEL1] or [HOWARD1]).

2.5   Privacy and Data Protection

There is no Privacy Law in Japan, but there was and still is a discussion about
privacy and data protection, mainly in connection with the introduction of a
unified individual code for all citizens.

In 1970 a "Liaison Council for a Unified Personal Code for Administrative
Processing among Ministries and Agencies" was established in the Administrative
Management Agency, and in 1971 this council published the "Survey and Report on
Protection of Privacy in an Information Society" (see JR No.36, pages 24-35).
This activity was related to plans of the government to implement a personal
code which, however, was abandoned in 1973 because of opposition from the
public. Under these circumstances the Administrative Management Agency submitted, in 1974, an inquiry to the Commission for Administrative Management and
Inspection on the "Measures to be Taken to Protect Privacy in Relation to the
Utilisation of Computers in Government Agencies" (see [AMA17]). The commission
limited its examination to the public sector and concluded that legislative
steps were not required at this stage. But the interim report submitted by the
commission in 1975 listed several items for further inquiries:

- Regulation of the establishment of personal information systems and the entry of information

- Notice of personal information systems

- Regulation of dissemination of information

- Regulation of the operation of systems including maintenance of files

- Granting individuals the right of access, the right to have one's information corrected or deleted, and the right of appeal

- Creation of a special regulatory authority

- Regulation of government contractors

(from [AMA1] pages 37,38).

Discussions, however, are still in progress and according to the press the government recently set up a consultative body of cabinet ministers to reflect on the legislation of a law protecting the privacy of the individual (see Daily Yomiuri, English edition, March 10th, 1980).

Contrary to discussions about privacy, concrete measures have been issued concerning data protection. Following the interim report on privacy the Administrative Management Agency prepared the "Guidelines on EDP Security" which was agreed upon by the interministerial meeting of the vice-ministers in January 1976. The Guidelines, intended to establish a framework of security measures to be followed by ministries and agencies, cover the following items:

- Organisation of data security management

- Control of input/output sheets and other media

- Control of documents

- Control of operation of computers and terminals

- Control and safeguard of computer rooms and file storage

- Commission of services and transfer of data

(from [AMA1] page 38).

According to the guidelines, ministries and agencies with installations started activities to establish respective rules and, to date, almost all ministries and agencies have established their own rules.

The Ministry of Home Affairs sent the guidelines to all prefectures, cities, towns and villages which then used these guidelines as a basis for issuing their own rules. Some municipalities also issued their own rules of privacy in order to demonstrate that the personal data of their citizens would not be misused.

In 1975 MITI established the "Computer Systems Security Committee" which issued the "Guidelines of Security Measure Standards for Electronic Computer Systems"

in 1977. These Guidelines, distributed to the information processing service industry, contain standards for the installation and operation of computers,
totalling 368 items (see JR No.30, page 18). The standards are classified by
three grades.

After issuing the guidelines MITI urged dp users to implement the safety
measures, and since 1978 MITI has been granting loans through the Japan
Developing Bank for general companies which implement them (see Chapter
2.2.2.6 (5)). As from 1980 MITI has also been granting subsidies for the preparation of an Information Processing Service Company Register (see Chapter
2.2.2.4 (5)) which contains information about the data security measures of
each individual data processing centre, and which refers to the safety standards
and grades defined in MITI's guidelines.

3. THE COMPUTER INDUSTRY

3.1 Domestic and Foreign Computer Manufacturers in Japan

The total output of the machine industries in 1978 was 33.5 trillion Yen which is about 18% of the GNP, out of which the output of the electronic industry was 6.4 million Yen. In detail the output of the electronic industry was (in billion Yen):

—	consumer equipment	1,993
—	industrial equipment	2,571
	* communication equipment	810
	* electronics applied equipment (including computer and related equipment, 910 billion Yen)	1,323
	* electronic measuring equipment	224
	* office machines	200
—	parts and accessories for communication equipment	1,025
—	semiconductors, integrated circuits and receiving tubes	822

(see [JEIDA2] page 6).

The six major Japanese computer manufacturers are:

- Fujitsu Ltd.

- Hitachi Ltd.

- Nippon Electric Company (NEC, NICHIDEN)

- Tokyo Shibaura Electric Co. (TOSHIBA)

- Mitsubishi Electric Corporation

- Oki Electric Co.

Table 14 shows the total and EDP-related revenues of these companies. Concerning the production of information processing equipment Fujitsu is the biggest company and recently even overtook IBM Japan in the share of the Japanese computer market (see EJR Vol.6, page 136, and EJR Vol.8, page 1). In the statistics supplied by Datamation for the financial year 1977 (see Table 16), Hitachi is the biggest Japanese firm in the DP industry, and the fifth biggest in the world after IBM, Borroughs, NCR and CDC. The discrepancies between Table 14 and Table 16

Unit: million Yen, ( ) increasing rate

Makers	Revenue	Operating Profit	Ordinary Profit	Net Profit	Revenues from EDV Business
Domestic Makers					
Fujitsu	501 000 (13,6%)	38 072 (70,1%)	33 424 (102,9%)	15 645 (45,8%)	326 752 (7,9%)
Hitachi	1 698 130 (13,0%)	138 234 (29,0%)	106 652 (30,0%)	53 088 (41,0%)	216 000 (13,7%)
NEC	719 773 (17,0%)	39 598 (56,9%)	23 514 (104,0%)	13 131 (72,5%)	200 800 (20,3%)
Toshiba	1 427 670 (15,0%)	133 522 (71,0%)	75 322 (108,0%)	41 039 (112,0%)	50 400 (17,2%)
Mitsubishi	1 075 446 (15,1%)	80 015 (39,4%)	48 733 (45,8%)	25 106 (73,1%)	53 000 (17,7%)
Oki	165 501 (21,1%)	17 656 (200,0%)	9 881 (799,1%)	3 061 (--)	62 800 (31,1%)
Foreign Based Makers					
IBM Japan	324 245 (2,8%)		72 982 (4,5%)	36 242 (5,1%)	324 245 (2,8%)
Univac Japan	73 607 (2,8%)	4 208 (29,7%)	3 181 (51,8%)	1 340 (27,1%)	73 607 (2,8%)
Burroughs	54 600 (16,1%) Estimate	Not available	Not available	Not available	54 600 (16,1%) Estimate
NCR Japan	77 834 (5,6%)	8 782 (207%)	10 273 (227%)	5 283 (239%)	34 285 (-0,1%)

Table 14   Financial result of major mainframe makers, FY 1979 (March 79-April 80)
(Source: Computopia Magazine, November 1980)

Unit: 100 million Yen

Rank	Makers	FY 1976	FY 1977	FY 1978	FY 1979	FY 1980 Estimate
1	Fujitsu	2 396	2 745	3 030	3 268	3 530
2	IBM Japan	2 755	2 938	3 153	3 242	--
3	Hitachi	1 420	1 600	1 900	2 160	2 500
4	NEC	1 140	1 376	1 669	2 008	2 410
5	Univac Japan	704	678	716	736	770
6	Oki	483	444	479	628	653
7	Burroughs	435	450	470	546	--
8	Mitsubishi	320	380	450	530	620
9	Toshiba	592	591	430	504	580
10	NCR Japan	343	369	343	343	--

Table 15   Revenue trend of EDP business of major mainframe makers
(Source: Computopia Magazine, November 1980)

result from the fact that it is difficult to distinguish dp related revenues from the others. (In the case of Toshiba Datamation equates the dp revenues with the revenues of the Industrial Electronic Product Sector which are 22% of the total revenue (see [TOSHIBA2] page 5), while Table 14 refers only to the computer revenues, which are 3.5%).

Hitachi, Toshiba and Mitsubishi Electric are general electric machinery manufacturers, the portion of dp revenues being quite small (Hitachi 12.7%; Toshiba 3.5% (total Industrial Electronic Product Sector 22%); Mitsubishi 4.9%). NEC is mainly a telecommunications equipment manufacturer, the revenues of this product group being 39%, while the dp revenues are 28% of the total revenue. NEC is the biggest vendor of equipment for NTT. Fujitsu is almost a pure computer manufacturer, the dp revenues in FY 1978 being about 68.8% of its total revenue, (in 1979: 65.2%), while telecommunication equipment was 24.8%, semiconductors 3.7%, and electronic components 2.7% in FY 1978 (see [FUJI15]; [NEC8]; and [TOSHIBA2], page 5).

Table 17 shows the market share of the major Japanese and foreign computer manufacturers at the end of June, 1979. IBM has the biggest market share of the computers installed, but as can be seen from Table 15, Fujitsu overtook IBM in the sales of computers in 1979. However, IBM is still the strongest company concerning the sale of very-large-scale computers. Manufacturers of small computers are not listed because this table is restricted to computers which cost more than 30 million Yen. Oki is not mentioned because its computers are produced by Oki Univac, and these computers are listed under Univac.

Rank	Company	Country	DP Revenues ($M)	DP Revenues as % of Total Revenues	Total Revenues ($M)	Year Ending	No. of Employees
1	Hitachi Ltd.	Japan	$1,830	17%	$10,804	3/78	138,690
2	Toshiba	Japan	$1,633	22%	$ 7,847	3/78	113,800
3	Fujitsu Ltd.	Japan	$1,248	71%	$ 1,761	3/78	32,062
4	Cii-HB	France	$1,061	100%	$ 1,061	12/78	NA
5	ICL	Great Britain	$1,019	100%	$ 1,019	9/78	33,978
6	Olivetti	Italy	$ 789	42%	$ 1,879	12/78	66,073
7	Siemens AG	Germany	$ 703	5%	$15,675	9/78	322,000
8	Nippon Electric	Japan	$ 672	21%	$ 3,249	3/78	60,554
9	Philips N.V.	Netherlands	$ 602	4%	$14,000	12/78	400,000
10	Nixdorf AG	Germany	$ 554	100%	$ 554	12/78	9,200
11	Oki Electric	Japan	$ 200	35%	$ 575	3/78	14,201
12	Mitsubishi	Japan	$ 190	5%	$ 3,960	3/78	NA

NA = Not Available

Table 16   The top non-American firms in the DP-industry in FY 1977
(from Datamation, May 25th, 1979, page 79)

(value in million Yen)

name of manufacturer	amount of money	market share	number of installations
IBM	564,213	27.8%	1,075 systems
Fujitsu	415,767	20.5	2,748
Hitachi	320,615	15.8	1,260
NEC	296,181	14.6	1,490
Univac	237,782	11.7	628
Burroughs	86,253	4.3	494
NCR	49,218	2.4	331
Mitsubishi	44,230	2.2	472
other foreign manufacturers	15,740	0.8	104
domestic systems	1,076,793	53.0	5,970
foreign systems	953,206	47.0	2,632
total	2,029,999	100.0	8,602

Table 17 Computer installations at the end of June, 1979
(from Computopia 1, January 1980, page 22)

Besides the above mentioned six domestic manufacturers of general purpose computers there are several Japanese manufacturers of mini-computers, process control
computers, small business computers (SBC) and peripherals (see EJR Vol.6, page
128), the most important being:

Canon Inc.

Casio Computer Corporation

Japan Business Computer

Maruzen

Matsushita

Sharp Corporation

Uchida Yoko Co. Ltd.

The manufacturers of general purpose computers, however, are also leading in the
production of small-scale computers and peripherals. For example, the MELCOM
system of Mitsubishi is the best selling office computer on the Japanese market.

a) Method of entry = Acquisition of stock

Foreign investor	Japanese corporation	Japanese investor	Foreign capital participation rate (%)	Month and year of establishment	Line of business
IBM WTC	IBM Japan	-	100	10/50	Manufacturing, import/export, sale and maintenance of computers
NCR	NCR Japan	Japan Securities Service Co., Toyo Trust Bank, individuals	72.2	1/51	Manufacturing and sale of cash registers and accounting machines; import/export, sale and maintenance of computers
Sperry Rand Co.	Oki-Univac	Oki Electric, Mitsubishi Electric	36	3/58	Manufacturing of computers
Sperry Rand Co.	Nippon Univac	Mitsui & Co., Oki Electric, Mitsubishi Electric	34.2	3/58	Sale and maintenance of computers
Mincom Corp. Ltd.	Sumitomo 3M	Nippon Electric, Sumitomo Electric	50	9/61	Manufacturing, import/export and sale of magnetic tape and magnetic disk packs
Hewlett-Packard Co.	Yokogawa Hewlett-Packard	Yokogawa Electric	49	8/63	Manufacturing, import/export, sale and maintenance of measuring instruments, advanced-model desk computers and mini-computers
Memorex Corp.	Memorex Japan	-	100	7/68	Import and sale of magnetic tape and magnetic disk packs; maintenance of peripherals
Control Data Corp.	CDC Japan	C. Itoh	40	4/71	Sale and maintenance of computers
HISI (Yamatake Honeywell)	Nippon Electric Honeywell Information Systems	Nippon Electric	50	10/72	Manufacturing, sale and maintenance of key-to-tape units
The Singer Company	Hitachi Singer	Hitachi, Ltd.	50	7/73	Sale and maintenance of POS terminals and other devices
Nashua	Nashua Japan	-	100	12/73	Import/export and sale of magnetic disk packs
Burroughs	Burroughs	Takachiho Koeki	95	12/73	Sale of computers
Olivetti	Olivetti Japan	-	100	9/61	Sale and maintenance of mini-computers, peripherals and terminals

Table 18   Entry of foreign capital into the Japanese computer and related industries
(from JR No.33, March 1978, page 12)

b) Method of entry = Establishment of branch

Foreign investor	Japanese corporation	Japanese investor	Foreign capital participation rate (%)	Month and year of establishment	Line of business
IBM World Trade Asia Corp.	-	-	-	3/60	Coordination of activities of IBM subsidiaries in the Asian region
Control Data Far East Inc.	-	-	-	11/66	Research and liaison concerning computers
Digital Equipment Corp. International	-	-	-	7/68	Sale and maintenance of mini-computers
Recognition Equipment Japan Inc.	-	-	-	8/68	Sale and maintenance of OCR devices
Memorex Pacific Corp.	-	-	-	9/69	Export surveys and liaison of magnetic tape and magnetic disk packs
Honeywell Electronics Inc.	-	-	-	9/69	Liaison concerning technical support
Electronic Memories & Magnetic Corp.	-	-	-	4/71	Surveys and liaison concerning magnetic disk packs
Calcomp Pacific Corp.	-	-	-	-	Sale and maintenance of plotters
Texas Instrument Asia Ltd.	-	-	-	-	Sale and maintenance of mini-computers

Table 18   Entry of foreign capital into the Japanese computer and related industries (from JR No.33, March 1978, page 12)

Matsushita (market names National, Panasonic, Technics and Quasar) is the
biggest consumer electronics maker in Japan, and in 1979 was also Japan's top
industrial earner. In the past Matsushita also produced computers, the MADIC IIA
mainly for scientific calculation, but it withdrew from the computer market
because it thought that there were too many computer manufacturers in Japan.
Recently Matsushita introduced its National Business Computer BC-5000 into the
Japanese SBC market where already more than 50 domestic and foreign suppliers
are vying in heated competition (see EJR Vol.6, pages 9ff.)

Table 18 shows the foreign computer manufacturers on the Japanese market, as of
March 1978. All of the listed companies have been established before the
liberalisation of capital import in 1974 and 1975 (see Chapter 2.2.4). Before
the capital liberalisation the establishment of foreign capitalised companies
had to be approved by MITI. Normally the permission was granted on the condition
that the domestic industry would benefit from the technical knowledge of the
foreign company.

3.2   Manufacturers of General Purpose Computers and their Co-operation

3.2.1   The Computer Series of the Japanese Computer Manufacturers

By the end of the 1960s most of the Japanese computer manufacturers had licence
contracts with American manufacturers:

     NEC   with Honeywell

     Hitachi   "   RCA

     Toshiba   "   GEC (General Electric Co.)

     Mitsubishi   "   XEROX

     Oki   "   Univac

     Fujitsu   "   none.

The former computer series of the Japanese manufacturers were mostly based on
the series of , or were even identical with, their American partners. The former
Japanese general purpose computer series were

     FACOM 230 series of Fujitsu

     HITAC 8000 series of Hitachi

     MELCOM series of Mitsubishi

     NEAC 2200 series of NEC

     TOSBAC series of Toshiba

     OKITAC series of Oki

     OUK series of Nippon Univac   (see JR General Survey, Nov. 1971, page 17).

OKITAC and OUK series are identical computers which are produced by Oki Univac
and marketed by Nippon Univac as OUK series, and by Oki as OKITAC series.

However, the later models of these series and the present computer series have
been developed by the Japanese manufacturers themselves. Besides the knowledge
gained from their American partners they also gathered technical knowledge by
participating in the Project on the Development of a High Performance Electronic
Computer. This was the first "Large-scale Project" relating to electronic computers (see also Chapters 2.2.2.3 and 2.2.3,c) directed by AIST and financed fully
by MITI to the sum of 10.05 billion Yen from 1966-71 (see JR General Survey,
Nov.1971, pages 43-48; and CWP 1973, page 22).

Furthermore Fujitsu, Hitachi, NEC and NTT's Electrical Communications Laboratory
have co-operated in developing the DIPS computer system (Dendenkosha Information
Processing System) for NTT. The DIPS system is a general purpose computer which
is used by NTT in its networks for communication control (see also Chapter
2.3.3).

The present Japanese series of general purpose computers were developed under
the Technology Research Association of Advanced Computers Series from 1972-76
(see also Chapter 2.2.2.1). In this research association subsidised by MITI to a
total of 62.1 billion Yen, the six major Japanese computer manufacturers were
re-organised into 3 groups, each of which developed a computer series competitive with the IBM/370 series:

        Fujitsu-Hitachi group: M-series

        NEC-Toshiba group: ACOS series 77

        Mitsubishi-Oki group: COSMO series

a) M-Series

The M-series were jointly designed by Fujitsu and Hitachi. After the design
phase the two companies developed their product series separately, Fujitsu its
FACOM M-series and Hitachi its HITAC M-series. Initially Fujitsu developed the
M-160 and M-190 models and Hitachi the M-170 and M-180 models. But in addition
both companies introduced their own version of the other's models so that each
company has its own complete M-series computer production line, including small
to medium scale models originally called the V-series. According to the development history the semi-conductor devices of the HITAC and FACOM M-series are different, but their internal structure and software interface are very similar.
Nevertheless the two series are not plug-compatible because of differences in
structure sets, interfaces, etc.

In order to be successful on the international market the M-series has the same
architecture as the IBM/370 series. The change was more abrupt for Fujitsu than
for Hitachi because the HITAC 8000 series was already IBM compatible (because of
Hitachi's co-operation with RCA) while the FACOM 230 series was not IBM compatible at all. However, Fujitsu emphasised the IBM compatibility more than Hitachi
and the FACOM M-series is IBM compatible with relation to job control language,
source programs, load modules, and data sets. Thus most software written for
IBM/370 can run on the FACOM M-series computers. The co-operation between
Fujitsu and Amdahl was very helpful for the realisation of the IBM compatibility
(e.g. the first Amdahl computers were produced in the Fujitsu factories, see EJR
Vol.3, Nos 2 & 3, page 9; and EJR Vol.2, Nos.16 & 17, page 5).

The HITAC M-series is less IBM compatible than the FACOM M-series, since Hitachi has different marketing policies and a different user spectrum. While Fujitsu emphasised the aim to replace IBM computers by their own M models, Hitachi concentrated on using their M-series as upgrades for their 8000 series. It is estimated that nearly 80% of the M-series computers sold by Fujitsu replaced competing IBM models, while only 20-30% of Hitachi M-series computers were IBM replacements (see EJR Vol.4, No.21, page 3).

Fujitsu's operating systems for the M-series are OSIV/F2 and OSIV/F4 which are interface compatible with OSII/VS and OS/MVS of IBM. Their internal structure, however, is different by which Fujitsu claims to have improved the performance by about 20% according to benchmark tests. Fujitsu has another OS, the OSIV/X8 for migrators from FACOM 230 series.

Hitachi's operating systems are VOS1 (corresponding to OSIV/F2), VOS2, and VOS3 (corresponding to OSIV/F4). VOS1, VOS2 and VOS3 are completely upward compatible. Furthermore the OS of the 8000 series, EDOS-MSO, can run on some models of the M-series.

(For further information about the M-series computers see EJR Vol.3, Nos.2 & 3; EJR Vol.2, Nos.16 & 17, and Auerbach Report).

b) ACOS Series 77

ACOS Series 77 was jointly developed by NEC and Toshiba and was called 'ACOS Series 77 NEAC' when supported by NEC and 'ACOS Series 77 TOSBAC' when supported by Toshiba. The series had the models 100 to 900, which were introduced between 1973 and 1976. The NEAC and TOSBAC series are fundamentally the same in terms of main-frame and operating systems, differing only in peripherals. However in 1978 Toshiba withdrew from the large- and medium-scale computer business, so further development of the ACOS Series 77 is now carried out by NEC alone. Marketing and development of basic software is done by NEC-Toshiba Information Systems Inc. (NTIS), established in 1974 and owned 60% by NEC and 40% by Toshiba. The new models 50, 150, 250, 350, 450 and 550, introduced in 1978 and 1979, were developed by NEC alone using the newest technology, while Toshiba's computer business concentrates on mini-computers, small business computers, peripherals and terminal equipment – mainly TOSBAC system 15, TOSBAC system 55 and TOSBAC series 7.

Contrary to the M-series, ACOS Series 77 is not IBM compatible; e.g. it has a word structured memory. Because NEC is especially strong in the public administration market (38.8% of the market share in the first half of 1979) the replacement of IBM computers is not their main aim although ACOS Series 77 computers happened also to have replaced IBM machines. Therefore the compatibility with former series is quite important. The ACOS Series 77 has emulation functions in order to be compatible with the NEAC 2200 series; and ACOS 600 and 700 are even compatible with the TOSBAC 5600 system in terms of hardware and software. Compatibility of other TOSBAC systems with ACOS Series 77 requires conversion programs. Furthermore each model of the ACOS Series 77 is upward-compatible.

The operating systems of ACOS Series 77 are ACOS-2 for model 200, ACOS-4 for models 300 and upwards, and ACOS-6 for models 600 and upwards.

c) COSMO–Series

The MELCOM–COSMO / OKITAC–COSMO Series were jointly developed by Mitsubishi Electric Corporation, Oki Electric Company, and Mitsubishi Research Institute. Oki, however, has never announced any sales of the OKITAC–COSMO Series. The COSMO Series has the smallest market share of the three Japanese large–scale general purpose computer series (M, ACOS 77, and COSMO–series).

The COSMO–Series is not IBM compatible. It is based on the preceding MELCOM and XEROX Series, and application software developed for MELCOM and XEROX systems can be run unchanged on the COSMO Series after conversion.

The operating systems for the COSMO Series are Universal Multiprogramming System / Virtual Storage (UMS/VS), Universal Timesharing System / VS (UTS/VS), Balanced Processing Monitor (BPM), Relative Batch Monitor (RBM), and Dynamic Processing System (DPS) (see Auerbach Report).

Figure 19 is an overview of the series of Japanese computer manufacturers in comparison with IBM series. Recently further models have been introduced which are not listed, e.g. ACOS series 77, models 50, 150, etc., or COSMO 1000.

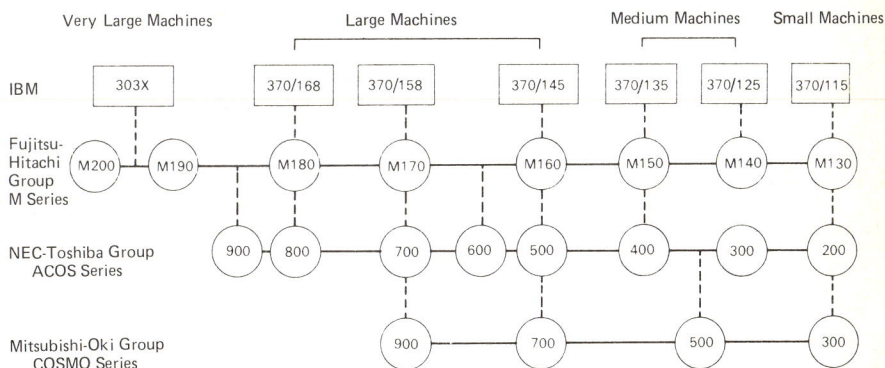

Figure 19   Comparison of IBM series and the series of the three groups of Japanese computer manufacturers (from CWP 1978, page 15)

3.2.2   The VLSI Technology Research Association

The VLSI Technology Research Association existed from 1976 until 1979. Its aim
was the development of large-scale integrated circuits for a next generation
computer in competition with IBM's future system. In this association the five
major Japanese computer manufacturers were organised into two groups (see Figure
20), the group laboratories being:

- the Computer Development Laboratories Ltd. (CDL) established by Fujitsu,
  Hitachi and Mitsubishi Electric

- and NEC-Toshiba Information Systems Inc. (NTIS) established, in 1974, by NEC
  and Toshiba for the development and marketing of basic software for the
  ACOS 77 Series.

Oki Electric was excluded from the research association because it had no experience in the development of super large-scale computers. Instead Oki
specialised in peripherals and small-scale computers.

The R & D costs for the 4 year period were 72 billion Yen, about 50% of which
equalling 30.54 billion Yen being the subsidy from MITI. The participating companies also paid 50% of the R & D expenditures plus management costs.

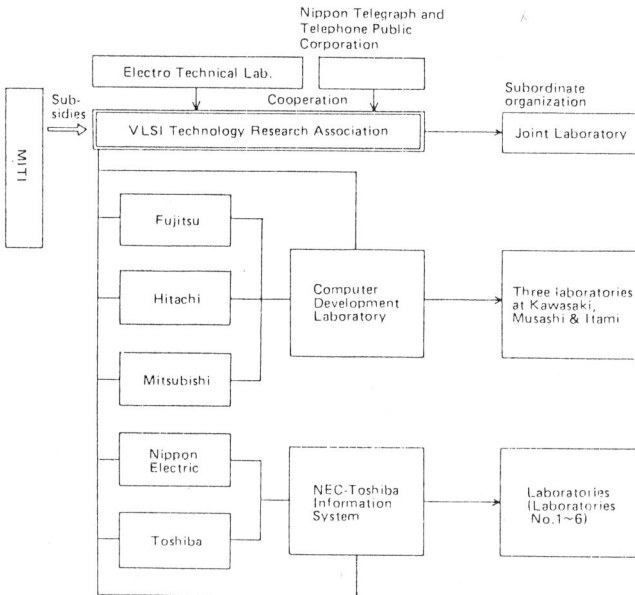

Figure 20   VLSI research and development system (from JR No.34 page 15)

The VLSI Technology Research Association co-operated closely with the Electrical Communications Laboratory (ECL) of NTT and with the Electro-technical Laboratory (ETL) of MITI (see Figure 20). Furthermore, ECL carried out a three-year development program for ultra LSI from 1975 until 1978 with a total R & D budget of 20 billion Yen, the research being carried out jointly by Fujitsu, Hitachi and NEC (see EJR Vol.3, Nos.2 & 3, page 8).

The VLSI Technology Research Association carried out its R & D activities at its joint laboratory and the group laboratories of CDL and NTIS. The joint laboratory was responsible for basic research, its researchers being transferred from the above mentioned five companies and from MITI's ETL. The group laboratories carried out research on the application of the technology and its practical use, the researchers being transferred from their parent companies.

The R & D activities can be subdivided into the following six items:

- microfabrication technology (down to a sub-micron level using electron beam, X-ray exposure, etc.)

- crystal technology (crystal growing, especially of defect-free large diameter silicon crystals)

- design technology (in order to accomodate many small size elements in a small size chip area)

- process technology (suitable for processing a pattern down to sub-micron levels)

- test and evaluation technology

- device technology.

The research association was very effective and by its results the Japanese computer industry became very advanced in the field of VLSI technology. For example, NTT and NTIS were the first in the world to develop (but not as yet to produce) 256K bit RAM chips by different technologies - i.e. electrical beam technology by NTT and optical technology by NTIS.

The research association developed about 600 patents, most of which are owned by the participating companies. Companies which were not members of the VLSI Technology Research Association can purchase the patents; also many foreign companies, which have cross-licencing contracts with the five Japanese companies concerned, acquired these patents. Recently MITI also decided to open its own patents (approximately 30) for international licencing (see EJR Vol.6, page 111).

Besides the five companies which were members of the VLSI Technology Research Association there are many other companies which developed VLSI technologies. While the research association developed integrated circuits for use in computers only, the aims of the non-participating companies were sometimes different, e.g. Nikon developed integrated circuits for use in cameras, and NTT circuits for data communication.

In September 1979 the production value percentages of semi-conductors (by product category) was:

- computer memory   31%

- desk-top computer 16%

- mini computer   15%

- watches   16%

- TV sets   7%

- game machines   15%

(from EJR Vol.6, page 114).

Because of the current worldwide shortage of semi-conductor parts, Japanese semi-conductor parts manufacturers continued to produce at full capacity with a total value of 914 billion Yen in FY 1979. For FY 1980 they planned high invest-ments for production facilities listed in Table 21. The amounts include invest-ments in foreign countries. NTT is not listed because it does not produce semi-conductor parts, but only develops them (see also EJR Vol.8, page 19).

Manufacturers	Major Applications	Amount ($ Million)
NEC	Computers, Communication Equipment	99
Fujitsu	Computers, Communication Equipment	61
Hitachi	Computers, Consumer Electronics	48
Sharp	Office Equipment	42
Matsushita Electronic	Electronic Devices	42
Toshiba	Consumer Electronics	42
Ricoh	Office Equipment	35
Mitsubishi Electric	Computers, Consumer Equipment	34
Oki Electric	Communication Equipment	25
Casio	Office Equipment	21
Sanyo Electric	Consumer Electronics	46 *

* Three years total from 1980-1982.

Table 21   Investments in semi-conductor plants and facilities by
            major Japanese manufacturers (for FY 1980), (from EJR
            Vol.6, page 115)

3.2.3   The Computer Basic Technology Research Association

While former research associations promoted mainly hardware, research of software is the main aim of the Computer Basic Technology Research Association
(CBTRA, in Japanese DENSHI KEISANKI KIHON GIJUTSU KENKYU KUMIAI). The budget for
the total 5 year period 1979-1983 is 56.4 billion Yen, of which 23.5 billion
Yen, i.e. 50% of the R & D costs, being the subsidy from MITI. The participating
companies also pay 50% of the R & D expenditures (23.5 billion Yen) plus 9.4
billion Yen management costs (see also Chapter 2.2.2.1).

Only mainframers or closely related companies are members of the research association. The association is organised in two groups:

1)   basic software technology (operating systems)

2)   technology for new peripheral devices.

The members of the first group are:

- Computer Development Laboratory (CDL)
- Fujitsu
- Hitachi
- Mitsubishi Electric
- NEC
- NTIS
- Toshiba.

The members of the second group are:

- Fujitsu
- Hitachi
- Matsushita
- Mitsubishi Electric
- NEC
- Oki
- Sharp
- Toshiba.

The subjects of research of the basic software technology development group are:

- basic technology
- network management technology
- data base management technology
- virtual machine technology
- very high level language processor technology
- Japanese text processing technology.

The research subjects of the development of the new peripheral devices group
are:

- Kana to Kanji conversion technology (especially text input devices)
- Japanese voice input technology

- Japanese OCR technology including handwritten text
- Japanese printer technology, in particular for Kanji
- very large disk device technology
- very large bubble device technology.

In contrast with the VLSI Technology Research Association, CBTRA does not have its own laboratories. The R & D work is carried out in the laboratories of the participating companies. Because of the difference between the existing operating systems of the members, only the principles of new basic software is to be researched, and the member companies will realise these principles in their own software products. This does not mean, however, that the research is merely theoretical; real technology and its evaluation is the subject of research.

The presidency of the research association changes every year. In 1980 the president was from Mitsubishi, and the two Vice-Presidents were from Hitachi and Oki.

CBTRA is not the first large nation-wide project for the promotion of software. In 1966 the Nippon Software Co. (NSC) was established by Fujitsu, Hitachi, NEC and the Industrial Bank of Japan, with full governmental backing. It received a 3 billion Yen order from MITI for the development of an operating software for a new super-large-scale computer from ETL. But in 1972 NSC went bankrupt and left basic software for a prototype computer model which was not compatible with the specifications of any manufacturer. However, it left a well-trained staff of about 300 software experts who helped raise the level of software of the Japanese information industry (see EJR Vol.6, page 43).

3.2.4   The Structure of the Japanese Computer Industry

Figure 22 shows the structure of the Japanese computer industry excluding the manufacturers of mini-computers, small business computers and peripheral equipment. The computer industry is centered around the three groups of manufacturers: NEC/Toshiba, Hitachi/Fujitsu and Mitsubishi/Oki. NEC-Toshiba Information Systems (NTIS), owned 60% by NEC and 40% by Toshiba, is the marketing and software development company for the ACOS series 77. Nippon Peripheral is a joint venture of Fujitsu and Hitachi for the development of magnetic devices, and FACOM HITAC for the marketing of M-series computers on the government market. CDL is the Computer Development Laboratory established by Fujitsu, Hitachi and Mitsubishi (see Chapter 3.2.1). For information about the 'tie-ups' between Japanese and foreign manufacturers see Chapter 3.4.

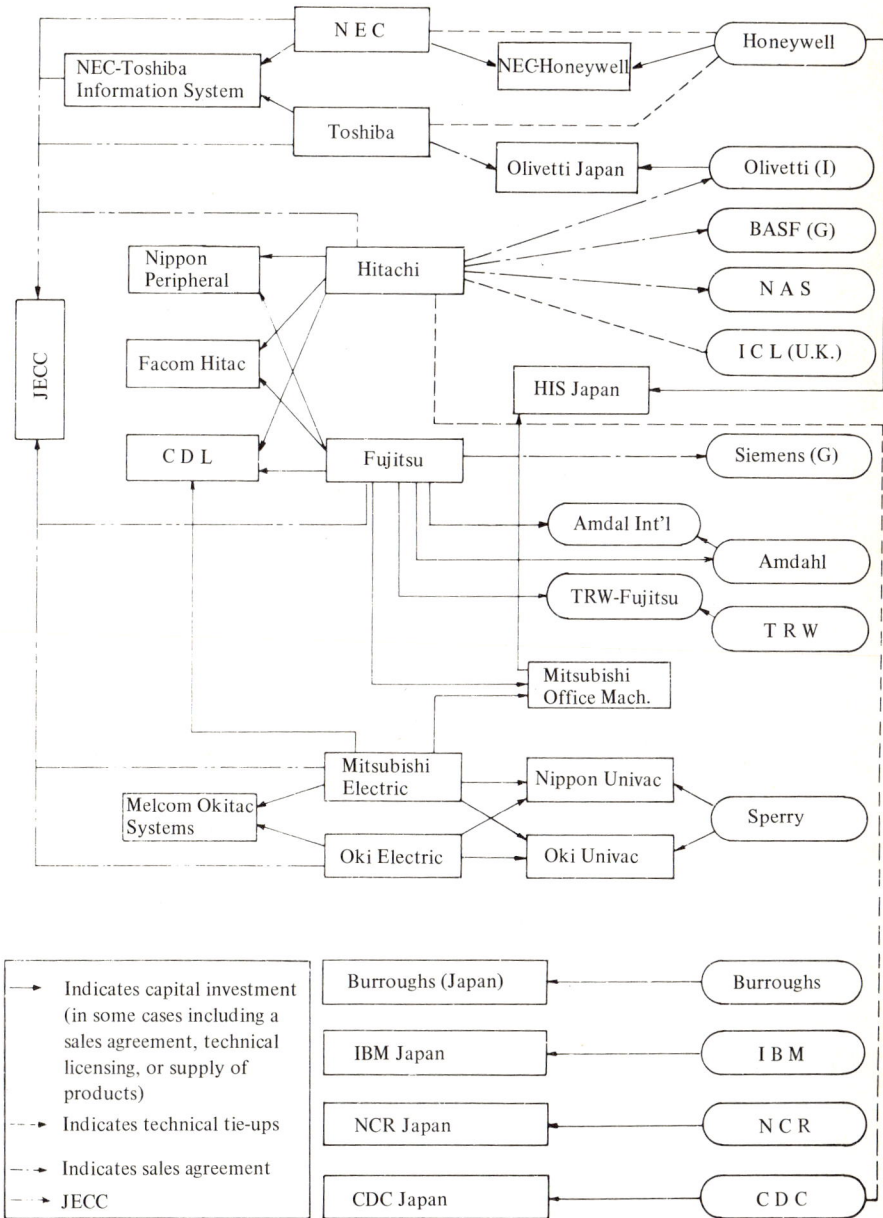

Figure 22   Major joint ventures and tie-ups of computer manufactures (from [JIPDEC17], page 9)

3.3   Organisations of the Japanese Computer Industry

3.3.1   Japan Electronic Computer Co. (JECC)

The Japan Electronic Computer Co. (JECC) is a joint rental and sales firm of the
Japanese computer manufacturers. It was established in 1961 by the Japanese computer manufacturers under the guidance of MITI. The JECC stockholders   include
the main Japanese computer manufacturers (see e.g.   JR No.34,   page 4; or CWP
1977, page 17).

The main task of JECC is the rental business for the computer manufacturers. If
a client wishes to rent a Japanese manufacturer's computer, the manufacturer
sells the computer to JECC and JECC rents the computer to the client. The
capital for the rental business is financed out of capital paid by the
shareholders, by loans from the Japan Development Bank (JDB), (see also chapter
2.2.2.6), and by financial institutions, insurance companies and foreign banks
(in Japan).

(in Yen 100 million)

Year	Computer Purchases	Loans from Japan Development Bank	Capital
1961	11	4	11
1962	32	8	21
1963	59	15	32
1964	117	25	47
1965	208	55	71
1966	269	70	106
1967	368	70	142
1968	666	90	189
1969	825	155	284
1970	922	215	425
1971	874	390	534
1972	892	150	597
1973	1,014	215	597
1974	1,244	325	597
1975	1,264	530	597
1976	1,340	430	597
1977	1,342	490	647

Japan electronic computer finance (from CWP 1977, page 17)

Further activities of JECC also aim to support the Japanese computer industry:

-   JECC compiles a program register of programs developed by the Japanese compu-
    ter manufacturers.

-   Since 1968 JECC has been conducting an annual survey on data centres and software houses, the "Japan Data Centre and Software Houses Directory" (see CWP 1977, page 18).

- JECC collects the propositions for tax reductions from the computer manufacturers in connection with the General Purpose Software Package Registration System (see also chapters 2.1.3.2 d; and 2.2.2.6).

- JECC promotes joint activities of the computer manufacturers, e.g. it participated in organising the Committee for Study and Research on Fifth Generation Computers.

- Since 1978 JECC has been carrying out the software rental business of the Japanese computer manufacturers (see EJR Vol.6,page 49).

3.3.2   Japan Electronic Industry Development Association

The Japan Electronic Industry Development Association (JEIDA) was established in 1958 as a non-profit making organisation by the leading manufacturers in the Japanese electronic industry. By the end of 1979 it had 88 regular members and 43 associate members. (A list of members is included in [JEIDA1].)

The following activities are carried out by its General Affairs Department and its Development Department:

- study of the patent and tax system

- investigation of important subjects relating to the electronic industries

- the issuing and distribution of monthly journals and other publications

- research and development of electronic computers, automated equipments and systems, and other applied electronic apparatus as well as electronic components and materials, rationalisation of production and promotion of computer utilisation

- technical research and standardisation of electronic components and devices

- management of the Electronic Materials Development Centre

  (from [JEIDA1] page 1).

Furthermore, JEIDA has set up various technical committees organised under its Board of Directors. A list of these committees is shown in Table 23.

Two important documents of these committees in the field of information processing are

a) an investigation about software engineering in Japan (of which parts have been translated into English, see [JEIDA3]), and

b) a study about the future of the electronic industry in Japan (also translated into English, see [JEIDA4]).

```
Board of Directors
  ↓
    (Sub-Board of Directors)          (Committees)
               ↓                           ↓
     _____      ┌--Business Administration
    |                        |     |--Taxation Systems
                                   └--Future of Electronic Industry

                                   ┌--Co-ordination of Computers
                                   |--Technology of Computers
                                   |--Standardisation of Computers
      _____             |--Safety of Data Processing Equipments
  __ |Policy Board |_____      |--Patent of Computers
     |on Computers |            |--Technology of Software
     |_____|           |--Co-ordination of Peripheral
                                   |    Equipment & Terminals
                                   |--Co-ordination of Office Computers
                                   |--Co-Ordination of Minicomputers
                                   └--DATA SHOW '79

                                   ┌--System Planning
                                   |--Research on Future Office Systems
                                   |--Co-ordination of Industrial Computer
                                   |    Systems
                                   |--Technology of Industrial Computer
      _____             |    Systems
  __ |Policy Board |_____      |--Standardisation of Industrial Computer
     |on Systems   |            |    Systems
     |_____|           |--Technology of Microcomputers
                                   |--Development of Microcomputers
                                   |--Co-ordination of Microprocessors
                                   |--Research for Instrumentation Systems
                                   |--Research for Computing-Instrumentation
                                   |    Systems
                                   └--Research for Rehabilitation Equipment
                                        Systems

      _____
     |Management Board|
  __ |on Electrical   |-----Technology of Electronic Materials
     |Materials       |
     |_____|

     _____      ┌--Technology of Electronic Devices
    |                        |     └--Standardisation of Silicon Technology
```

Table 23: Committees of JEIDA organised in 1979
         (from "Guide to JEIDA" published by JEIDA, 1980, see [JEIDA1]).

3.3.3   Centre of the International Co-operative for Computerisation

The Centre of the International Co-operative for Computerisation (CICC) was established in 1976 within JEIDA as a non-profit making organisation supported by the Japanese government. Its members are leading computer manufacturers and software houses, including Fujitsu, Hitachi, Mitsubishi Electric, Matsushita, NEC, Oki Electric, Omron Tateisi Electronics, Sharp, Toshiba, Computer Applications Co. (CAC), Nippon Algorithm Co. (NALGO) and Nippon Electronics Development Co. (NED).

The aim of CICC is to promote the business activities of the Japanese information industry in the developing countries in accordance with the scientific technological co-operation between Japan and these countries. The strategies are:

- provision of information material about Japanese information technology

- performance of seminars and training courses

- dispatch of technical advisers

- establishment of dp service centres and training centres

- inclusion of computerisation into bilateral co-operation apreements

- co-operation with various international organisations

       (see [CICC1]).

Through CICC the Japanese information industry has an efficient organisation which supports their activities in the developing countries. For example, a delegation from CICC recently visited China and gave a series of lectures on Chinese character processing technologies (see EJR Vol.6, page 133).

3.4   Imports and Exports of Computers

Japan imports more computers and related equipment than it exports. In 1978 the ratio of export to import was 0,63 but, as shown in the table below, this ratio was higher than in previous years. In 1977 the ratio had been 0,28 and in 1976 0,30.

The main recipients of Japanese exports were USA (31.2% of the total in 1977), Australia (12.7%), and West Germany (6.7%). The amounts include exports by foreign capitalised companies manufacturing in Japan, e.g. IBM Japan. The overwhelming majority of imports came from USA amounting to 63.1% of the 1976 total (see JR No.37, pages 12-14; and JR No.41, pages 42-43).

a) exports of computers   (value in million Yen)

	digital main- frames	digital periph- erals	sub- total	related equip- ment	total	annual increase (%)
1975	11,089	9,628	20,717	834	21,551	14.5
1976	11,396	27,296	38,692	587	39,279	82.3
1977	17,866	22,135	40,001	999	41,000	4.4
1978	21,834	47,251	69,085	601	69,686	70.0

b) imports of computers   (value in million Yen)

	main- frames	periph- erals	sub- total	parts	total	annual increase (%)
1975	45,504	51,870	97,374	33,285	130,659	− 9.8
1976	49,793	46,174	95,667	36,954	132,121	1.5
1977	54,491	54,755	109,246	37,225	146,471	10.4
1978	36,346	45,199	81,545	29,455	111,000	− 24.2

Table 24   Exports and imports of computers
            (from JR No.41, pages 42 and 43)

Exports to Asian developing countries are still low in comparison with exports
to America and Europe. But Japan recognises this region as being an important
market for the future, and Japanese companies are actively developing this
market. The Centre of the International Co-operative for Computerisation (CICC)
co-ordinates these activities. Because Japan developed the Kanji processing
facilities for its own language (which has no Latin characters) it has important
advantages in exporting computer systems with Kanji processing facilities to
those countries which have similar language problems, especially to China (see
also Chapter 6.3). Recently, however, foreign companies have also developed
Kanji text processing systems, among others IBM, CDC and Burroughs.

Japan's large exports to Australia show today's importance of the pacific
market.

In order to enhance their exports the Japanese computer manufacturers founded
various subsidiaries abroad and made business 'tie-ups' with foreign companies.
Below are listed such activities (but the list is not exhaustive):

a) subsidiaries of Japanese companies abroad

- NEC Information Systems Inc. (NECIS): sales company for USA and Canadian markets for the SBC computer ASTRA

- NEC Systems Laboratory Inc. (NECSYL): market research and laboratories in USA and Europe

- NEC Microcomputers Inc. for the production of semi-conductors and micro-processors in USA

- NEC Computers Singapore Ltd. (NECOS): sales of the SBC NEAC System 100 in SE-Asian market

- Fujitsu America: for sale of electro-mechanical parts, discrete components, semi-conductors, sub-assembly of 470/V6 and other Amdahl computers, etc. (see EJR Vol.6, page 63)

- FACOM Korea

- FACOM Australia PTY Finance

- Fujitsu do Brasil

- Fujitsu Espana

- Okidata for marketing of peripheral equipment, printers and disk drives

- MELCOM Business Systems Inc. for the sale of SBC in USA

- Toshiba America for marketing electronic computers

- Hitachi America Ltd. for sale of electronic equipment including computers in USA

- Hitachi Semi-conductors (America) Inc.

b) joint ventures between Japanese and foreign companies (see Figure 22)

- HIS Japan: Honeywell and Mitsubishi Office Machines

- Amdahl International: Amdahl and Fujitsu (see EJR Vol.6, page 63)

- TRW-Fujitsu: Fujitsu and TRW for the sale of Fujitsu computers in the American market under the Fujitsu brand name

- Nippon Univac: Sperry Rand, Mitsubishi Electric and Oki Electric

- Oki Univac: Sperry Rand, Mitsubishi Electric and Oki Electric (see EJR Vol.3, Nos.2 & 3, Page 11)

- FACOM Computer Philippines Inc.: Fujitsu and the Martel Group in the Philippines (see EJR Vol.3, No.10, page 8)

- Fuji Electronic Components: Fuji Electric Co. and Siemens AG of West Germany for the production of semi-conductor parts (see Journal of the

Asian Electronic Union, June, 1980, page 31)

c) sales of Japanese computers and peripherals to foreign companies on OEM basis

-   FACOM M Series, large models to Siemens

-   HITAC M Series, large models to Olivetti

-   Hitachi's computers to National Advanced System, a subsidiary of National Semi-Conductors

-   Hitachi's disk controllers to BASF (Germany)

-   Fujitsu's magnetic tape drives to Memorex (see EJR Vol.6, page 63)

-   Fujitsu computers to Amdahl

-   HITAC M180 to Itel Corp.

d) agreements in technical co-operation

-   Fujitsu and ICL concerning micro-processor technology and large-scale computers (M380 and 382)

-   NTT and IBM concerning telecommunication technology

4. THE INFORMATION PROCESSING INDUSTRY

The figure below shows the structure of the information industry.

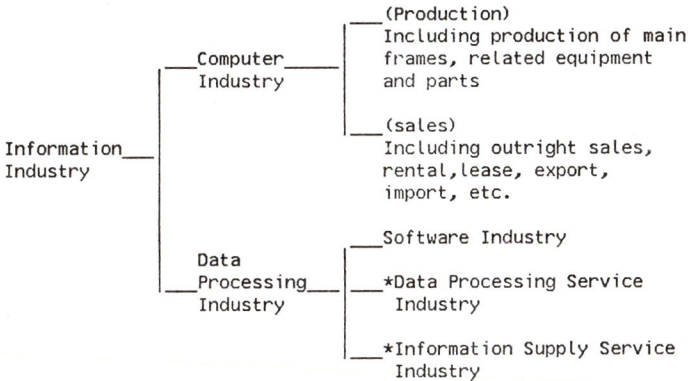

```
                                            ___(Production)
                                            |  Including production of main
                    ___Computer_____        |  frames, related equipment
                    |  Industry             |  and parts
                    |                        |
                    |                        |___(sales)
   Information___   |                           Including outright sales,
   Industry         |                           rental, lease, export,
                    |                           import, etc.
                    |
                    |                        ___Software Industry
                    |  Data                  |
                    |__Processing___    _____|___*Data Processing Service
                       Industry             |     Industry
                                            |
                                            |___*Information Supply Service
                                                 Industry
```

* The businesses which provide on-line data processing services and on-line
information supply services via communication circuits are sometimes referred
to jointly by a single term such as "Data Network Industry" or "Data Communications Industry".

(from CWP 1978, page 13).

The specifications, however, are ambiguous because sometimes the data processing
industry (DP industry) is called the information processing industry or the computer service industry. In addition to the listed types of industry there are
also system houses which are selling turnkey systems consisting of hard- and
software.

The difference between the above listed types of information processing companies is not very clear because many companies are carrying out software development as well as data processing and other services. This is illustrated by the
fact that 26 members of the Software Industry Association (SIA) are also members
of the Japan Information Processing Centre Association (JIPCA).

According to the annual "Survey on the State of Special Service Businesses"
published by MITI there were approximately 1300 information processing companies
with about 1640 establishments at the end of 1977 (see JR No.39, page 1). Their
annual sales amounted to 412 billion Yen which are about 0.22% of Japan's Gross
National Product (GNP). However, the total sales of the top 50 companies (see
table 26) amount to 151 billion Yen which is about 40% of the sales of the whole

75

data processing industry. This means that there are many small companies. In 1977 the annual sales per employee was only 7.75 million Yen (for 71,641 employees), which is not very high. These figures show that the data processing industry has a low productivity rate.

The following table (Table 25) shows a breakdown of sales by activities of the data processing industry for 1977.

	million Yen	
business calculations	123,927	30.0 %
other calculations	14,650	3.6 %
software development and programming	77,307	18.7 %
card punching	55,410	13.4 %
machine time sales	17,348	4.2 %
personnel dispatch	52,564	12.7 %
information supply services	23,811	5.8 %
various surveys	31,148	7.6 %
others	16,415	4.0 %
total sales (of 1309 companies with 1640 establishments)	412,581	100.0 %

Table 25   Breakdown of sales by operation for computer service
           firms for 1977 (from JR No.39, page 2)

The highly qualified activities are comparatively low, especially software development, which is less than 20% of the activities. On the other hand, low quality activities such as card punching, machine time sales and personnel dispatch amount to almost 30% of the total sales.

The computer service companies can be distinguished according to their origin:

-        affiliated companies of computer manufacturers

-        affiliated companies of large-scale users

-        independent companies

-        jointly established companies

-        affiliated companies of public institutions

(compare JR No.37, page 22).

In Table 26 the largest companies are affiliates of computer manufacturers and large-scale users, e.g. Nippon Business Consultant and Hitachi Software Engineering (Hitachi), NEC Information Service and NEC Software (NEC), Facom Information Processing Co. (Fujitsu), Nomura Computer Systems (Nomura Securities Co.), Japan Information Service and Sumisho Computer Service (Sumitomo Bank), Century Research Centre (C. Itoh & Co.), M.S.K.Systems (Mitsubishi).

Rank	Company	Sales (million Yen) 1978	Sales per Employee (Y10,000) 1978	Increase over 1977 (%)	FY 1977 Sales (million Yen)	FY 1976 Sales (million Yen)
1	Nippon Business Consultant	11 725	1 016	16,9%	10 030	8 094
2	Computer Service Corporation	8 060	536	81,7%	4 437	NA
3	Mitsui Knowledge Industry	7 889	3 034	5,0%	7 516	6 200
4	Nomura Computer System	7 874	2 072	19,3%	6 600	5 861
5	Japan Information Processing Service	7 165	877	11,2%	6 444	6 022
6	NEC Software	7 083	1 331	63,1%	4 342	NA
7	Japan Information Service	6 000	1 087	25,0%	4 800	4 250
8	NEC Information Service	5 960	2 413	0,3%	5 940	4 180
9	Hitachi Software Engineering	5 655	467	17,3%	4 795	3 580
10	Intec	5 186	532	14,0%	4 550	3 728
11	Facom Information Processing Co. Ltd.	4 800	823	-	NA	4 735
12	Century Research Centre	4 758	753	7,2%	4 440	3 650
13	Koyoei Information Processing Service Centre	4 543	851	30,1%	3 493	2 854
14	M.S.K. Systems	4 534	4 489	6,3%	4 267	3 390
15	Toyo Information Systems	4 301	935	13,2%	3 800	2 730
16	Sumisho Computer Service	4 245	1 740	20,3%	3 529	3 034
17	T.K.C.	4 223	1 860	21,1%	3 487	2 533
18	Diawa Computer Service	4 182	2 698	4,7%	3 994	3 457
19	Japan Business Automation	3 965	911	-	NA	2 995
20	Nippon Electronics Development	3 964	531	-	NA	NA
21	Marketing Intelligence Cooperation	3 875	999	7,3%	3 611	2 845
22	Central Systems	3 712	775	15,9%	3 203	2 432
23	Fujigin Computer Service	3 602	1 078	5,8%	3 403	2 870
24	The Daiko Electronic & Communication Co., Ltd.	3 317	1 040	10,3%	3 007	2 668
25	Tokyo Security Computer Centre	3 035	2 550	11,0%	2 734	2 340
26	Nissei Computer Service	2 781	746	63,3%	1 703	1 317
27	Kansai Electronic Computing Centre	2 446	1 015	29,7%	1 886	1 699
28	NCR Japan	2 369	1 112	1,4%	2 336	2 157
29	Tsuzuki Denki Kogyo	2 323	1 249	14,0%	2 038	1 601
30	C.E.C.	2 313	598	-	NA	NA
31	Nippon System Development	2 024	370	25,9%	1 608	1 258
32	Chuo Computer Systems	2 023	1 005	6,9%	1 892	1 614
33	Hokkaido Business Automation	1 853	904	11,2%	1 666	1 285
34	Data Process Consultant	1 832	353	25,8%	1 456	1 128
35	Seibu Johu Centre	1 800	783	12,8%	1 596	1 400
36	Computer Applications	1 715	917	18,9%	1 442	NA
37	Tohoku Computer Service	1 675	941	13,8%	1 472	1 320
38	The Kaihatsu Computing Centre Ltd.	1 663	1 131	13,2%	1 469	NA
39	Kozokeikaku Engineering	1 656	1 104	11,4%	1 487	1 286
40	Tokyo Data Centre	1 650	825	11,5%	1 480	1 500

Table 26 The top 40 information processing service firms in Japan
(from "Register and General Survey of the Information Processing Industry", published in [JIPDEC17], page 13)

The largest independent company in Table 26 is Intec (No.10) which mainly offers time-sharing services. Most independent data processing companies are small or medium sized firms which are working subsidiarily for computer manufacturers, large-scale users, organisations and their affiliated companies. The affiliated companies are organised according to the needs of the parent firm. The affiliates of general companies are mostly former data processing companies of their parent firm which have become independent. For example, Kaihatsu Computing Service Centre (KCC, No.38 in Table 26) is owned 90% by the Electric Power De-velopment Co. (EPDC), and 10% by banks; and approximately 50% of its activities are contracts from EPDC.

The information processing activities of the dp divisions of Japanese and foreign computer manufacturers in Japan are not listed in Table 26. If they had been taken into consideration they would have taken the first places (see JR No.39, page 3).

4.1   Data Processing Service Industry

It is difficult to distinguish between information processing service companies and software houses because the business activities may include software devel-opment and information supply services as well as data processing services. There are supposed to be (a) about 1300 information processing companies, (b) about 1000 dp service companies and (c) 600 to 1000 software houses, which means that between 300 and 700 dp companies are supposed to belong to both types of industry.

The dp service companies (or computer centres) are usually bigger than normal software houses because they chiefly have computers and equipment, while many software houses merely sell their programming services.

NTT is a special type of competitor for the dp industry. On the one hand NTT rents communication circuits, while on the other hand it also provides various computing services by the following services - DEMOS (multi-access on-line sys-tem), DRESS (real-time sales-management system) and DIALS (arithmetic and library system). Furthermore there is competition from general enterprises. Ac-cording to a survey by JIPCA (Japan Information Processing Centre Association) 15% of enterprises which have computers constantly accept outside work and 5% occasionally accept work.

The chief purposes of the service bureaus owned by computer manufacturers, how-ever, are to promote the computer sales of their parent company and to support their users. The computer centres are organised by the parent manufacturer which encourages, or insists on, the use of its own computers (see Table 27).

Name (secretariat)	Date of founding	Nature of business	Number of members
TOSBAC Service Bureau Council (c/o Computer Business Department, Tokyo Shibaura Electric Co., Ltd.)	August, 1973	• Exchange of business and technical information, studies of standardization. • Joint utilization of equipment, personnel and software. • Development and joint bidding for large-size projects. • Publication of organ "TOSBAC Computing Center Council News".	19 companies (25 places of business)
NEAC Data Processing Service Business Group (NEC Information Service Ltd.)	September, 1972	• Nation-wide bidding for contracts for service jobs. • Development work for joint systems. • Concentrated personnel education. • Publication of organ "NEAC Center Reports." • Development of "inhabitants' living information system" under commission of Ministry of International Trade and Industry. • Development of "comprehensive information system on housing tracts for wholesalers" under commission of MITI.	25 companies (38 places of business)
HITAC Information Center Network Council (Nippon Business Consultant Co., Ltd.)	July, 1968	• Education: advice for new graduates and beginners, courses for intermediate and advanced levels. • Joint bidding for contracts for large-size jobs from the Ministry of Agriculture and Forestry. • Distribution of "HITAC Network News" (a monthly organ).	35 companies (52 places of business)
Service Bureau Univac Group (Japan Univac, Ltd.)	April, 1970	• Liaison, collaboration, and mutual assistance in business matters. • Education, lectures, research, study trips. • Publication and distribution of necessary materials.	30 companies (46 places of business)
FACOM Computer Service Network (F.I.P.)	September, 1973	• Research in software and exchange of information. • Joint research and development of software. • Technical guidance and training of members. • Mutual dispatching of specialists, joint use of computers.	37 companies

Table 27   Organisations of manufacturer-affiliated service bureaus (from JR No.37, page 23)

4.1.1   Japan Information Processing Centre Association

The Japan Information Processing Centre Association (JIPCA) is the organisation
of the dp service industry. Founded in 1970 by 60 dp service companies it has
now over 120 member companies, representing 12% of all DP service companies but
more than 60% of their sales (see Table 28).

	No. of Enter- prises	Sales Amount	Total No. of Employees	Annual Sales per Enterprise	Number of Employees per Enterprise	Annual Sales per Employee
Industry total	1,009	306.9 bill. Yen	59,025	(A) 305 mill. Yen	(C) 58	(E) 5.2 mill. Yen
Members	122	192.3 bill. Yen	24,722	(B) 1,576 mill. Yen	(D) 203	(F) 7.77 mill. Yen
Members share	12%	62.6%	41%	(B)/(A)=5.2	(C)/(D)=3.5	(E)/(F)=1.5

Table 28   Shares of JIPCA members (from JR No. 39, page 11)

JIPCA's main activities involve the setting up of committees for research,
surveys, exchanges of information, etc. An important activity in the past few
years was the implementation of MITI's safety measures in order to build up the
confidence of users. In 1977 MITI had proposed safety standards for computer
centres which have the rankings of A, B, and C. It is expected that by the end
of 1980 the dp service industry will achieve the B ranking which covers over 280
items (see also Chapter 2.5).

4.1.2   Japan Punch Centre Association

The Japan Punch Centre Association, founded in 1970, has about 50 members. It
co-operates with JIPCA and SIA in order to promote the interests of the information processing industry.

4.2   The Software Industry

Because of the problems already discussed, the situation of the software industry is not yet very stable. Table 29 shows the business distribution of major
software companies.

	FY 1975	FY 1976	FY 1977	FY 1980 (Est.)	FY 1984 (Est.)
Software development	54.7%	61.7%	64.6%	59.0%	56.9%
Development and sales of software packages	0.3%	0.5%	0.6%	2.1%	4.8%
Centre services	37.5%	30.9%	27.8%	26.7%	26.0%
System houses (turnkey systems): including sales of equipment	2.7%	2.7%	3.2%	6.8%	8.4%
Other	4.8%	4.2%	3.8%	5.4%	3.9%
Total	100.0%	100.0%	100.0%	100.0%	100.0%

Table 29   Sales distribution of major software companies
by type of business
(from a SIA survey, published in JR No.39, page 13)

The portion of software development is quite high (about 60%), but the portion
of development and sales of software packages is very low, only about 3%. This
fact shows the lack of independent business activities of the software industry.
In fact, most of their software development is subsidiary work for computer
manufacturers and large companies. Figure 30 shows the hierarchy of software
companies which are working for Nippon Electric Co. (NEC).

NEC Software Ltd., a software company fully owned by NEC, receives orders for
software development from NEC, then distributes them to the first hierarchy of
software houses for execution, which in their turn give sub-contracts to the
next level of software houses, etc. About 70 software companies are working in
this way for NEC Software Ltd. Furthermore NEC gives contracts for software development directly to about 10 software companies. Other computer manufacturers,
general companies and industrial organisations also have their subsidiary software companies which are working mainly for them. This can be confirmed by
reading Table 31 which shows that computer manufacturers are the main customers
of the software industry. The portion of software development orders from computer manufacturers, however, is supposed to decrease in the future.

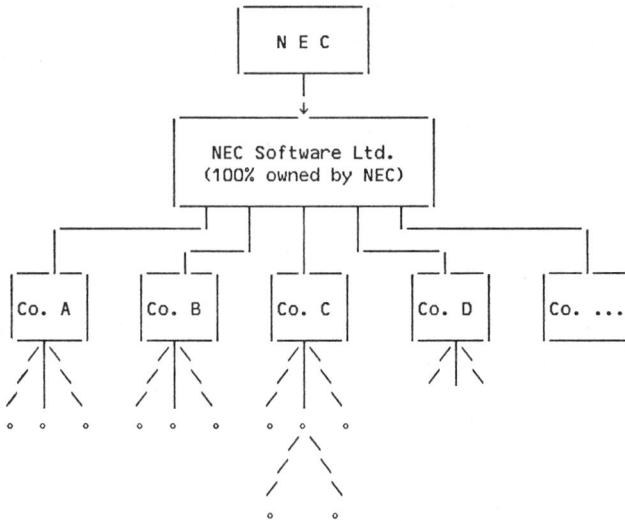

Figure 30   Subcontractors for software development of NEC

dp departments of customers possessing computers	24.2%
non dp departments of customers possessing computers	3.8%
customers not possessing computers	3.7%
computer manufacturers	59.5%
software industry and information processing service industry	3.3%
others	5.0%

Table 31   Software sales ratio by customers in 1977
(from JR No.39, page 16)

In many cases the computer manufacturers and general companies tend to do the basic design and concept themselves and to give only the programming and coding work to their subsidiary software companies. This is a fundamental problem for the future of the software industry because it influences the income of the software houses and hinders them from becoming qualified for independent development of software. Table 32 shows that almost 50% of their software development

work is only program design, programming and testing. The portion of system
design and concept work, however, is supposed to increase in the future.

	FY 1975	FY 1976	FY 1977	FY 1980 (Est.)	FY 1984 (Est.)
total consignment	36.3%	40.1%	41.9%	45.8%	53.2%
basic design, system design	8.5%	10.2%	11.2%	14.1%	14.4%
program design,programming, testing	55.1%	49.7%	47.0%	40.1%	31.8%

Table 32   Breakdown of software consignment development sales
             (from JR No.39, page 14)

The main reason for the poor situation of the software industry is the attitude
of the users towards software. They regard it as part of hardware and are not
willing to pay for it separately. Even the Ministry of Finance grants financial
support for the acquisition of hardware in government departments more readily
than for software, although the Japanese government is making a great effort to
promote the development of the software industry. However, since computer
manufacturers have decided to unbundle their software costs, the situation of
the software industry is supposed to improve.

Another reason for this situation is the fact that ordinary users are not very
willing to use general-purpose software. Most companies, organisations, ministries, agencies and municipal bodies have large data processing divisions which
are developing the software for their own use and are sceptic towards the use of
software packages which are "black boxes" and which they do not understand as
much as their own programs. A further impediment against the use of software
packages is the absence of standardisation of business in Japanese companies.
For example, Fujitsu tried to develop an accounting system, but since every
customer wanted to make major modifications, it discontinued this development.
After the oil crisis, however, financial considerations have become more important in Japanese companies and they are becoming much more willing to
purchase software packages.

Furthermore, the software industry has the following problems:

- There is a shortage of computer specialists, because fewer specialists are
   being trained than are needed by the various industries. This shortage will
   prove a handicap, especially for the computer service industry, because
   computer manufacturers — and also many users — are more profitable and
   reliable, and are much more appreciated by employees than the computer
   service companies. According to a study by MITI's Industrial Structure
   Council, there will be a shortage of 179,000 computer specialists by 1985.
   The computer manufacturers and users will require around 513,000 computer

specialists, and the computer service industry around 65,000 specialists, but there will only be around 399,000 trained people to fill these posts. According to SIA's estimation the requirements of the software industry will be even greater.

- The average age of the employees in the software industry is higher than that of the employees in the computer industry. Because of the seniority principle the younger managers of the computer industry do not want to meet the older ones of the software industry; (in this context "old" means over 35 years old).

- Many software houses lease personnel to their clients, mainly to computer manufacturers. According to the opinion of SIA, this personnel dispatching service should be prohibited in pursuance of Chapter 44 of the Labour Law.

- The profit margin of the software companies is very small. The total revenue of the whole computer service industry (including software and data processing service industries) is increasing by 20% each year, but the profit margin is increasing only by about 5%.

- Because of their poor financial situation the software companies are not strong enough to take the risk of developing general-use software on their own and to offer software packages on the market.

4.2.1 Japan Software Industry Association

The Software Industry Association (SIA), established in 1970 by 32 software companies, is a non-profit making organisation (SHADAN HOJIN) aiming to promote the information processing industry. In June 1980 membership was limited to 107 from an estimate of 600 to 1000 software companies. (For a list of members see [SIA4], part 3, page 6.) These members represent on the one hand about a tenth of the software companies and on the other hand about a sixth of those employed. This is because relatively more of the larger software companies are represented than the smaller ones. For example, in Figure 30 only NEC Software Ltd. and the software companies of the next level are members of SIA, but the companies of the lower level are not.

The main points of SIA's policy are:

- to establish the "software industry" as a third sector of industry separate and independent from the other two sectors, i.e. hardware supply and final user sector

- to make a wide range of technical contributions to society as system consultants, for designing systems and solving problems

- to actively promote all plans and projects needed for member firms to improve their corporate structure, technological level and administrative methods, and establish a management concept common to all member firms

- to give information and to propose demands to MITI, other government offices and agencies, (compare JR No.39, page 16 and [SIA4], part 3, page 1).

In 1980 the main activities of SIA were:

-   The holding of the Software Convention '80 during Information Week.

-   Research and studies (11 items), e.g.

    *   MITI's software advancement plan
    *   meetings on technological problems of software development
    *   the study of software pricing problems (see [SIA7])
    *   the publication of SIA's reports.

-   Activities subsidised by the Bicycle Racing Association

    (1) technological field, e.g. :
        *   survey on software production data
        *   survey on software documentation techniques
        *   survey on software protection techniques

    (2) studies made by member companies, e.g. :
        *   study on production management systems
        *   study on program portability
        *   study on equipment for software development (compare [SIA2], page 3).

Among other reports SIA publishes a detailed list of its members containing ex-
act data about their capacity (see [SIA3]). Furthermore SIA publishes reports
about the situation of the software industry (see e.g. [SIA5] and [SIA6]), but
unfortunately most of these reports are written in Japanese.

4.2.2   Software Product Centre

The Software Product Centre (SPC) was established in June 1979 by MITI's
Electronics Policy Division in order to promote the dissemination of general-use
software. It's main activity is to accept, and then to submit to IPA, applications for tax relief from software houses, data processing service companies,
general users of data processing, and Japanese juridical persons partly financed
by foreign main-frame manufacturers in connection with the general-purpose software registration fund (see Chapter 2.1.3.2 d).

SPC publishes newly submitted software packages in its quarterly journal, SOFT-
WARE RYUTSU (Software Circulation), and also publishes annually a list of all
registered software systems in which all functions of the software products are
described. Futhermore SPC publishes reports about the situation of software in
Japan, (see e.g. [SIA17]).

SPC is part of SIA, but its members, which in 1980 totalled 66, need not be
members of SIA.

4.3   Information Supply Service Industry

According to a survey conducted by MPT (Ministry of Posts and Telecommunications), a total of 45 firms were offering data communication services (dc
services) as of the end of 1976. (1975 : 39, 1974 : 35.) They offered 80 service
systems, 62 of which were available for general users while 18 were exclusive
systems for the use of the parent company only (see CWP 1978, page 20).

The information supply service companies (or data base service companies) can be
classified as follows (according to JR No.39, page 18):

- producers
  * public organisations
    ₒ information from government organisations
    ₒ information other than from government organisations
  * private organisations

- distributors
  * facility service vendors
  * information retailers or brokers

- on-line service bureaus.

Many data base service companies are producers of data bases as well as being
vendors. The Japan Patent Information Centre (JAPATIC), which closely co-
operates with MITI's Patent Office, produces a data base containing its own data
(PATOLIS) and retails data bases of the International Patent Document Centre
(INPADOC) (see JR No.39, page 29).   JICST (Japan Information Centre of Science
and Technology) of STA (Science and Technology Agency) collects scientific data
for its JICST file and and retails the foreign Chemical Abstracts (CA), MEDLARS
and TOXLINE files (see [JICST1] and [GID1]). The largest data bases are those of
private companies containing economic and financial data. The largest data base
service regarding the contents of the data bases is that of the NIKKEI Economic
Electronic Databank Service (NEEDS) of the Nihon Keizai Shimbun, a leading
Japanese business periodical. The Quotation Information Centre, however, has the
largest turnover of sales, and the greatest number of terminals connected to its
on-line real time system QUICK. Table 32 lists the most important data bases in
Japan (see also JR No.39, page 24; EJR Vol.4, No.8; and EJR Vol.7, page 28).

At present there are about 20 on-line service companies, the 6 most important
being:

  - Information Services International Dentsu (Dentsu / GE, Mark III-network)

  - Tymshare / Marubeni

  - Data Service Far East of CDC

  - CALL / 370 of IBM

  - Fujitsu FACOM

  - Japan Information Processing Service (JIP).

These companies offer the following services:

- data transmission

- handling and manipulation of data by higher programming languages and data management systems

- supply of software packages (Dentsu / GE: Network Software Service and Author System)

- data base services mainly of financial and economic data

- some of them also offer international on-line services.

Through the supply of software by the above mentioned TSS services, the client has access to Japanese made as well as foreign made software. For example, Information Services International Dentsu, who operate General Electric's Mark III network in Japan, offer in their "Author System", in addition to their own, all software systems which are available through the American Mark III network (see [REPORTS], report about Information Services International Dentsu, and [DENTSU2]). Japanese companies tend to use American and European software packages because they consider these systems to have been proved efficient and reliable.

Under the provisions of Japan's Public Telecommunication Law, private vendors are not allowed to own communication equipment. They are only allowed to own centres and must rent domestic circuits from NTT and international circuits from KDD (Kokusai Denshin Denwa, Japan's international telegraph and telephone company), (see Chapter 2.3.1).

NTT, however, also offers on-line services, and with its systems DEMOS, DRESS and DIALS it occupies about 25% of the Japanese on-line service market. The biggest private on-line service bureaus are IBM and Dentsu / GE, and each have about 25% share of the market.

MITI is afraid of the large market share of strong information supply companies which are financed from abroad, particularly because additional foreign firms want to establish subsidiaries in Japan. MITI wants to build up a Japanese information service industry and would like it to be included in the Machinery and Information Industry Law.

The information supply industry also makes efforts to upgrade the level of Japan's data base services. In 1979, 21 key data base service enterprises, including the Quotation Information Centre, organised a liaison council which worked out the "Appeal for Promotion of the Data Base Service Industry" and presented it to several ministries and agencies. The demands

- help in improving the foundation of Japan's data base service industry, including clear rights and distribution procedures;

- assistance in the building and maintenance of an adequate scale of data bases;

- policy measures to promote the distribution of data base service information.

It is likely that the council may develop into a fully-fledged association of all Japanese data base service enterprises (see EJR Vol.7, page 38).

	Name of Data Base	Name of Producer	Main Fields	Information Source	Commencement of Compilation	Data Quantity	Updated	No. of Items	Distributor
	NEEDS-IEE	Nihon Keizai Shimbun Ltd.	Energy & economy statistics	24 publications of government, Bank of Japan, Nikkei Statistical materials; about 1,000 affiliated are as of energy (petroleum, gas coal, electric power, nuclear power) and general economic data.	1/1960	180,000	Monthly	12,000	Nihon Keizai Shimbun Ltd.
	JAPATIC Comprehensive Retrieval File	Japan Patent Information Center (JAPATIC)	Patent information	Summary of patents disclosed in Japan	1971	675,000	Bi-weekly	150,000	JAPATIC
Natural Sciences and Engineering	JAPATIC Primary Retrieval File	Japan Patent Information Center (JAPATIC)	Patent Information	—Japanese patents (disclosed & published), Utility models (disclosed & published) —U. S. Patents —Foreign patent information from International Patent Document Center (43 countries)	1955 overseas, from 1973	2,684,000 (Japan)	Bi-weekly	400,000	JAPATIC
	JICST Science & Engineering Documents File	Japan Information Center of Science & Technology (JICST)	Science & technology	8,500 journals, conference materials, reports. Concerning JICST "Science & Technology Latest Literature"	4/1975	1,080,000	Three times monthly	360,000	JICST
	Clearing file	Japan Information Center of Science & Technology (JICST)	Science & technology	Research subjects being conducted by 400 public testing & research institutions in Japan	1976	45,000	Annually	15,000	JICST

Table 33   Principal Data Bases in Japan (collected by Ashai Research Centre Ltd., published in JR No.39, pages 24-26)

Category	Database	Organization	Type	Description	Date	Number	Frequency	Number	Source
Humanities & Social Sciences	Minryoku Data Base	Asahi Shimbun Ltd.	Regional statistics (regional economy, industry, culture)	Based on Asahi Shimbun's "Minryoku", economy, Industry & culture of 47 prefectures and 750 regions.	1966	539,000	Annually	49,000	Information Services International Dentsu. Ltd.
	NEEDS-IR	Nihon Keizai Shimbun Ltd.	Newspaper Information	Articles from Nihon Keizai Shimbun, Nikkei Sangyo Shimbun, Nikkei Ryutsu Shimbun, Nikkei Business.	5/1975	231,000	Monthly	80,000	Nihon Keizai Shimbun Ltd.
	NRI/E	Nomura Research Institute	Macro-economic, Industrial	About 300 types of materials on macro-economy, Industry, trends, published by government offices, agencies and industrial organizations. (2,000 affiliated, of which 800 are concerned with industry.)	1/1965	338,000	Weekly	26,000	Information services International Dentsu. Ltd.
	NEEDS-TS/I Nikkei financial data Nikkei stock price file	Nihon Keizai Shimbun Ltd.	Micro-economic	Financial data (267 items) based on stocks & bonds reports of 1,700 companies listed on the first section of the stock exchange. Stock price data of first section companies.	4/1968	{ 5,000,000 { 5,000,000	{ Monthly { Daily	{ 500,000 { 510,000	Nihon Keizai Shimbun Ltd
	NEEDS-TS/II Nikkei Genenal Economic File	Nihon Keizai Shimbun Ltd.	Macro-economic	Statistical materials put out by 10 government ministries & agencies, Bank of Japan, etc. (about 70 in all) (about 3,300 affiliated)	4/1968	300,000	Weekly	30,000	Nihon Keizai shimbun Ltd.
Management & Economy	QUICK Video 1	Quotation Information Center (QUICK)	Stock price information	Stock price data of companies listed on the first section of the stock exchange, accounts settlement reports, market information (Dow, share price indexes, etc.)	4/1974	—	Instantaneous (Real time)	—	QUICK
	TSR Enterprise Information, Financial Data Bank	Tokyo Shoko Research Ltd	Basiness, finance	Stocks & bonds reports of 1,500 companies listed on the first section of the stock exchange and 13,500 companies not listed on the first section. (About 80 items.)	The most recent three terms are kept on record	3,960,000	Monthly	1,320,000	Information Services International Dentsu., Ltd.
	Trade Statistics of Each Nation	Institute of Developing Economies	Trade statistics	Trade statistics put out by about 80 nations, with emphasis on OECD countries. (import & export data by country and item; preparation of world trade matrices, etc.)	1962	180 reels of magnetic tape	Annually	12 reels of magnetic tape	Institute of Developing Economies

Table 33   Principal Data Bases in Japan (collected by Ashai Research Centre Ltd., published in JR No.39, pages 24-26)

	Name of Data Base	Name of Producer	Main Fields	Information Source	Commencement of Compilation	Data Quantity	Updated	No. of Items	Distributor
	Japanese Trade Statistics Data	Institute of Developing Economies	Trade Strartistics	Japanese Trade Statistics annual (listings of import/export quantities, values, and country, by item)	1951	50 reels of magnetic tape	Annually	2 reels of magnetic tape	Institute of Developing Economies
	U. N. Population Data	Institute of Developing Economies	Population Statistics	United Nations "Demographic Year Book"	1950	25 reels of magnetic tape	Annually	1 reel of magnetic tape	Institute of Developing Economies
	S. E. Asia Trade Statistics Data	Institute of Developing Economies	Trade Statistics	Reports on statistics put out by 18 Southeast Asian nations.	1950	80 reels of magnetic tape	Annually	3 reels of magnetic tape	Institute of Developing Economies
	Legal Data Relating to Investment in Developing Nations	Institute of Developing Economies	Investmen' laws & regulations	Laws relating to Investment, companies, contracts, labor, industrial rights and taxes in the Philippines, Indonesia, Singapore, Malaysia, Thailand, Hong Kong, and Korea.	1977	200,000	Annually	200,000	Institute of Developing Economies
Management & Economy	Fresh Foodstuffs Distribution Information	Ministry of Agriculture, Forestry & Fishery	Distribution information (Market & place of origin information)	-Green produce market information (77 markets, 58 items) -Livestock market information (22 markets, major cities) -Information on origin of green produce (production & shipping forecasts) -Information on livestock origin (information on calf & piglet transactions in major markets)	11/1976		Daily (market information) Monthly (area of origin)	As required	Ministry of Agriculture, Forestry & Fishery
	Industrial Bank Financial Data	Industrial Bank of Japan	Business finance	Reports on stocks & bonds of 1,600 companies listed on the first section of the stock exchange (381 ~ 600 items)	1963	12,800,000 (20 terms)	Quarterly	640,000	Nihon Keizai Shimbun Ltd.
	COMPASS Long-term Credit Bank Enterprise Financial Data	Long-Tern Credit Bank of Japan	Business finance	Reports on stocks & bonds, and semi-annual business reports, on 1,500 companies listed on the first section of the exchange and 900 not listed on the first section.	1965	10,940,000	Quarterly	910,000	Nihon Keizai Shimbun Ltd. Nihon Portfolio Service Ltd.

Table 33   Principal Data Bases in Japan (collected by Ashai Research Centre Ltd., published in JR No.39, pages 24-26)

4.4 Measures to solve the Problems of the Information Processing Industry

After the successful development of computer hardware the Japanese government and Japanese industry recognised that software could be a bottleneck to further computerisation. As a result of this estimation, the importance of the infor- mation processing industry is increasing and, as from 1978, the information processing industry was granted more subsidies than before, because it was recognised as a separate branch of industry (in addition to the computer in- dustry and the end users) in the Machinery and Information Industry Law (KIJOHO) of 1978.

Although software is the main field of promotion, the computer industry still receives the largest portion of financial aids offered. Only computer manufacturers and affiliated companies are participating in the largest promoted project in the field of software development – the Computer Basic Technology Research Association (see Chapter 2.2.2.1). The computer manufacturers also receive the greatest benefit from tax relief through the General Purpose Soft- ware Package Registration System because they register more packages than soft- ware companies. The information supply service is not even included in the promotion law because it is not yet clear whether MITI or MPT is responsible for this industry, which includes data processing and data communication.

Nevertheless the economic situation of information processing is changing in favour of the information processing industry (compare EJR Vol.6, page 42-49). The decision of the foreign and domestic computer manufacturers to "unbundle" their software prices is supposed to ease the business activities of software houses, because the manufacturers will no longer be competitors which offer software free of charge. Furthermore, because of industry's difficult financial situation after the oil crisis and because of the growing complexity of software systems, end users are becoming more and more willing to use software packages. Thus SIA supposes that about 30 out of their approx. 100 members are going to become independent companies.

SIA proposes the following measures to ameliorate the situation of the software industry:

- Software houses should accept well-established specialised software packages from general companies and generalise them. This assures that software packages satisfy the needs of the potential users (see [SIA5], pages 114,115). E.g. Software AG of Far East purchased the prototype of its Advanced Automatic Computer Operation System (A-AUTO) from Fuji Photo Film Co. and re-modelled it into a general purpose software system (see [REPORTS], report about Software AG of Far East).

- Even small software houses can survive in the software market if they specialise in a few subjects; e.g. the Tool Software Co., which has about 35 employees but does not own a computer, gets about 60% of its income from only one simulation project on the effects harbours have on the environment (see [REPORTS], report about Tool Software Co.).

- Because the financial situation is a critical point for the information processing industry, SIA emphasises its pricing policy. This is difficult, however, because of the monopoly act and the observance of the Fair Trade Commission.

4.5   Export of Japanese Software

As the Japanese software companies are becoming more self-reliant they plan on
establishing subsidiaries overseas. At present there are Japanese-led software
houses operating in Taiwan, Malaysia, Singapore, Great Britain and the United
States (see The Japan Economic Journal, 19.2.1980, "Computer Firms are trying to
expand overseas software jobs"). Recently the subsidiaries of two Japanese software companies have started operating in the U.S. - DPC America Inc., a daughter
company of Data Process Consultant Ltd. (which also has another subsidiary company in London), and Management Information Science International (see Datamation, February 1980, page 58). At first they sold software mainly to Japanese
companies in the U.S., but they want to do business with American companies as
well. Furthermore, they inquire after software packages on the American market
which might be marketable in Japan.

The American subsidiaries of the hardware manufacturers, however, have the chief
purpose of supporting their sales activities.

The East-Asian market is important because of two aspects: on the one hand subsidiary software companies of the Japanese hardware manufacturers in these
countries are helping to prepare the market for Japanese computers; and on the
other hand software development is cheaper in this area. For example, Computer
Application Corp. of Tokyo has its programs coded and debugged by CAC Taiwan,
its joint venture with Systex Corp. of Taiwan, which reduces the costs by
30-40%. Facom Korea Ltd., a joint venture of Fujitsu and a Korean company, supports Fujitsu's computer sales and produces software that has been subcontracted
out from Tokyo.

Because the Chinese market is expected to become especially important, Fujitsu
and NEC intend to open software specialist training centres in several principal
Chinese cities. As the Japanese written language uses similar characters as in
Chinese, Japanese computers have some advantages over their American competitors
because of their capacity to process Japanese and Chinese characters. According
to "Business China" (of Hong Kong), from 12th December 1980, Fujitsu and the
Chinese Science Commission of Tientsin are negotiating a joint venture for the
development of a computer hardware and software system for the Chinese language.

5. USERS OF DATA PROCESSING

According to the quarterly "Survey on Computer Deliveries and Trade-Ins" from MITI, the number of operating computer systems at the end of June 1979 was 61,687 sets, having a purchase price value of 3,315 billion Yen (see Table 34).

	No. of sets	Value
large	2,753 sets	1,997,177 mill. Yen
medium	7,485 sets	787,408 mill. Yen
small	17,590 sets	328,524 mill. Yen
very small	33,859 sets	202,873 mill. Yen

large	: more than 250 million Yen
medium	: 40 Million − 250 million Yen
small	: 10 million − 40 million Yen
very small	: less than 10 million Yen

mini-computers are not included

Table 34 Computer installations as at the end of
         June 1979 (from [JIPDEC17], page 1)

The various branches of industry, however, are not equally automated. Tables 35 and 36 show the number of computers installed, classified by industry.

	Value (bill. Yen)	Percentage
manufacturing	1,026	31%
(electric machinery)	(360)	(11%)
banking, insurance and securities	740	22%
government and municipal bodies	489	15%
wholesale and retail	419	13%
service bureaus	183	6%
education	106	3%
transportation and communication	86	2%
others	264	8%

Table 35 Market structure by industry sectors at end
         of June 1979 (from [JIPDEC17], page 4)

(Value: in million yen)

Industrial Category	Set	Value	Value per Set
Agriculture	59	1,098	18.6
Forestry and hunting	26	293	11.3
Fisheries, fishing and pisciculture	128	2,452	19.2
Mining	105	3,742	35.6
Construction	1,191	38,768	32.6
Foodstuffs	2,149	50,132	23.3
Textiles and textile products	1,371	30,186	22.0
Pulp, paper and paper products	504	11,937	23.7
Publishing and printing	510	23,024	45.1
Chemicals and petroleum refining	2,114	115,721	54.7
Ceramics	443	17,845	40.3
Iron and steel	708	106,575	150.5
Fabricated metal products	966	36,247	37.5
Machinery	1,222	57,666	47.2
Electric machinery	2,815	360,140	127.9
Transport equipment	1,055	140,439	133.2
Precision machinery	535	26,455	49.4
Other manufacturing	2,103	49,603	24.6
Wholesale and retail, trade firms	23,761	419,426	17.7
Finance	5,198	583,953	112.3
Security	232	47,111	203.1
Insurance	244	109,308	448.0
Real estate	140	3,040	21.7
Transportation and telecommunications	1,860	86,380	46.4
Electricity, gas and water	234	48,882	208.9
Service	4,875	245,974	50.5
(General Service)	(2,468)	(62,530)	25.3
(DP Service)	(2,407)	(183,444)	76.2
Hospital	289	11,834	40.9
Universities	830	81,483	98.2
Senior high schools	331	7,132	21.5
Other schools	142	6,548	46.1
Municipal bodies	1,087	74,320	68.4
Government departments and agencies	534	127,482	238.7
Governmental organizations	793	287,312	362.3
Cooperative association and organizations	3,002	95,529	31.8
Religious organizations	24	979	40.8
Not elsewhere classified	107	6,917	64.6
Total	61,687	3,315,982	53.8

Table 36   Computer use classified by industry sectors, at the end of June 1979
           (from a MITI Survey, published in [JIPDEC17], page 3)

As can be seen from Table 36, the wholesale-retail-trade industry is the business category having the most computer installations, whereas the installations of the finance business are valued the highest, followed by the electric machinery industry. It is worth mentioning that government organisations and government departments are already in the 4th and 5th positions. The degree of automation within the manufacturing industry, however, is higher than one would suppose from the table, because process control computers (just as minicomputers, analog computers and small business computers) are not included in Tables 35 and 36.

5.1   Private Companies

An attempt is made here to outline the situation in private industry by using examples of some companies and branches of industry.

Banking was one of the first business sectors to introduce data processing into its business. Bank automation in Japan started more than 20 years ago as batch processing, and on-line systems were also introduced very early. At present most banks have their individual inter-branch on-line real time systems for their intra-bank business (see e.g. EJR Vol.5, No.20); furthermore there are the following on-line inter-bank networks (see NAKAMURA1):

-   The Nationwide Bank Data Communication System (ZENGIN system) processes all inter-bank domestic transactions.

-   The Nippon Cash Service System serves off-premises cash dispensers which are connected on-line to the computers of several banks.

-   The Mutual Vicarious Service mainly serves the smaller banks.

-   The TOCS system, recently introduced by the city banks and the SICS system introduced by the regional banks, for off-premise cash dispenser service.

The largest financial network, however, will be MPT's Postal Saving System which will have terminals in every post office (see EJR Vol.5, No.20, page 4).

An example of a trading company is Nippon Yusen Kaisha (NYK), one of Japan's largest shipping companies which operates 305 vessels and about 60,000 containers. Having installed its first computer in 1965 most of its activities — about 500 application businesses — are transacted by computers, mainly:

    - Management of finance and accounts

    - Shipping documentation

    - Container inventory control

    - Vessels movement control

    - Analysis of business statistics

- Computation of charterage for adjustment

- Computation of salaries and personnel management

- Computation of the vessel's technical matters

- Management planning for efficient investment.

Figure 37 is a diagram of NYK's total information system. Almost all application software (totalling more than 5000 programs) has been developed by NYK's Information System Chamber employing about 50 members under assistance of NYK's subsidiary software company, Nihon System Centre (NSC) employing about 150 people (NSC is working approx. 50% for NYK). The main application systems are the Container Inventory Control System and the Documentation System. Like many companies which introduced data processing very early, NYK has an IBM system and, for its terminal on-line networks, uses IBM SNA network architecture (see also [REPORTS], report about NYK, and [NYK3]).

Asahi Chemical, a chemical company with 13,000 employees, also started data processing very early. Its application software includes strategic planning, finance and accounting, purchasing, order entry, sales, personnel information and production control. The application software was developed by Asahi Chemical's System Control Department, while Asahi Chemical only purchased IMS, MPSX (for linear programming), DSS (distribution system simulator), and some engineering packages. The non-standard basic software was developed in co-operation with NEC, for example Asahikasei's Communication and Teleprocessing Network (ACT).

ACT is a packet switching network, the trunk of which is formed by three NEAC 3200-70 packet-switching processors, to which 3 large-scale computers (2 X IBM/370-158 and 1 X FACOM M-160) are connected. Through 6 NEAC 3200 communication processors are further connected 31 small computers or intelligent terminals; 24 non-intelligent terminals; and 32 telex-lines. Most of the remote processors and terminals are domestic products. The data transmission procedures specially designed for ACT are based on BSC. ACT has been designed for batch use only, and the IMS terminals are connected to the IBM/370 systems by special lines (see [REPORTS], report about Asahi Chemical).

The Mitsubishi Oil Company (MOC), a joint venture between the Mitsubishi-Group and Associated Oil Co. of USA, had in 1977 3000 employees and sales of 750 billion Yen. MOC's data processing has the following aims:

- to process the actual results of its business activities

- to provide the management with timely information

- to assist the management decision making by using modern techniques of management science.

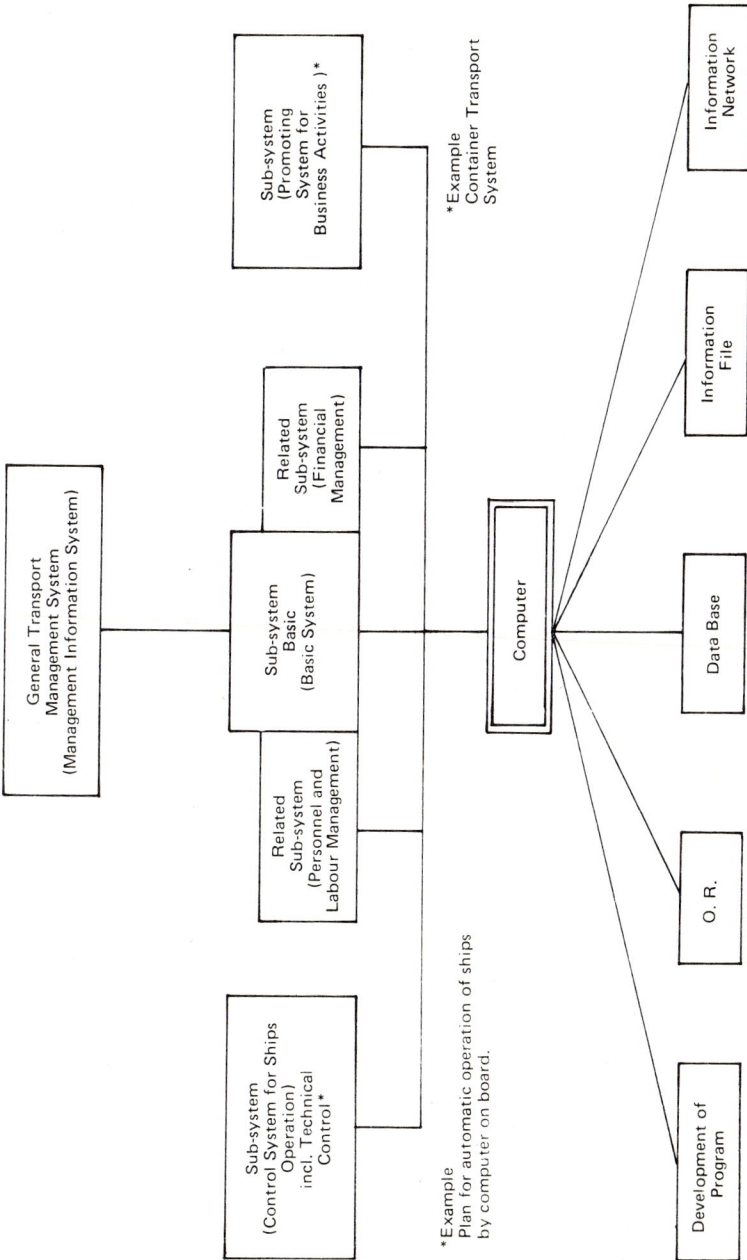

Figure 37 Information system of NYK (outline of the total system) (from [NYK3], page 8)

General Transport Management System (Management Information System)

Sub-system (Control System for Ships Operation) incl. Technical Control*

Related Sub-system (Personnel and Labour Management)

Sub-system Basic (Basic System)

Related Sub-system (Financial Management)

Sub-system (Promoting System for Business Activities)*

*Example
Plan for automatic operation of ships by computer on board.

*Example
Container Transport System

Computer

Development of Program

O. R.

Data Base

Information File

Information Network

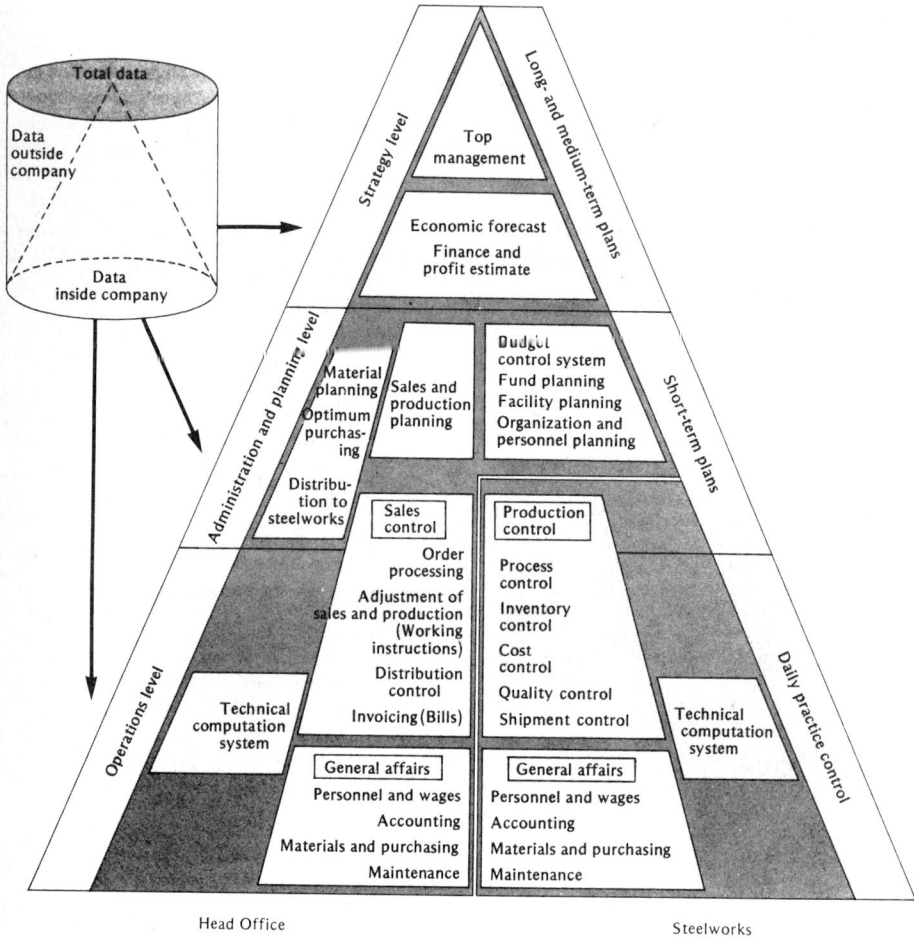

Figure 38   Information systems in the steel industry (from [TETSU1], page 25)

Thus the overall application system consists of the following parts:

- middle and long range planning (5 to 10 years)
    * capital investment; sales and distribution; crude oil import and ocean tankers

- operation planning and budgeting (half to 1 year)
    * manufacturing planning; income forecast; sales and distribution planning; tanker and import planning

- monthly planning
    * crude oil assignment; tanker allocation; monthly manufacturing program; monthly income forecast; monthly sales and distribution program; inventory control

- implementation and activity records
    * accounting records; sales and distribution records; plant operation reports; inventory reports.

Most of the application software has been and is being developed by MOC's Oper- ation Research and Computer Department, with software houses doing subsidiary work. Concerning economic studies MOC co-operates with the Mitsubishi Research Institute (MRI) — a think tank of the Mitsubishi Group, other research institu- tions, and government organisations. The refinery computerisation, however, is being performed separately by the Refinery Computerisation Development Group together with the computer sections of the refineries.

The central computer is a Burroughs System B6800, installed at the head office in Tokyo; furthermore, MRI's computer system is being used for most of the oper- ations research work. In the three refineries 2 IBM 8100 systems and 1 IBM/370-125 system are installed. At the three refineries, the three oil depots and the nine branch offices MELCOM M70 terminal computers are installed which are connected to the central computer by a circuit switching network. The net- work architecture, based on Burroughs' architecture, has been developed by Burroughs like most of MOC's system software (see also [REPORTS], report about MOC).

The steel industry has seen a rapid increase in the use of computers in recent years. Steel makers now rely on integrated computerised information systems. These systems feature a pyramidal structure consisting of a strategy level at the top, aimed mainly at providing top management with long- and medium-term plans; an administration and planning level in the middle, mainly for making short-term operational plans; and an operational level at the bottom for execu- tion and control of daily work. With a complete network of sub-systems to cover individual operations at head office, steelworks and local sales offices, the data processing hierarchy functions as an organically combined, integrated sys- tem for the benefit of corporate management.

At the bottom level the information system is divided into two major branches — the sales control system, and the production control system. These two systems function interdependently (see Figure 38).

As of January 1979, there were 853 computers in operation at 41 steel companies. Of this total, 152 were business computers and 673 were process computers, the former being operated by all 41 companies and the latter by 18 of them. Through communication lines, 65 on-line systems were in operation at 22 companies. Today an increasing number of orders from trading firms, wholesalers, and steelmaker-affiliated companies are received in the form of magnetic tapes. Utilisation of communication lines will be extended to include these external organisations in the future (see [TETSU1] pages 24,25).

The Japan Iron and Steel Federation (JISF, in Japanese TETSUREN) co-ordinates the exchange of information about the total systems of the steel makers. Furthermore, JISF developed the Steel Information System (SIS) providing statistics about iron and steel as well as other related fields, mainly collected from member companies, other industries, Japanese ministries, and Japanese and international statistics. The time series statistical data base of SIS was put into partial use in 1973, and the on-line data retrieval and analysis system was put into operation in 1978 (see also [REPORTS], report about JISF, and EJR Vol.6, page 100).

SIS is also structured to be a sub-system of MITI's Policy Planning Information System which is planned to contain data bases of several industry sectors (see Chapter 5.2.1).

5.2   Government and Public Institutions

As can be seen from Tables 34 and 35, the government and government organisations are very advanced in using data processing. In some areas the government or public institutions were even the pioneers of computerisation, e.g. MITI's Policy Planning Information System was developed earlier than other economic data bases, and the developers of the NEEDS system, the SIS of the Japan Iron and Steel Federation, and others studied MITI's system before developing their own.

5.2.1   Ministries and Agencies

In 1958 an IBM computer was already installed at the Meteorological Agency and was the first computer at a Japanese administrative body. In 1968 a Cabinet Resolution was declared to pursue computerisation positively in Japanese government offices in order to expand its use in new fields of application rather than to limit computer usage entirely to clerical work (see, for example, CWP 1978, page 7).

The Administrative Management Agency (AMA) was given, among other tasks, the responsibility to promote and co-ordinate data processing in ministries and agencies. It acts in co-operation with other co-ordinative bodies (which have been described in Chapter 2.1.2.3, see Figure 4). Important decisions, however, are made by the cabinet, the vice ministers or the Council of Directors in charge of ADP. Such decisions are, e.g.:

-        rules for the acquisition of computers, called the "Requests for Proposals"

- the decision in 1978 to "unbundle" the software when purchasing computer systems for the Japanese Government

- the decision in 1978 not to continue handicapping foreign computer manufacturers when purchasing computers for the Japanese government

- the publication in 1976 of the "Guidelines on EDP Security" (see Chapter 2.5).

With regard to the standardisation of documentation within the government, AMA proposed some standards for names and items, but extensive standards for software development do not yet exist.

When a ministry or agency wants to purchase a computer it must act according to the "Request for Proposal": it calls for proposals from JECC or the hardware manufacturers, and evaluates their proposals according to these rules. But there is no co-operation between ministries or agencies in order to use the same computer and software systems, therefore the variety of computers is very great in central government. The portion of foreign manufacturers, however, is smaller than in the private industry.

The Administration Management Agency tends to make the data processing facilities of the central government accessible to all ministries and agencies (see also JR No.38, page 24). For this purpose it made a list of all existing data base systems and it promotes the development of an inter-ministerial network, called "Resource Sharing System" (RSS).

Furthermore the Administrative Management Agency established the Joint Use Computer Centre for use by ministries and agencies. But because virtually all ministries and agencies have their own large computer systems only the Ministry of Finance uses the centre, and this only occasionally. The following application systems developed by AMA in the Joint Use Computer Centre, however, are being used by the whole central government:

- Legal Retrieval System

- Proceedings Retrieval System

- Payrolls and Mutual Aid System

- Government Pension Administration System (compare [AMA1], pages 41,42).

Table 39 shows the number of computers in ministries and agencies and their applications. The Defence Agency, MPT, the Ministry of Transport and MITI are the leading computer users among the ministries.

According to the cabinet decision of 1968 Japanese ministries are using information processing not only for their daily clerical work but also for supporting their policy and decision making, and many ministries have large data banks containing the relevant information. For example, MITI's Policy Planning Information System contains mainly economic, financial and technical data (see Table 40). Data which have been collected primarily for statistical purposes have also been used in the MITI data-bank; furthermore, data are being collected from Japanese and international institutions (see [MITI1] page 12):

- Economic Planning Agency : Macro economic statistics, etc.

- Ministry of Finance   : Japan trading statistics, etc.

- Statistics Bureau   : Consumer's price index, etc.

- Bank of Japan   : Wholesale price index, etc.

- Japan External Trade   : Trading statistics of foreign
  Organisation (JETRO)   countries

- Japan Industrial Bank   : Enterprise financial data

- Japan Iron and Steel   : Data of steel and iron .
  Federation (JISF)

The Policy Planning Information System (PPIS) consists of the Information Retrieval System and the Data Analysis System. The Information Retrieval System consists mainly of the MITI End User Language (MEU) which is identical to INQ of NEC (modelled after ADABAS). The Data Analysis System enables the user to analyse the data according to econometrical models. Economic and financial data bases and analysis systems are quite numerous in the Japanese economy, and they seem to be relied on more deeply than in USA or Europe.

PPIS consists of two categories of systems:

- important policy fields

    * Enterprise Information System
    * Economic Co-operation Information System
    * International Trade Information System
    * Energy Information System
    * Technology Information System (by the Patent Office)
    * Mineral Resources Information System

and

- important industry sectors, at present:

    * Iron and Steel Information System
    * Paper and Pulp Information System.

MITI wants to establish such information systems, like the Iron and Steel Information System (SIS, developed by JISF, see Chapter 5.1) and the Paper and Pulp Information System, for all branches of industry. It prefers decentralised data bases to large data centres because they can be quite easily managed by their producers. All these data bases will be integrated into the Resource Sharing System (RSS) which will share computer resources among ministries and agencies. The network software for RSS is being developed by MITI, the Economic Planning Agency (EPA) and JIPDEC. As for the first step the computers of MITI's DP Administration Division and of EPA have been linked.

Department	No. of sets	Main applications
Prime Minister's Office	2	Statistics
National Police Agency	6	Fingerprint enquiries, Vehicle enquiries, Driver administration
Administrative Management Agency	1	Statute searches, Salaries
Hokkaido Development Agency	2	Technical calculations, Calculation of construction costs, Salaries
Self-Defense Agency	49	Supplies administration, Technical calculations, Communications, Weather
Economic Planning Agency	1	Economic analyses
Science & Technology Agency	11	Technical calculations
Environment Agency	1	Analyses, Pollution measurements
Ministry of Justice	6	Administration of criminal records, Immigration/Emigration control, Calculation of deposits
Ministry of Foreign Affairs	6	Information retrieval, Issuance of Passports, Telex message exchange, Copying
Ministry of Finance	14	Statistics, Information retrieval, Taxes
Ministry of Education	11	Statistics, Information retrieval, Analyses
Ministry of Health and Welfare	10	Statistics, Social insurance, Pensions
Ministry of Agriculture, Forestry and Fishery	16	Statistics, Inventory control, Technical calculations, Information retrieval
Ministry of International Trade & Industry	29	Statistics, Information retrieval, Technical calculations
Ministry Transport	51	Statistics, Vehicle test registration, Weather, Air traffic service
Ministry of Posts and Telecommunications	63	Savings, Insurance, Statistics
Ministry of Labor	7	Statistics, Employment insurance, Workers' accident insurance, Labor insurance, Employment bureau
Ministry of Construction	20	Statistics, Technical calculations
Ministry of Home Affairs	1	Statistics
Total	307	

Source: Administrative Management Agency "Report on Basic Survey of Computer Usage"

Table 39   Number of computers and their major applications in government ministries and agencies at the end of 1979 (from an AMA survey, published in CWP 1980, page 48)

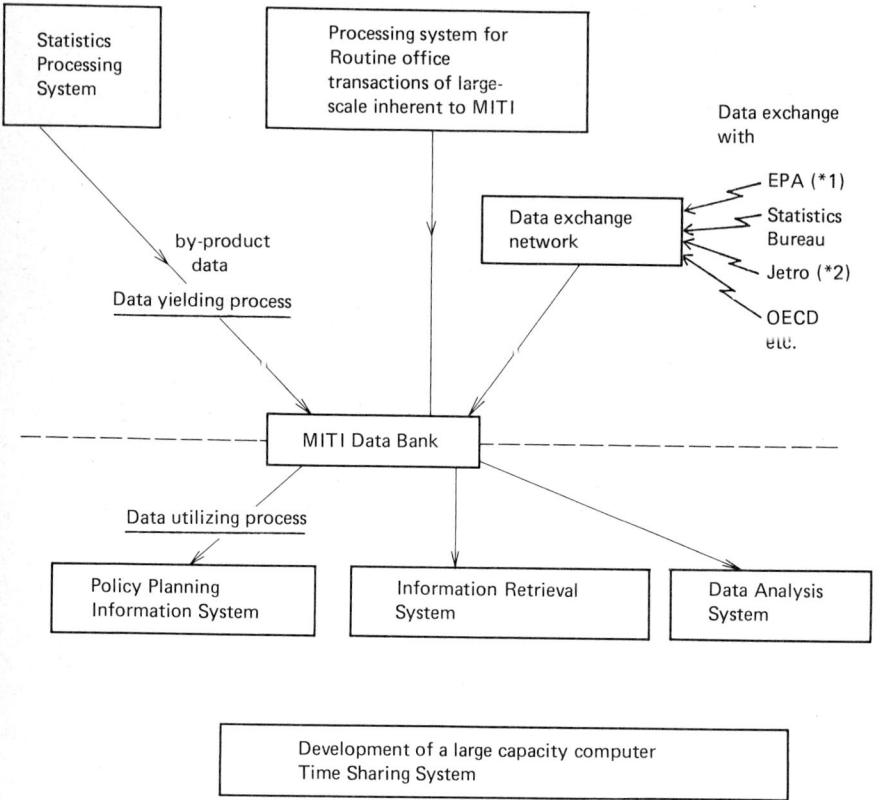

Figure 40 Outline of the administrative information processing system at MITI
            (from [MITI1], page 3)
    (*1)   Economic Planning Agency
    (*2)   Japan External Trade Organisation

Another important application of computer usage in MITI is the Patent Application Business System. The total business procedure from the proposal to the investigation and decision has been automated, and MITI also wants to use the collected data in order to get information about the newest technological developments. The Patent Office co-operates with the Japan Patent Information Centre (JAPATIC) which developed the Patent On-line Information System (PATOLIS).

Of the 29 computers mentioned in Table 39, MITI has 6 general-purpose computers at its head office:

- the Data Processing   : ACOS 77/900II,
  Administration Division   NEAC 2200/575

- the Export Insurance   : ACOS 77/500,
  Planning Division   ACOS 77/800III

- The Patent Office   : two HITAC M-170.

The rest are installed at research institutes supervised by AIST.

Other ministries also have very advanced application systems. As an example the following on-line networks systems are listed:

- Automobile Registration System of the Ministry of Transport

- Fresh Food Distribution System of the Ministry of Agriculture, Forestry and Fishery

- Automated Meteorological Data Acquisition System of the Meteorological Agency

- Labour Market Centre On-line System of the Ministry of Labour

- Nippon Air Cargo Clearance System (NACCS) of the Ministry of Finance

- Post Office Deposit Savings System of MPT

- National Life Insurance System of MPT.

The Post Office Deposit Savings System, which will have terminals in all post offices, will be Japan's largest on-line system.

5.2.2   Government Organisations

Japan has a total of 111 government-related organisations, 56 of which in 1978 had general purpose digital computer systems valued at over 10 million Yen (3 "kosha" public corporations, 8 "kodan" public corporations, 9 "jigyodan" public corporations, 7 public finance organisations, 4 co-operative and special banks, 1 "eidan" public corporation, 7 special companies and 17 others, see Table 41).

The organisation using the biggest number of computers is the Japanese National Railways (JNR) which operates the Railway Seat Reservation System (see JIP Vol.2, No.1, 1979, pages 37-52). This system is one of Japan's largest on-line

Names	Number of sets

Kosha

Names	Number of sets
Japan Tobacco and Salt Public Corp.	4
Japan National Railways (JNR)	102
Nippon Telegraph and Telephone Public Corp. (NTT)	73

Kodan

Names	Number of sets
Water Resources Development Corp.	3
Japan Petroleum Development Corp.	2
Japan Railway Construction Corp.	1
New Tokyo International Airport Corp.	2
Japan Housing Corp.	1
Japan Highway Public Corp.	5
Tokyo Expressway Public Corp.	3
Hanshin Port Development Authority	2

Jigyodan

Names	Number of sets
Power Reactor and Nuclear Fuel Development Corp.	2
National Space Development Agency	11
Japan International Cooperation Agency	1
Coal Mining Industry Rationalisation Corp.	1
Coal Mine Damage Corp.	3
Smaller Enterprise Mutual Aid Projects Corp.	1
Small Business Promotion Corp.	1
Smaller Enterprise Retirement Allowance Mutual Aid Project Corp.	1

Koko

Names	Number of sets
Hokkaido and Tohoku Development Corp.	1
Okinawa Development Finance Corp.	1
People's Finance Corp.	4
Agriculture, Forestry and Fishery Finance Corp.	1
Small Business Finance Corp.	2
Small Business Credit Insurance Corp.	1
Housing Loan Corp.	1

Kinko, Tokushuginko

Names	Number of sets
Japan Development Bank	1
Export-Import Bank of Japan	1
Central Cooperative Bank for Agriculture and Forestry	6
Shoko Chukin Bank	6

Table 41   Number of computers installed at government organisations
(from [AMA1] page 19

Names	Number of sets

Eidan

Names	Number of sets
Teito Rapid Transit Authority	1

Tokushugaisha

Names	Number of sets
Tohoku District Development Co., Ltd.	1
Electric Power Development Co., Ltd.	1
Nihon Aeroplane Manufacturing Co., Ltd.	1
Okinawa Electric Power Co., Ltd.	2
Japan Airlines Co., Ltd.	10
Japan Motor Terminals Co., Ltd.	1
Kokusai Denshin Denwa Co., Ltd. (KDD)	12

Others

Names	Number of sets
Overseas Economic Cooperation Fund	1
Better Living Information Centre	1
Japan Atomic Energy Research Institute	2
Japan Information Centre of Science and Technology	1
Institute of Physical and Chemical Research	1
Japan Foundation	1
Japan Scholarship Society	1
Private School Personnel Mutual Aid Association	1
Japan School-Lunch Society	1
Japan School Safety Association	1
National Theatre	1
Social Insurance Medical Fee Payment Fund	37
Japan Racing Association	157
Agriculture, Forestry and Fishery Organisation Employees Mutual Aid Association	1
Japan External Trade Organisation	1
Institute of Developing Economies	1
Japan Broadcasting Corp. (NHK)	46
TOTAL	535

Table 41   Continued

network systems handling a million seats per day for the two-month reservation
period, and having installed about 1800 terminals. It also includes a telephone
reservation system by which any telephone user who has a push button apparatus
can automatically make his own reservation.

Nippon Telegraph and Telephone Public Corp. (NTT) and the International
Telegraph and Telephone Company (KOKUSAI DENSHIN DENWA Co., KDD) use most of
their general-purpose computers in their networks for data communication and
data processing (see Chapters 2.3.3 and 4.3, and [NTT1] page 45); NTT uses them
also in its large laboratories. Many of the computers are DIPS-11 systems
developed by NTT in co-operation with Fujitsu, Hitachi and NEC (see, e.g.
[NTT2], page 24).

The Japan Horse Racing Association uses its computers for compiling data on its
ticket sales for pari-mutuel betting.

The Japan Broadcasting Corporation (Nippon Hoso Kyokai, NHK) operates its Total
On-line Program and Information Control System (TOPICS) which executes all NHK's
business activities including programme network planning, programme performing
schedule and production, and management of programmes and transmission.
Developed since 1963, put into operation in 1968 and continuously improved since
then, it is said to be one of the most advanced total business systems in Japan
(see [NHK2]).

5.2.3   Local Governments

Japan is organised into 47 prefectures (KEN) including the metropolis (TO) Tokyo
and the city districts (FU) Kyoto and Osaka. At the municipal level there are
approximately 3300 cities (SHI), towns and villages, and in the metropolis Tokyo
there are also special wards (KU). According to the Local Autonomy Law the local
governments have the right of self administration, and they are assisted and
advised in their tasks by the Ministry of Home Affairs, which is by far the
smallest of all Japanese ministries.

Computer utilisation by local authorities started in 1960 with the city of
Osaka, followed by the city of Kyoto, Kanagawa prefecture and metropolis Tokyo.
At present all 47 prefectures and about 83% of all municipal bodies are using
computers (2726 municipal bodies out of 3279 in April 1978, see [LASDEC3] page
5). But only approximately 20% of the municipal bodies have computers of their
own, about 60% of them are using the computers of outside organisations.

Table 43 shows the application systems used by prefectures and municipal bodies.
Most of the systems here listed have been developed by the local governments
themselves. For example, the metropolis Tokyo did not use any application system
developed by other institutions until 1979. There is almost no co-operation
between local governments, nor even between different districts or divisions of
the same city, in the purchase and operation of computers and in the development
of software. Most of the software being utilised is special application software.

In 1970, however, the local governments founded the Local Authorities Systems
Development Centre (LASDEC). The Ministry of Home Affairs assisted the
establishment of LASDEC, but is not a member. LASDEC's task is to assist the local governments in their data processing business, to develop standardised sys-

Type of authority	Intro-ducing	Contract-ing	Total	Number of installed computers
Individually utilizing				
Special ward	19	4	23	22
Designated city	9	-	9	68
City	238	352	590	338
Town and village	133	1,557	1,690	139
Sub-total	399	1,913	2,312	567
Joint utilizing				
Sub-total	294	120	414	43
Total	693	2,033	2,726	610

Table 42   Computer utilisation by municipal bodies as of 1st April, 1978
(from [LASDEC3], page 26)

tems and programs for the use of municipal bodies, to disseminate information concerning information processing of local governments, and to train local government personnel. LASDEC made the concepts for the automobile taxation, the residents' taxation, the fixed property taxation, the industrial statistics and the population registration systems. Most local governments programmed their own systems while some even modified LASDEC's concept. The local allocation tax system, however, which was developed and programmed by LASDEC in 1978, is being used by all 47 prefectures.

LASCEC established the Administrative Information System which is a system library containing reliable and proved software systems developed by LASDEC or the local governments. In 1978 this library contained 420-430 systems.

Many cities, towns, villages and wards are developing inhabitants' information systems (JUMIN JOHO system) containing all relevant information about the residents. In 1980 approximately 100 municipal bodies used such a system, most of which had already introduced a personal identification number for their residents. About 800 municipalities used a basic registration system containing personal data, e.g. name, date of birth, sex, relation to householder, place of birth, registration date, former address, election permission, personal insurance, pension, childrens subsidies, car insurance, etc. (see [LASDEC9], page 30). Some municipalities used a DBMS, of which most were AIM of Fujitsu. Many systems processed only alpha-numeric characters and Kana. But because names on documents must be written in Kanji (Chinese characters) some municipalities recently introduced Kanji input and output systems.

a) Metropolitan districts and prefectures

Computer-processed operation	Number of munici- pal bodies
Payrolls	47
Statistical surveys of Ministry of Home Affairs	47
Automobile taxes	47
Specified statistics	46
Afforestation planning	46
Personnel management	45
Bond issue control	41
Clerical work related to personnel committees	40
Various statistics	40
Atmospheric pollution monitoring	39
Administration of various subsidies (agriculture, forestry and fishing)	37
Clerical work concerning various types of welfare funds	37
Various types of surveys (related to commerce and industry)	35
Various types of financial work (related to agriculture, forestry and fishing)	35
Clerical work concerning educational committees	34
Forecasting and planning	32
Public housing management	32
Clerical work related to public safety committee	32
Individual business taxation	31
Accounting	31
Street ledger management	31
Construction and design calculations (related to civil engineering and construction)	30
Corporate taxation	23
Construction and design calculations (related to agriculture, forestry and fisheries)	23
Cooperate and prefectural residents' taxation	22
Automobile income taxation	20
Hospital clerical work	18
Construction progress management	17
Hospital treatment	17
Education	16
Water turbidity measurements	15
Clerical work for election management committee	15
Livelihood protection	14
Merchandise management	13
Various types of financial work (related to commerce and industry)	13
Water service and sewerage	10
Consumers taxatation on food and drink etc.	9
Mine-lot taxation	8
Real estate and income taxation	6
Various types of medical examinations	5
Sound and vibration measurements	5
Agriculture cooperative work	3
National pensions	3

Table 43   Objectives of computer processing by municipal bodies as of 1st April 1978 (from [AMA1], pages 26-29)

b) Cities, towns and villages

Computer-processed operation	Number of munici- pal bodies
Residents' taxation	2,572
Fixed property taxation	2,342
National health insurance	2,034
Light vehicle taxation	1,548
Payroll	1,318
Water service and sewerage	1,077
National pensions	1,049
Urban planning taxation	712
Statistical surveys of Ministry of Home Affairs	686
Residents' records	684
Clerical work for election management committee	485
Clerical work for educational committees	438
Various types of medical examinations	431
Personnel management	330
Agriculture cooperative work	270
Bond issue management	184
Public housing management	166
Clerical work concerning various types of welfare funds	106
Livelihood protection	104
Specified statistics	101
Education	80
Accounting work	79
Hospital clerical work	65
Atmospheric pollution monitoring	52
Forecasting and planning	44
Various types of surveys (related to commerce and industry)	36
Merchandise management	26
Hospital treatment	22
Street ledger management	18
Clerical work related to personnel committee	16
Construction and design calculations (related to civil engineering and construction)	11
Administration of various types of subsidies (related to agriculture, forestry and fisheries)	10
Water turbidity measurements	7
Noise and vibration measurements	7
Administration of various funds (commerce and industry)	6
Construction and design calculations (agriculture, forestry and fisheries)	4
Construction progress management	3
Administration of various funds (agriculture, forestry and fisheries)	2

Table 43   (part 2)

5.2.4   Data Exchange within the Government

In 1968 the cabinet issued a decision concerning the computerisation of government work including the efficient use of data. Nevertheless the exchange of
machine readable data within the government is not very great.

In particular, the exchange of personal data is limited since the government
cancelled the introduction of a personal identification number. The following
are the main cases of exchange of machine-readable media containing personal
data:

- car registration
  The 80-90 branch offices of the Ministry of Transport transmit the data about
  car registration on-line to the ministry. The ministry sends the data on tape
  to LASDEC, about 4 or 5 reels daily. LASDEC sorts the data according to the
  prefectures and sends the tapes to the prefectures. The transmitted data are
  about 2.5 million cases per month

- vital statistics
  The 47 prefectures transmit their population data (birth, death, stillbirth,
  marriage, divorce, change of address) monthly to the Ministry of Health and
  Welfare by marksheets. The Ministry adds the coded name of the illness and
  sends the data on tape to LASDEC, which sorts the data according to the
  prefectures and sends the tapes or total tables to the prefectures.

- The Ministry of Law sends data about Japanese entering Japan to the Ministry
  of Foreign Affairs, the Immigration Office, the Public Prosecuter and the
  police.

- The Ministry of Transport sends data about car accidents to the police.

Besides these data flows there are only small amounts of exchange of personal
data.

5.2.5   Universities

In 1975 Japan had 81 national, 34 public and 305 private colleges and universities offering at least a four-year programme. The private universities are
financed mainly by the students' fees which are very high. National and public
universities claim no or comparatively low fees. The University of Tokyo (TOKYO
DAIGAKU, abbreviated to TODAI) is a national university and is the best and most
wealthy of Japanese universities. It gets special support from the Ministry of
Education. The University of Tokyo is the most important in the field of computer science. Next in importance in the field of computer science come the
universities of Kyoto and Osaka, then the Tokyo Institute of Technology. Out of
the private universities Keio University is the most important in computer
science, and although Waseda and Sofia Universities are also famous they do not
offer computer science. Generally speaking, national universities are more important in the field of information science and, because they have more financial support and relatively fewer students, they have more opportunities for
research.

- Tokyo University

    Prof. KUNII   : data bases

    Prof. WADA   : operating systems, advanced programming languages, e.g. they
                      are now implementing ADA - the programming language used by
                      the US Department of Defence

    Prof. MOTOOKA   : data flow hardware systems using micro-processors

    Prof. GOTO   : Parametron, a specific language for symbol manipulation

- Kyoto University

    Prof. HAGIWARA : Micro programming

    Prof. NAGAO   : natural languages, picture processing

    Prof. SAKAI   : voice recognition

- Osaka University

    All staff are doing theoretical research.

    Prof. HASAMI   : automata theory

    Prof. TANAKA   : fuzzy automata theory

- Keio University

    Prof. AISO   : multi-processor systems, simulation of complex systems

In principle universities have no duties to industry but they will often be
asked to make contributions. Industry often needs some neutral person to check
their concepts, or assigns special research projects to a university institute.
For example, Keio University's Laboratory of Computer Engineering receives
allowances for research projects from industry which are higher than its official budget. But not all universities have contracts with industry like Keio.
From industry's viewpoint, the research of most universities is too theoretical.
The main research is being made by the industries themselves.

The duties of a professor can be illustrated in this example from Keio
University: Normally a professor has to teach two classes of undergraduate
students and one class of graduates per semester, but the graduate class is held
in only one semester per year (1 class = 1.5 hours). He may use the rest of his
time for any purpose: research, outside activities in committees etc., special
lectures, etc. Because of their knowledge, professors are members of many committees and bodies, e.g.:

- the Information Industry Sub-committee of MITI's Industrial Structure Council

- the Research Committee on Fifth Generation Computers organised by JIPDEC

- the advisory committee of JSD's Software Engineering Project

(see also [REPORTS], reports about Keio University and University of Tokyo).

5.2.6   Research Institutes

In Japan most R & D activities in the technological field are carried out by the laboratories of private companies and also most government expenditures for the promotion of research are in favour of industry. Therefore there are only a few public research institutes, mainly the laboratories of MITI and NTT. The main R & D institutes in the field of information processing are:

- AIST's Electro-technical Laboratory :
  theoretical and practical research; fundamental research on optical fibres, semi-conductors, computer architecture, advanced peripherals, software engineering, artificial intelligence; supervision of and research activities for Large-Scale Projects of the National R & D Programme; also other fields than information technology, e.g. research on energy; staff of over 700 employees, budget about 46 million Dollars in 1980 (see also Chapter 2.2.3, [AIST1] and [AIST6]).

- NTT's three Electrical Communication Laboratories :
  theoretical and practical research; staff of over 3000, one third for computer science; development of the DIPS computer system, computer networks based on CCITT standards, network architecture DCNA in competition with IBM SNA, budget fully financed out of NTT's own reserves (see also Chapter 2.3.3).

- JIPDEC :
  practical research mainly in the field of software technology, network architecture (e.g. Resource Sharing System (RSS)), distributed data bases, computer architecture (5th generation computer), application software, surveys and studies; education of dp experts; staff of about 150, budget 2.3 billion Yen in 1980 (see also Chapter 2.1.3.4).

- Kansai Institute of Information Systems :
  research institute similar to JIPDEC but for the Kansai region (West Japan, around Kyoto and Osaka).

- Information Processing Society of Japan :
  theoretical research; partner of IFIP, ISO and other international committees.

6. JAPANESE SOFTWARE

6.1   System software

System software seems to be the most advanced of Japanese software. The Japanese manufacturers of general-purpose computers have much experience in developing system software, in particular for operating systems. Most of them had licence contracts with American manufacturers in the 1960s, and their first system programs were based on those of their foreign partners. However, they developed independently the system software for their present series, which is nevertheless so designed to compete with IBM's systems, and the interfaces of the system programs of Fujitsu and Hitachi are even identical to IMB/370 system programs.

As the new computer systems needed good system software, MITI's promotion measures in favour of software were mainly concerned with basic software. The most important public projects for the development of system software were:

- Nippon Software Co. (NSC) operated from 1966-72 and developed the basic software for the "Project on the Development of a High Performance Electronic Computer", directed by AIST (see Chapters 3.2.1 and 3.2.3).

- Fujitsu, Hitachi and NEC co-operated with NTT's ECL in developing the system software for NTT's DIPS computer system (see Chapter 3.2.1).

- The Computer Basic Technology Research Association (1979-1983) will develop system software for a future computer system.

- Most of the packages registered in the General Purpose Software Package Registration System are system programs, which have mostly been developed by the main-frame manufacturers (see Chapter 2.1.3.2 d).

- Furthermore about 30% of the subsidies from IPA for software development have been granted for system programs.

a) operating systems

The operating systems (OS) of the Japanese general purpose computer series are: (see Chapter 3.2.1)

- FACOM M-series :   OSIV/F2, OSIV/F4, OSIV/X8

- HITAC M-series :   VOS1, VOS2, VOS3

- ACOS series 77 :   ACOS-2, ACOS-4, ACOS-6

- COSMO series   :   UMS/VS, UTS/VS, BPM, RBM, DPS.

These operating systems have high speed and throughput and compete well with IBM OS. According to speed, throughput and reliability users consider them to be as

effective as IBM OS. But they think that Japanese computer manufacturers do not
have modern OS for medium sized computers like the UNIX system of Digital Equipment (DEC). Scientists of research institutions and universities mentioned the
UNIX system as the main reason for the purchase of a DEC computer system
especially because of its good editing functions. The OS of Japanese mini- and
office computers, however, are estimated to be very advanced.

b) compiler and utilities

All computer manufacturers have various compilers and utilities.

c) data base management systems

Table 44 shows the data base management systems (DBMS) of the Japanese computer
manufacturers. Most of them were announced during 1976 and 1977 and came on the
market later than IBM's IMS.

AIM, Fujitsu's DBMS for its M-series, has been modelled in order to compete with
IBM's IMS. In contrast to IMS, however, it is integrated into the OS in order to
be more effective and to avoid double functions. For former users of IMS Fujitsu
offers its IMS Interface and Support System (IISS) by which the former IMS user
can change his IMS data base into an AIM data base and use his IMS programs
which are being interpreted by IISS.

Supplier	DBMS	Product Type	Computer Model	Price in Yen	Users (as of)
Fujitsu	AIM	CODASYL	M160, 180II, 190	–	20 (4/78)
	INIS	based on RAPID	FACOM "8" Series	–	60 (2/77)
	RICS	based on RAPID	FACOM "8" Series FACOM 230-75	–	5 (2/77)
Hitachi	PDM	Network	HITAC 8250-8700, M150 – 180	–	130 (2/77)
	ADM	Hierarchical	HITAC 8350-8700, M160II, 170, 180	–	26 (2/77)
NEC	ADBS	CODASYL	ACOS 300-500	–	50 (6/78)
	IDS	CODASYL	ACOS 600-900	–	60 (6/78)
	RIQS/INQ	CODASYL / Relational	ACOS 600-900	–	9 (6/78)
Mitsubishi	EDMS	CODASYL	COSMO 700, 900	170 000/Mo	19 (2/77)
	DMS-5	CODASYL / EDMS-Subset	COSMO 500	80 000/Mo	2 (2/77)

Table 44   DBMS packages offered by Japanese computer makers
             (from EJR Vol.5, No.11, page 5)

RIQS or INQ of NEC, and ADM of Hitachi, have been modelled after ADABAS of Software AG. PDM of Hitachi which is modelled after TOTAL of Cincom Systems is the
number one DBMS package of the systems offered by domestic manufacturers according to the number of installations.

The most successful DBMS, however, is IBM's IMS. The reason for this success is
the loyalty of IBM users to IBM products and services, and the fact that IBM was
on the market earlier than its competitors. DMSII of Borrough's was also very
successful penetrating 99% of Borrough's medium to large scale computer market
in Japan.

Regarding the fact that the DBMS of the computer manufacturers are comparatively
cheap or even free of charge, the success of the DBMS of foreign software houses
is astonishing. The customers for which the software houses mainly developed
their DBMS are IBM users and users of IBM compatible systems. Although ADABAS is
the most expensive of all listed DBMS, its success stemmed from a very careful
market strategy, and by the end of 1979 it already had 27 installations and 8
test installations. However, software houses still have some problems because
users have more confidence in the computer manufacturers than in the software
houses, especially since the licence right for TOTAL was recently transferred
from Cincom Systems to another company.

Supplier	DBMS	Product Type	Computer Model	Price in Yen	Users (as of)
IBM Japan	IMS	Hierarchical	370/138-168, 370/145-195	230,000/Mo	100+(6/78)
Burroughs	DMS II	CODASYL	B1700-B7700 B1800-B7800	–	80 (6/78)
Nippon Univac	DMS-1000	Network	Univac 1100 Series	free	–
NCR Japan	NCR-TOTAL	CODASYL	Century Series, N8450 & Up	9 Million	–
DEC Japan	DBMS 11/10/20	CODASYL	PDP-11 Series, System 10 & 20	–	10 (6/78)
CDC Japan	DMS-170	CODASYL	CYBER170 Series, 70/1000 Series	–	–

Table 45   DBMS packages sold in Japan by US computer makers
(from EJR Vol.5, No.11, page 4)

Software House	Japanese Sales Agent	DBMS	Product Type	Computer Model	Price in Yen	Users (as of)
CINCOM Systems	CINCOM Systems Japan	TOTAL	Network	IBM, Univac, Burroughs, CDC, DEC, F-H M-series	270,000- 600,000/Mo	27 (6/78)
Cullinane Corp.	JMA Systems	IDMS	CODASYL	IBM 360/370, 303X, F-H M-series	15 Million	1 (6/78)
MRI System	CJK	SYSTEM 2000	CODASYL	IBM 360/370, Univac 1100 series, F-H M-series	600,000-1.1 Million/Mo	1 (6/78)
Software A.G.	Software A.G. of Far East	ADABAS	Inverted File Structure	IBM 360/370, F-H M-series, Siemens 7000	36 Million	15 (6/78)

Table 46   DBMS packages offered by major foreign software firms
              (from EJR Vol.5, No.11, page 7)

d) computer network architecture

Table 47 shows the network architectures of computer manufacturers in Japan.
They can be classified into two groups: those which are designed in order to be
compatible with IBM's SNA, and those which (like DCNA) adapt the standards of
ISO and CCITT, principally X.25 and HDLC. Most of the Japanese computer
manufacturers co-operated with NTT in developing DCNA, and their own network
architectures are compatible with DCNA. Fujitsu and Oki, however, made their
respective network systems FNA and DONA compatible with SNA in order to meet the
needs of the IBM users. Figure 48 illustrates NTT's DCNA concept.

Most of the existing networks, however, have been developed by the users
themselves, mostly in co-operation with NTT or the computer manufacturers (by
March 1978 there were 2749 network systems, see JR No.37, page 46). Because they
have been developed before the announcement of NTT's DCNA and the international
standards of X.25 and HDLC, they are not compatible with DCNA. Even some of
NTT's services, e.g. DEMOS and DRESS, do not observe the DCNA concept, but new
protocols for DEMOS and DRESS are under development which will adopt this concept.

Maker		Network architecture	Issue
IBM	SNA	Systems Network Architecture	9/74
Toshiba	ANSA	Advanced Network System Architecture	12/76
NEC	DINA	Distributed Information Processing Network Architecture	12/76
NTT	DCNA	Data Communication Network Architecture	3/77
Fujitsu/Hitachi	MSNA	M Series Network Architecture	3/77
Fujitsu	FNA	Fujitsu Network Architecture	5/77
Hitachi	HNA	Hitachi Network Architecture	5/77
Mitsubishi Electric	MNA	Multi-share Network Architecture	3/77
Oki Electric Ind.	DONA	Decentralized Open Network Architecture	3/77
Nippon Univac	DCA		
Burroughs Japan	DNS		
Toshiba	TOSWAY		

Table 47   Network architectures of mainframe makers
(from "Continuing Progress of Computerization in Japan 1977–78"
published by CICC, page 47)

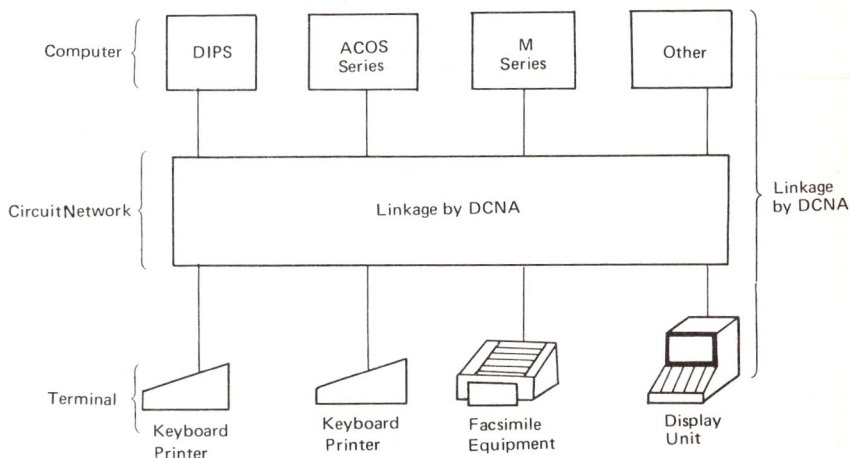

Note:
ACOS Series: Computer Systems developed jointly by NEC and Toshiba.
M Series: Computer Systems developed jointly by Hitachi and Fujitsu.

Figure 48   NTT's concept of a future data communication system based on DCNA
(from "Continuing Progress of Computerisation in Japan 1977–78",
published by CICC, page 47)

NTT has four authorised public networks: the public telephone exchange network,
the TELEX network, the telegraph exchange network, and the digital communication
network DDX (Dendenkosha Data Exchange System), (see JR No.37, pages 46ff.; EJR
Vol.4, Nos.6, 11 and 14; EJR Vol.6, pages 86-93; and Chapter 2.3.3). DDX, consisting of a circuit and a package switching system, adopts the DCNA concept but
it is also supposed to serve SNA users (see Figure 49).

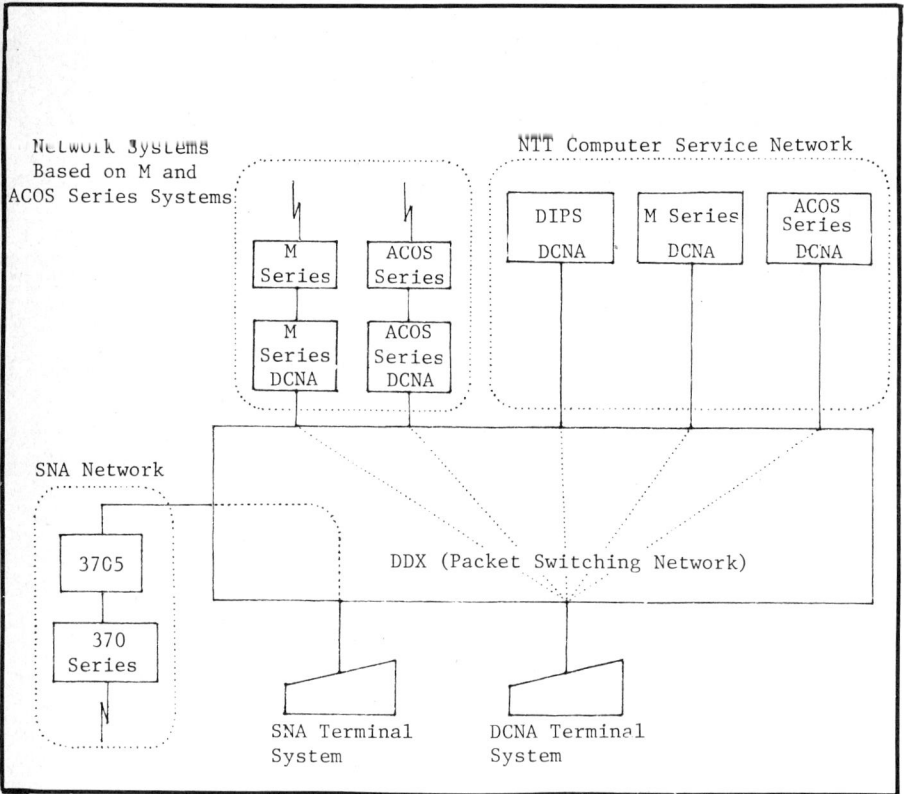

Figure 49 DCNA and SNA in the DDX network (from EJR Vol.4, No.14, page 5)

6.2   Application Systems

A lack of application software is supposed to be the greatest impediment for a
further expansion of the market share of the Japanese computer manufacturers,
e.g. many IBM users in Japan mentioned the large variety of IBM's application
software to be one of the important reasons for purchasing an IBM computer system. This is a great problem for Japanese computer manufacturers, because the
area of application software is very large. The capacity of the computer
manufacturers is almost covered by the development of system software, e.g. the
quantity of application software made by Fujitsu is only about one sixth of that
of basic software.

Most software systems at present being used are for special purposes. The systems have usually been developed by the users themselves under the assistance of
and co-operation with the computer manufacturers. Large users usually have large
dp divisions employing many skilled experts who want to develop their own application software. Furthermore the computer manufacturers offered their software
development assistance at a very low cost and sometimes, because of the strong
competition, even free of charge. But because of the rising software development
costs and the growing complexity of software systems, the computer manufacturers
had to promote the use of general purpose software. Their decision to "unbundle"
software was a step in this direction. Good software packages are especially important if the Japanese computer manufacturers want to enter the US market. At
present all Japanese computer manufacturers offer a large variety of general
purpose software systems. As an illustration, NEC's application systems for its
ACOS series 77 model 450 are listed below (from "NEC system 450", a booklet, by
Nippon Electric Co.):

- Management Science

    * Mathematical Programming System MSP
    * Statistics Analytic System STATPAC
    * Cluster Analytic System CLUSTER
    * Cross Total System CROSS
    * Multiple Dimensional Data Analysis System MDAS
    * Forecasting / Computation Economic System FORES
    * Industry Related Analysis System 10A
    * Project Planning / Management System PMCS
    * Discrete Type Simulation Language GPSS/V
    * System Dynamics Language DYNAMO/F
    * Continuous Type Simulation Language CSPL
    * Continuous and Discrete Joint Purpose Simulation Library SIML

- Engineering

    * Mathematical Library MATHLIB
    * Graphic Display Library GDSP
    * Digital Plotter Library PGL
    * Automatically Programmed Tool System APT80
    * Construction/Engineering Works/Structure Package Library ICEP
    * Composite Structure Analysis System ISAP
    * Electronic Circuitry Network Analysis System ECAP

- Information Retrieval

    * Information Retrieval System IRS
    * The Japanese Language Information Retrieval System LRS.N
    * Code Retrieval System IRS/CODE
    * Pharmacology Document Retrieval System IRS/RING

- Management and Business Data Processing

    * Management Evaluation System MEDIC
    * Japanese Language Management Evaluation System MEDIC.N
    * Tax Calculation Library TAXLIB
    * Composite Accounting System CASY
    * Japanese Language Composite Accounting System CASY.N

- Production Management

    * Material Planning / Management System AMCS
    * Extended Material Planning / Management System AMCS.EX
    * Schedule Planning / Management System APCS

- The Japanese Language Processing

    * Japanese Language File Processing System NFPS
    * Japanese Language Document Designing System NFDS
    * Kana-Kanji Conversion System KKCS

The computer series like the FACOM M-series which are IBM compatible can use the application programs written for the IBM/370 system without being changed. But, because of small incompatibilities in special interfaces and because of a time gap of modification, Fujitsu usually confirms software packages originally written for IBM systems.

The use of general purpose software, however, is limited in Japanese companies for the following reasons:

- the business structure of Japanese companies is as yet less standardised than that of American or European firms

- text processing is more difficult for the Japanese language than for Western languages

- as mentioned before, Japanese users are not yet aware of the value of software, therefore they are not willing to pay separately for software

- the experts of dp divisions want to develop their own software systems.

For these reasons the software package market is not very advanced. In some areas of business, however, the software packages are already being used very frequently. According to Fujitsu's information, software packages are easily marketed in the business fields of management science, management planning and control, engineering, and information retrieval.

Generally speaking, numerical programs - such as scientific calculations, econometric modelling, process control, or operations research - are quite advanced, whereas text processing and general business programs – such as accounting and transaction data processing – are less advanced than in Europe and the US because of the difficulties of the Japanese language and the lack of standardisation of Japanese companies. For example, Fujitsu developed an accounting system but, because all users wanted so many modifications, they discontinued it. Japanese text processing is developing very rapidly, but in comparison with English word processing it is still lagging behind. One meets large numerical data bases containing technical, financial and economic data, etc., but data bases containing Chinese characters (Kanjis) are met more seldom, e.g. the bibliographical JICST file only started storing Kanji characters since 1977.

The Japanese computer manufacturers are also marketing many software packages which have been developed by foreign software houses. The Japanese users like using these foreign packages because they have already been proved effective. For example, Information Services International Dentsu Ltd., which supplies software packages through the "Author System" of its Mark III network, offers mostly foreign packages (see EJR Vol.7, page 82).

6.3   Kanji Processing

Japanese language processing is essential for an increasing computer usage in Japan. Written Japanese is composed of Chinese (KANJI) characters and phonetic (KANA, i.e. HIRAGANA and KATAKANA) characters. Hiragana and Katakana total only 47 characters, but there are well over 10,000 Kanji characters. The Ministry of Education issued a list of 1850 common use Kanjis, the so-called TOYO-KANJI, but some 3000 Kanjis are ordinarily used in newspapers and periodicals.

Former systems processed only Roman (Latin) characters or Kana characters. However, Japanese texts written in Kana or Roman characters are very difficult to read and are often ambiguous. Because of these problems the CAPTAIN system of NTT uses, for example, a keyboard containing only numbers since the use of Roman or Kana characters would offer only a little more ease of use but would be much more expensive. Both industry and government made a great effort to develop methods for Kanji processing, e.g. the National R & D Project "Pattern Information Processing System (PIPS), (see also Chapters 2.2.2.3(1) and 2.2.3).

Pace-setters for the use of Japanese word processing systems were newspapers, printing companies and data base suppliers, e.g.

- Newspaper Composition System ANNECS of Nihon Keizai Shimbun, a major economic journal (see JR No.36, page 51)

- Diet Processing Reference System of the National Diet Library (see JR No.25, page 28)

- JICST Science and Engineering Documents File (see Chapter 4.3)

- NELSON system of the ASAHI SHIMBUN, a leading vernacular newspaper

- Encyclopedia Editing System of Gakushu Kenkyu Sha (see EJR Vol.6, page 58).

However, recently various computer manufacturers have developed comparatively cheap Japanese word processing systems which are going to penetrate the Japanese market, mainly in the field of office work (see JR No.40). Most are stand alone minicomputers or small business computers; however, Fujitsu's Japanese Processing Extended Facility (JEF) has been integrated into the system software of its M-series computers (see, for example, AEU, June 1980, page 144; or EJR No.6, page 59). By using JEF the user can handle Chinese characters in high level programming languages as comfortably as other characters. Recently, other manufacturers have also introduced similar Japanese language processing facilities (see JR No.45, page 11).

Compared with Roman characters the handling of Kanji characters has some difficulties concerning data input, storage, retrieval and output, for which various solutions have been proposed. The difficulties arise from the large number of Kanji and their complicated structure. The JIS (Japanese Industrial Standard) code has a first level consisting of 2984 Kanji, and a second level of 3384 Kanji, totalling 6349 characters, which are arranged in a 14-bit system (compare JR No.36, pages 41ff.). Figure 50 shows a small detail of the JIS code. Since the JIS Kanji code was issued comparatively late, most existing systems do not apply it, using instead their own codes.

The methods of arranging Kanji characters which are in use are

- according to the radicals, similar to the methods used in Chinese character dictionaries

- according to representative readings which may be "Chinese" readings (ON – reading), or "Japanese" readings (KUN – reading)

- according to the number of strokes.

If Kanji are arranged according to their radicals or the number of strokes, searching for a character is very dificult. Arrangement according to representative readings is complicated because most Kanji have multiple Chinese and Japanese readings. In the JIS Code the Kanji of the first level are arranged according to the "Chinese" reading, but those of the second level are arranged according to their radicals.

							第2バイト b7	0	0	0	0	0	0	0	0	0	0	0	0	0	0	0	0	0
							b6	1	1	1	1	1	1	1	1	1	1	1	1	1	1	1	1	1
							b5	0	0	0	0	0	0	0	0	0	0	0	0	0	0	0	1	1
							b4	0	0	0	0	0	0	0	1	1	1	1	1	1	1	1	0	0
							b3	0	0	0	1	1	1	1	0	0	0	0	1	1	1	1	0	0
							b2	0	1	1	0	0	1	1	0	0	1	1	0	0	1	1	0	0
							b1	1	0	1	0	1	0	1	0	1	0	1	0	1	0	1	0	1
b7	b6	b5	b4	b3	b2	b1	区＼点	1	2	3	4	5	6	7	8	9	10	11	12	13	14	15	16	17
0	1	0	0	0	0	1	1	(SP)	、	。	，	．	・	：	；	？	！	゛	゜	´	｀	¨	＾	￣
0	1	0	0	0	1	0	2	◆	□	■	△	▲	▽	▼	※	〒	→	←	↑	↓	＝			
0	1	0	0	0	1	1	3																0	1
0	1	0	0	1	0	0	4	ぁ	あ	ぃ	い	ぅ	う	ぇ	え	ぉ	お	か	が	き	ぎ	く	ぐ	け
0	1	0	0	1	0	1	5	ァ	ア	ィ	イ	ゥ	ウ	ェ	エ	ォ	オ	カ	ガ	キ	ギ	ク	グ	ケ
0	1	0	0	1	1	0	6	Α	Β	Γ	Δ	Ε	Ζ	Η	Θ	Ι	Κ	Λ	Μ	Ν	Ξ	Ο	Π	Ρ
0	1	0	0	1	1	1	7	А	Б	В	Г	Д	Е	Ё	Ж	З	И	Й	К	Л	М	Н	О	П
0	1	0	1	0	0	0	8																	
0	1	0	1	0	0	1	9																	
0	1	0	1	0	1	0	10																	
0	1	0	1	0	1	1	11																	
0	1	0	1	1	0	0	12																	
0	1	0	1	1	0	1	13																	
0	1	0	1	1	1	0	14																	
0	1	0	1	1	1	1	15																	
0	1	1	0	0	0	0	16	亜	唖	娃	阿	哀	愛	挨	姶	逢	葵	茜	穐	悪	握	渥	旭	葦
0	1	1	0	0	0	1	17	院	陰	隠	韻	吋	右	宇	烏	羽	迂	雨	卯	鵜	窺	丑	碓	臼
0	1	1	0	0	1	0	18	押	旺	横	欧	殴	王	翁	襖	鴬	鴎	黄	岡	沖	荻	億	屋	憶
0	1	1	0	0	1	1	19	魁	晦	械	海	灰	界	皆	絵	芥	蟹	開	階	貝	凱	劾	外	咳
0	1	1	0	1	0	0	20	粥	刈	苅	瓦	乾	侃	冠	寒	刊	勘	勧	巻	喚	堪	姦	完	官
0	1	1	0	1	0	1	21	機	帰	毅	気	汽	畿	祈	季	稀	紀	徽	規	記	貴	起	軌	輝
0	1	1	0	1	1	0	22	供	侠	僑	兇	競	共	凶	協	匡	卿	叫	喬	境	峡	強	彊	怯
0	1	1	0	1	1	1	23	掘	窟	沓	靴	轡	窪	熊	隈	粂	栗	繰	桑	鍬	勲	君	薫	訓
0	1	1	1	0	0	0	24	検	権	牽	犬	献	研	硯	絹	県	肩	見	謙	賢	軒	遣	鍵	険
0	1	1	1	0	0	1	25	后	喉	坑	垢	好	孔	孝	宏	工	巧	巷	幸	広	庚	康	弘	恒

Figure 50　A small detail of the japanese graphic character set for information interchange, JIS C 6226-1978

Regarding Kanji input, several input methods have been developed which are listed in table 51.

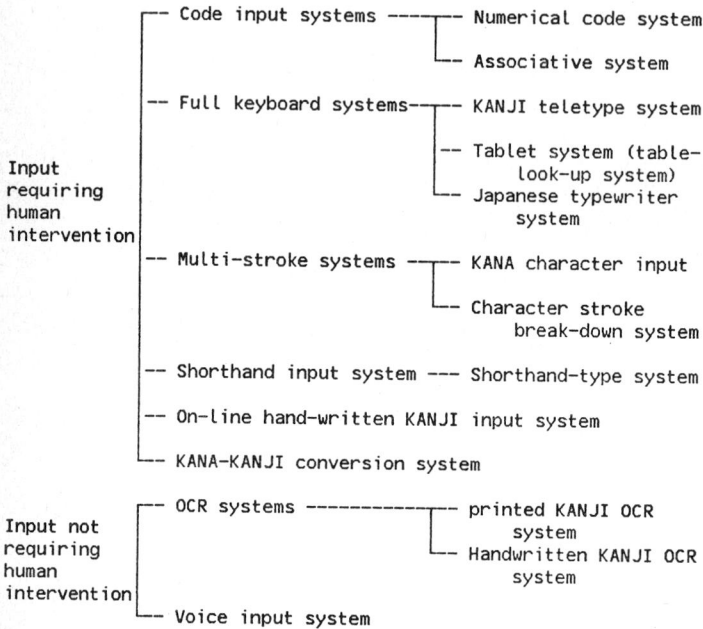

```
                   ┌── Code input systems ───┬── Numerical code system
                   │                          └── Associative system
                   │
                   │── Full keyboard systems──┬── KANJI teletype system
                   │                          │
                   │                          │── Tablet system (table-
Input              │                          │    look-up system)
requiring          │                          └── Japanese typewriter
human              │                               system
intervention       │
                   │── Multi-stroke systems ──┬── KANA character input
                   │                          │
                   │                          └── Character stroke
                   │                               break-down system
                   │
                   │── Shorthand input system ─── Shorthand-type system
                   │
                   │── On-line hand-written KANJI input system
                   │
                   └── KANA-KANJI conversion system

                   ┌── OCR systems ───────────┬── printed KANJI OCR
Input not          │                          │    system
requiring          │                          └── Handwritten KANJI OCR
human              │                               system
intervention       │
                   └── Voice input system
```

Table 51   Classification of input systems
             (from JR No.36, page 45)

Code input systems require a long training for the typist in order to memorise the codes of the frequently used Kanji, but it can attain the highest input speeds (around 100-120 characters per minute). In the Japanese typewriter system all Kanjis are depicted on the keyboard and every Kanji is input by one touch (by pen or finger). The Kanji teletype system is a multiple touch system in which the characters are arranged in blocks and are identified by two (or more) touches. On the tablet system the characters are arranged by pages of a booklet. By these full keyboard systems an experienced typist can input 50 ~ 60 characters per minute. The method which is most adequate for inexperienced persons is the Kana-Kanji conversion system. The typist types the phonetic Kana character and the computer will depict the Kanji characters which have the respective pronunciation in the order of frequency of use. Toshiba's Japanese word processor JW-10 can even select the Kanji according to the grammatical context.

The output of Kanji is complicated and expensive because of the complex structure. Kanji characters need at least a 18 x 16 dot matrix for printing but, in
order to achieve a good readability, even more dots are being used, e.g. 24 x 24
or 32 x 32 dot matrices. Taking a 24 x 24 dot matrix and a set of 2000 Kanji the
output device must have a memory of more than 1 million bits just for generating
these 2000 Kanji. Therefore Kanji terminals are much more expensive than normal
terminals and their use is often limited by financial reasons.

Table 52 is a list of small business computers incorporating Kanji processing
features and Table 53 is a list of Japanese word processors.

Japanese word processors are specially made for Kanji processing, while small
business computers also have versions which incorporate only Roman and Kana
Characters. The best selling system of those listed is Toshiba's TOSBAC Kanji
System 15, Model 3. As can be seen from Tables 52 and 53, non Japanese
manufacturers have also developed Japanese text processing systems. The Japanese
word processing technology is not only essential for handling the Japanese language, but for all languages which have non-Roman characters, and is therefore
very important for the whole of the Asian market (see e.g. EJR Vol.6, page 133).

The introduction of Japanese text processing will change the office work more
than text processing did in Western countries. Because of the complexity of the
Japanese language, typewriters were never popular in Japan and at present most
documents are still being written by hand (see EJR Vol.7, page 100).

Manufacturer	Model	Input Device		Output Device				Display Unit		Main Memory	Auxiliary Memory	Price (M Yen)	Date of Announce.
		Input Method	Char. Sets	Output Method	Printing Speed	#Chars/Line	#Matrix Format	#Chars.	Matrix Format				
Casio	8700 Model 130	Pen Touch / Tenkey	2,000	Dot Matrix	40cps	68cpl	16x16	40x10	16x16		243KBx2(FDD)	5.35	5/79
	8700 Model 135	Pen Touch / Tenkey	2,000	Dot Matrix	40cps	68cpl	16x16	40x10	16x16		1MBx2(FDD)	5.70	5/79
	8700 Model 140	Pen Touch / Tenkey	2,000	Dot Matrix	40cps	68cpl	16x16	40x10	16x16		243KBx2(FDD)	5.70	5/79
	8700 Model 145	Pen Touch / Tenkey	2,000	Dot Matrix	40cps	68cpl	16x16	40x10	16x16		1MBx2(FDD)	6.05	5/79
	8700 Model 170	Pen Touch / Tenkey	2,000	Dot Matrix	40cps	68cpl	16x16	40x10	16x16	224KB	243KB(FDD) 18.6MB(Disk)	8.50	8/79
	8700 Model 175	Pen Touch / Tenkey	2,000	Dot Matrix	40cps	68cpl	16x16	40x10	16x16	224KB	972KB(FDD) 18.6MB(Disk)	8.68	8/79
	8700 Model 180	Pen Touch / Tenkey	2,000	Dot Matrix	40cps	68cpl	16x16	40x10	16x16	224KB	243KB(FDD) 18.6MB(Disk)	8.85	8/79
	8700 Model 185	Pen Touch / Tenkey	2,000	Dot Matrix	40cps	68cpl	16x16	40x10	16x16	224KB	972KB(FDD) 18.6MB(Disk)	9.03	8/79
Canon	CANONAC 71	Pen Touch / Tenkey	46	Dot Matrix	90cps	68cpl	9x18	80x20	16x16	32KB	512KBx2(FDD) 256KBx2(FDD)	4.95- 15.00	9/79
Fujitsu	FACOM SYSTEM 80	Pen Touch	3,072	Dot Matrix	45cps	68cpl	16x16	40x24	16x16	192KB	10MB-40MB	10.18	4/79
IBM Japan	IBM Kanji System / 34	Full Keyboard	6,709	Dot Matrix	851pm 1401pm	66cpl 66cpl	18x18 18x18	40x12	18x18	48KB- 128KB	8.6MB(Disk) 13.2MB-128.4MB(Disk)	0.5/Mo	10/79
Japan Business Computer Japan	JBC System 1	Finger Touch / Tenkey	3,200	Dot Matrix	371pm	68cpl	16x23	384	24x24	64KB	2MB-4MB(FDD)	0.127/Mo	4/78
	JBC 100 Series	Pen Touch	6,500	Dot Matrix	20cps	64cpl	24x24	384	24x24	64KB	20MB-592MB (Disk)	0.2/Mo	5/79
Mitsubishi Electric	MELCOM 80 Super 8 Kanji	Finger Touch / Tenkey	2,965	Dot Matrix	20cps	88cpl	24x24	512	24x24	32KB	10MB(CDD)	7.18	7/79
	Nihongo Model 18	Tenkey / Phonetic / Book / Pen Touch / OCR / Associate / Bar Code	3,418	Dot Matrix	60cps	88cpl	24x24	40x25	24x24	192KB- 256KB	3.5MB, 8MB(Disk)	7.20-	3/80
	Nihongo Model 28	ditto	3,418	Dot Matrix	60cps	88cpl	24x24	40x25	24x24	256KB-	3.5MB, 8MB(Disk)	7.20-	3/80
	Nihongo Model 38	ditto	3,418	Dot Matrix	60cps	88cpl	24x24	40x25	24x24	-512KB	3.5MB, 8MB(Disk)	7.20-	3/80

Table 52   Small business computer models incorporating Kanji processing features (from EJR Vol.6, pages 129,130)

Manufacturer	Model	Input Device		Output Device				Display Unit		Main Memory	Auxiliary Memory	Price (M Yen)	Date of Announce.
		Input Method	Char. Sets	Output Method	Printing Speed	#Chars/Line	#Matrix Format	# Chars.	Matrix Format				
NEC	NEAC System 50II	Pen Touch / Tenkey	3,882	Dot Matrix	90cps	90cpl	24x24	40x16	24x24	256KB-512KB	1MBx4(FDD)	9.3-21.4	2/81
	NEAC System 100II, 150II	Pen Touch / Tenkey	3,882	Dot Matrix	90cps	90cpl	24x24	40x16	24x24	256KB-512KB	1MBx4(FDD)	9.3-21.4	2/81
OKI	OKITAC Model K30 S/9	Pen Touch	6,349	Dot Matrix	60cps	88cpl	24x24	40x16	24x24	128KB	1MBx2(FDD)	7.38	8/78
	OKITAC Model K50	Pen Touch	6,349	Dot Matrix	60cps	88cpl	24x24	40x16	24x24	128KB-256KB	1MBx2(FDD)	8.98	10/79
	OKITAC Model K55	Pen Touch	6,349	Dot Matrix	60cps	88cpl	24x24	40x16	24x24	128KB-256KB	10MB(Disk)	11.98	8/78
	OKITAC Model K60	Pen Touch	6,349	Dot Matrix	60cps	88cpl	24x24	40x16	24x24	128KB-256KB	1MBx2(FDD) 20MB(Disk)	10.48	10/79
	OKITAC Model K70	Pen Touch	6,349	Dot Matrix	60cps	88cpl	24x24	40x16	24x24	128KB-256KB	1MBx2(FDD) 40MB(Disk)	11.98	10/79
Toshiba	TOSBAC Model 10 S/15	Phonetic Book / Associate Code	3,340	Dot Matrix	35cps	90cpl	24x24	64x24	24x24	64KB	243KB(FDD)	6.8	5/78
	TOSBAC Model 20	Phonetic Book / Associate Code	6,688	Dot Matrix	35cps	90cpl	24x24	64x24	24x24	64KB	486KB(FDD)	7.0	5/78
	TOSBAC Model 30	Phonetic Book / Associate Code	11,186	Dot Matrix	35cps	90cpl	24x24	64x24	24x24	64KB	10MB(Disk)	8.7	5/78
	TOSBAC Model 60	Phonetic Book / Associate Code		Dot Matrix	35cps	90cpl	24x24	64x24	24x24	64KB			4/79
	TOSBAC S/65	Phonetic Book /		Dot Matrix	35cps	90cpl	24x24	64x24	24x24	246-1024KB	80MBx8	28.0	11/79
Uchida Yoko	USAC S/11	Pen Touch	3,072	Dot Matrix	45cps	68cpl	24x24	40x24	16x16	192KB	10MB-40MB	10.18	4/79
Nippon Univac	Series 8 Model 20	Tenkey / Phonetic / Book / Pentouch / OCR Associate Code	3,418	Dot Matrix	60cps	88cpl	24x24	40x24	24x24	146KB-262KB	3.5MB, 8MB(Disk)	7.20	3/80
	Series 8 Model 30	ditto	3,418	Dot Matrix	60cps	88cpl	24x24	40x24	24x24	262KB-524KB	3.5MB, 8MB(Disk)	16.00	3/80

Table 52   part 2

Maker	Product title	Model	Price (Yen)	Input system (No. of characters)	Output system	Dots	Output speed
Toshiba	Japanese Word Processor	JW-10	6.3 million	Kana-kanji auto-conversion (6,802)	Wire dot impact	24x24	35 characters/sec.
Pentel	Prose Producer	Petacon	5.5 million	Full-key, pentouch (3,800)	Thermal	24x24	20 characters/sec.
Alps Computer	Japanese Word Processor	CT-2500	7.4 million	Full-key, push (7,560)	Laser printer PPC printer Dot printer	24x24 24x24 24x24	10 pages/min. 10 pages/min. 20 Characters/sec.
Ricoh	Japanese Word Processor	TX-620	Not yet set	Two-touch (2,304)	Electrostatic printer	32x32	84 characters/sec.
Oki Electric	Japanese Electronic Typewriter	Word Editor 200	Master: below 1.2 million Slave: below 600,000	Kanji display selection (3,304)	Wire dot impact	24x24	25 characters/sec.
Nihon Word Processor	Japanese Word Processor	WP-10 WP-10D WP-20 WP-20D	3.2 million 4.8 million 3.7 million 5.4 million	Full-key, pen touch (2,600) Full-key, pen touch (2,600) Full-key, pen touch (4,000) Full-key, pen touch (4,000)	Type character impact	- - - -	10 characters/sec. 10 characters/sec. 10 characters/sec. 10 characters/sec.
Sharp	Japanese Word Processor	Sho-in	2.95 million	Full-key, pen touch (2,646)	Ink-jet	24x24	74 characters/sec.
Canon	Japanese Word Processor	CAT	Not yet set	Kana-kanji auto-conversion (2,965)	Thermal, plain paper	-	15 characters/sec.

Table 53   Japanese word processors (from JR No.40, pages 6,7)

6.4   Software Development

Software has become the bottleneck of further computerisation. Software costs are rising and although many computer users have large dp divisions, they cannot keep pace with the going demands. The solution to the problem is to rationalise software production processes and to utilise more general-purpose software packages. As it is a general situation in Japan's information processing, the mainframe manufacturers are also most advanced concerning the automation of software development. Most manufacturing firms are developing software production systems (SPS), e.g.

- Software Development Engineer's Methodology (SDEM) and Software Development Support System (SDSS) by Fujitsu (see [FUJI13])

- Software Work Bench (SWB) by Toshiba

- Standard Technology and Engineering for Programming Support (STEPS) by NEC (see [NEC17])

- Integrated Computer Aided Software Engineering System (ICAS) by Hitachi (see [HITACHI4])

- Customer Oriented Application Program Development System (CORAL) by Hitachi (see EJR Vol.7, page 63)

- Application Program Support System (APS) for the development of general purpose programs by NTT

- Application Program Generator for Business (APGB) for business applications by NTT

- Program Development System for Microprocessors (PMP) by NTT (see [NTT8]).

These systems are being designed in order to correct the sources of errors in the present process of software development:

- difference between specification and coded program

- difference between the program and its documentation

- lacking documentation

- side effects of modifications

- ill-defined interfaces between different modules.

The software development process has been structured into well-defined steps, the interfaces of which are standardised and are being supported and checked by automated procedures which may even create the documentation automatically. In Table 54, for example, are shown the nine phases in the software development process as in Fujitsu's Software Development Engineer's Methodology (SDEM). As can be seen, the programming and testing support tools of the System Development Support System (SDSS) are being used only beginning with the program design (phase No.4). For the support of planning and system design, however, Fujitsu applies the system ISDOS. The components of SDSS are shown in Table 55 (for further explanations see [FUJI13]).

	PLANNING (PN)			DESIGN (DN)			PROGRAMMING	TESTING (TG)		MAINTENANCE & EVALUATION

Phase / Stage / Step

(1) Survey & Planning (SP) (2) Project Planning (PP) (3) System Design (SD) (4) Software Requirements (5) Program Design (1D) (6) SDR (System Design Review) (7) Programming (8) Integration Test (9) System Test (10) TGR (Testing Review) (11) Operational Test (12) ME

Steps: SP | Basic PP | Detailed PP | Initial Design (ID) | Logical Design (LD) | Program Structure Design (PS) | Module Design (MD) | PG | IT | ST | OT | ME

(GO?) Software Requirements → Software Spec.
System Requirements → System Spec.
FDR (Program Design Review) PDR

Contents

- Survey of Trends
- Analysis of User's Requirements
- System concept

- Detailed System Concept
- Cost/Benefit Analysis
- Plan for Development
- Plan for Resource

- Initial External Design
- System Flow
- System Configuration
- Basic Common Interface

- Detailed External Design
- System Architecture
- Data Design (Logical)

- Specification of Module Structure within Programs
- Procedure for Processes within Module (outline)
- Definition of Module Interface
- Data Design (Physical)

- Procedure for Processes within Modules (Detail)
- Physical Data Design (intra-module)

- Coding
- Debug
- Module Test

- Integration Test
- System Test
- Functional Test Performance Test etc.
- Operational Test
- Total evaluation of Project

- Maintenance
- System Evaluation

Documents

- Survey Drafts

- Project Planning Document

- Initial Design Spec.

- Test Plan Document
- Logical Design Spec.

- Program Structure Specification

- Module Specification
- Module Integ. Test Specification
- User's Manual
- System Test Spec.

- Source List
- Results of Module Test

- Results of Integration/ System Test
- Maintenance guide
- Operation Manual

- Evaluation Report

Supporting Tools

ISDOS (ISL, PSA)

Project Library
MDL, MDA

Software Development Support System (SDSS)
Module Test Tool, Test Comparator, Path Tracer, (Stu, Driver) Test Case Selector

Standards for system development

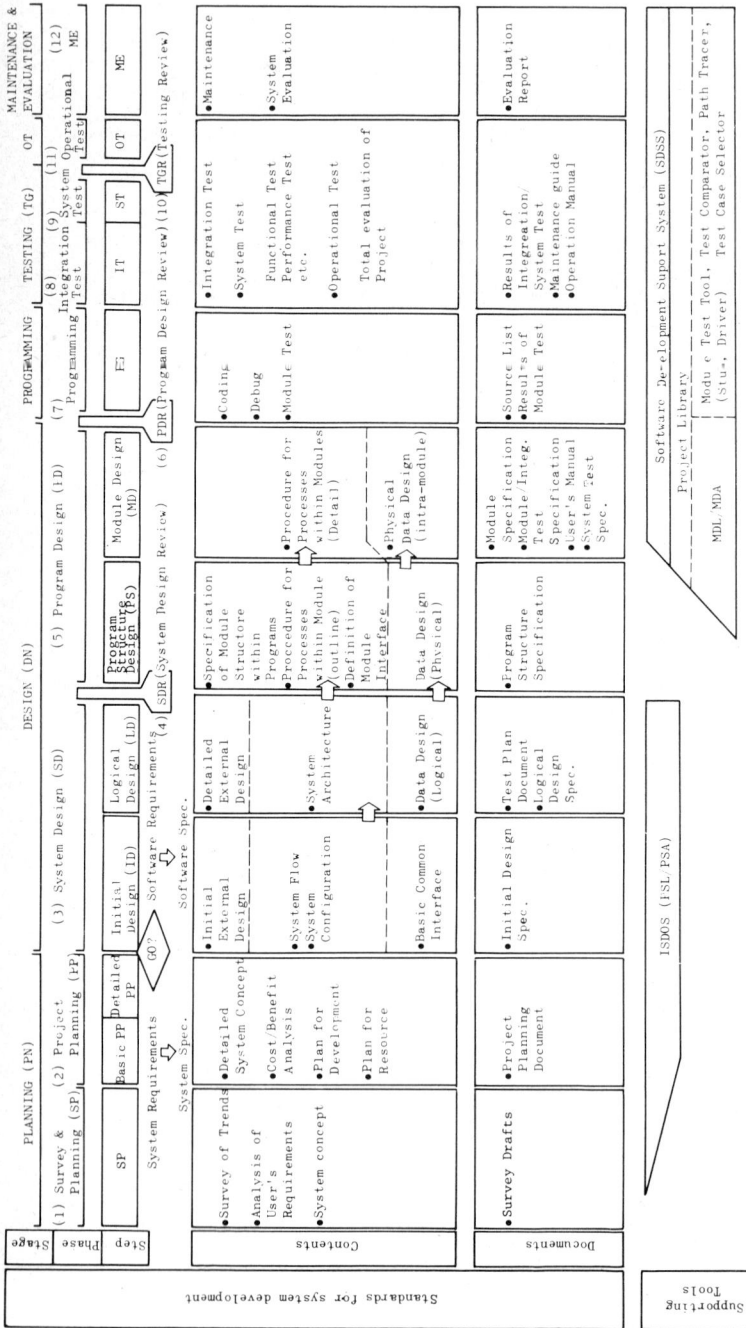

Figure 54   SDEM breakdown of the software development process and the tools and documentation necessary for it (from [FUJI13])

```
                                    ┌──────────────────────┐
                                 ┌──┤  LIBRARY MANAGER     │
          ┌──────────────────┐   │  └──────────────────────┘
       ┌──┤ PROJECT LIBRARY  ├──┤
       │  └──────────────────┘   │  ┌──────────────────────┐
       │                         └──┤  TEXT EDITOR         │
       │                            └──────────────────────┘
       │
       │                            ┌──────────────────────┐
       │                            │  DOCUMENTOR          │
       │                            │                      │
       │                            │  Module specification│
       │                            │                      │
       │                         ┌──┤  Common area map     │
       │                         │  │  Cross reference table│
┌────┐ │  ┌──────────────────┐   │  │  (Common area to module,│
│SDSS├─┼──┤ MDL / MDA        ├──┤  │   module to module)  │
└────┘ │  └──────────────────┘   │  │  Module structure chart│
       │                         │  └──────────────────────┘
       │                         │  ┌──────────────────────┐
       │                         └──┤  INTERFACE CHECKER   │
       │                            └──────────────────────┘
       │
       │                            ┌──────────────────────┐
       │                         ┌──┤ MODULE TEST SUPPORT TOOL│
       │                         │  └──────────────────────┘
       │                         │  ┌──────────────────────┐
       │                         ├──┤  TEST RESULT COMPARATOR│
       │  ┌──────────────────┐   │  └──────────────────────┘
       └──┤ TEST SUPPORT TOOLS├──┤  ┌──────────────────────┐
          └──────────────────┘   ├──┤  MODULE PATH TRACER  │
                                 │  └──────────────────────┘
                                 │  ┌──────────────────────┐
                                 └──┤  TEST CASE SELECTOR  │
                                    └──────────────────────┘
```

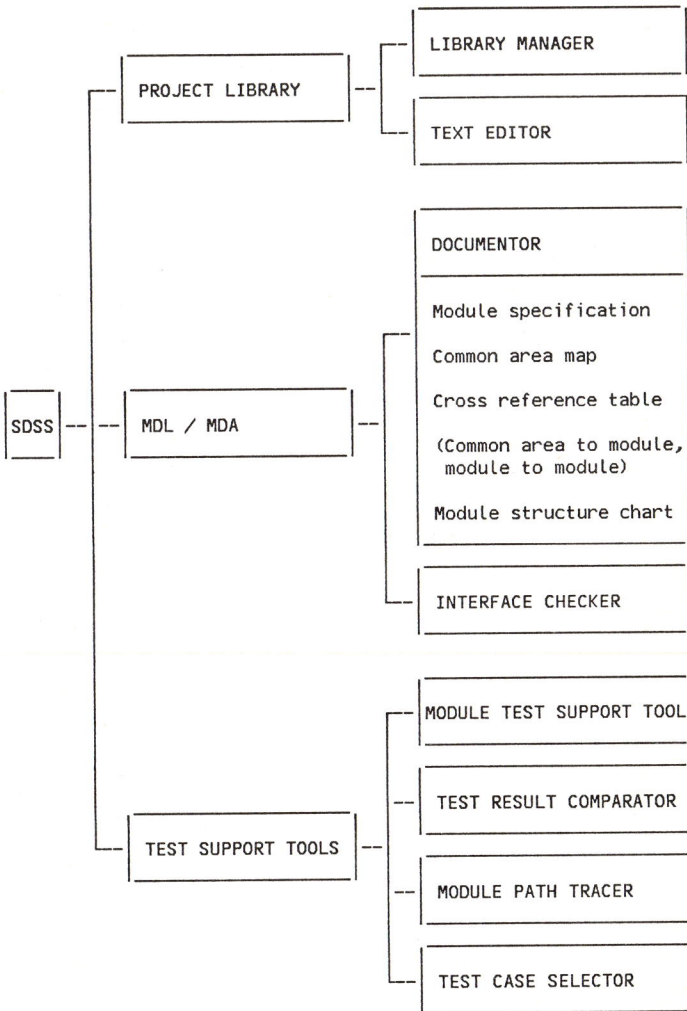

Table 55   Components of SDSS (Version 1) (from [FUJI13])

Concerning NTT's software production systems, it is worth mentioning that APGB uses the TSS services DEMOS and DRESS for file editing and management.

The above mentioned software production systems, however, are still under development and are not yet being used by all divisions. At present most of the computer manufacturers' software is still being developed by the conventional method, in which only some steps of software development have been automated. Hitachi practises the Software Production and Inspection Process, in which every step of software development is being monitored by an inspection department, the man-power being about 1/7 of that of the developing department. Normally one group carries out the development from beginning to end, but often the assistance of subsidiary software companies is used. In Fujitsu's software development divisions, however, the different stages of software development are normally made by different personnel. Also, in NEC, system analysis and concept, programming, test and maintenance, are usually done by different working groups. Analysis and test are always carried out by NEC's staff but subsidiary companies are often involved in the programming work and the maintenance is done by NEC Field Service Co. Toshiba's own staff normally carry out system analysis and concept, but programming, test and maintenance would be subcontracted out to subsidiary software houses.

Software houses and general companies do not apply software production systems yet. But they rationalised their software production process as far as possible by the use of self-made support tools, packages from the manufacturers of their computer system, or purchased software packages, e.g.:

- for requirement definition (analysis, design phase);

  * System Analysis Design Technique (SADT) of SofTech Boston
  * Information System Development and Optimising System (ISDOS) of Michigan University
  * Software Requirements Engineering Methodology (SREM) of TRW.

  In this phase, however, most software developers still work conventionally without automated support tools.

- for the programming and test phase

  * Most of the software developers (almost 50% of visited institutions) use IBM's HIPO for program description and documentation. Some developers use a modified HIPO, e.g Toshiba uses THIPO which has been modified for use on Toshiba's computers.
  * Dynamic Statement Analyser of Colorado University
  * SPEAKEASY by Argonne National Laboratory, Illinois
  * Software monitor SPARK by Burroughs

(the listed methods have been quoted by the institutions personally visited, see Appendix 3).

Furthermore, there are a lot of support tools for debugging, editing and program management.

The maintenance phase is usually supported only in software production systems.

Most of the software developers use high level programming languages. According to a 1978 JEIDA survey of 1306 companies the following languages were used:

Cobol	59.4 %
Fortran	7.4
PL/I	3.4
Algol	0.1
Other higher languages	8.2
Assembler	16.6
Generators	2.2
Machine and special languages	2.7

Other high level languages mentioned by those institutions visited are APL, BASIC and PASCAL. One user applied a pre-processor for COBOL, called Business Language BL/I, in which the programmer writes the programs by filling out decision tables.

Some computer manufacturers and also general companies have adopted special programming languages for basic software, e.g. System Programming Language (SPL) and SL/100 by Fujitsu; System Description Language (SYSL) by NTT (see [NTT16]); System Description Language (SDL) by Hitachi.

About half of the institutions visited apply the structured programming technique, which is often supported by structured documentation facilities like HIPO, or by structured compilers, e.g. Structured FORTRAN or COBOL (SFORTRAN, SCOBOL), or the structured programming language SIMPLE (developed by NTT).

In order to aid testing and maintenance, some developers apply IBM's Improvement Program Technique (IPT, including HIPO), the WALK THROUGH method and Burrough's software monitor SPARK. Software quality tests, like automatic software evaluation systems or program verification systems, do not exist and only some research projects are concerned with this subject, e.g. JSD's Software Engineering Project.

The organisation of software development differs greatly from one company to another. For example, in one company the whole development work is carried out by the same working team, while in another company each phase of software development is done by a different team. Most companies, however, are assisted by subsidiary software houses, mainly for coding, testing and maintenance. Although analysis and design are normally done by the developing company itself, often it is carried out with the assistance of the hardware suppliers.

The information concerning the portions of the different phases of software development differ very much. Some developers said that most of their software staff were occupied by maintenance work (i.e. up to 80%), while others said that analysis and concept needed most of their manpower.

The need for improving the productivity of software development is also very important for microcomputers. Therefore Mitsubishi Electric, NTT and NEC, for example, have developed software development tools for their own microcomputers (PL/I, PMP-C and TK80-BS, see EJR Vol.7, page 1).

It is astonishing that, in spite of the existence of time sharing systems (TSS), the use of punch cards is still very common in Japan. Because of their Kanji characters, Japanese staff (in contrast with Westerners) are not accustomed to

using typewriters and/or keyboards, and therefore prefer to remain using punch
cards. But because TSS are becoming more and more attractive and easy to use,
and as Kana and Kanji characters are being interpreted, there is a tendency to
use punch cards just for the first input of a coded program. Some companies use
optical readers for input of the hand-written coding forms.

JSD's Software Production Technology Development Project (see also chapter
2.1.3.3) is an interesting experiment to make software development more effective. This project aims at establishing a library of basic modules from which
any application program can be generated. The user defines his problem in a
generator type language called CPL-A and, according to the specifications, modules from this module library will be selected and a source program in a PL/I
type programming language, called CPL-B, will be generated. The project has been
completed but, as of 1980, not yet put into practice.

7. FUTURE DEVELOPMENTS

The future development of the Japanese economy is being discussed on a wide scale by the government, by industry, by public and private organisations and committees, and by the general public.

One of the important government bodies for the planning of the economic policy is the Industrial Structure Council (SANKOSHIN) which is organised by MITI. Its members from industry, public and private organisations, and universities authorised the vision of MITI's industrial policy for the 1980s (see also Chapter 2.1.2.1). This vision (see [AIST2] and Appendix 1) emphasises

- energy

- improving the quality of life and community facilities (e.g. by social systems)

- knowledge - intensive and innovative technologies

- next generation technologies.

Based on the "Visions of MITI Policies in the 1980s" MITI also publishes surveys for particularly important branches of industry. The report about the future of the information industry (see [AIST11] and Appendix 1) has been authorised by the Information Industry Sub-committee (JOHO SANGYO BUKA), which is a sub-committee of the Industrial Structure Council.Its members are: presidents of large computer manufacturers; representatives of industrial organisations in the information industry, e.g. JECC, JEIDA, JIPDEC, IPA, SIA and JIPCA; university professors. In the past the Information Industry Sub-committee issued several interim reports on the situation of the information industry, the first being in 1968.

MITI's advisory board which is concerned with MITI's industrial R & D strategy is the Industrial Technology Council which is organised within AIST (see Chapter 2.2.3 and Figure 8). The council receives proposals from several R & D committees organised by AIST, including the Information R & D Committee. The present target periods for industrial R & D are until 1985, from 1985 to 2000, and after 2000. Until 1980 there were nine R & D categories: energy, resources, city, environment, information, production systems, medical applications, disaster, and food, but the categories were later reviewed.

Besides MITI other ministries and agencies are also concerned with future technological developments. For example, the Science and Technology Agency (STA) of the Prime Minister's Office conducts studies about technological innovations and publishes annually the "White Paper on Science and Technology".

Several public organisations also make contributions to the development of an information society. The Research Institute of Telecommunications and Economics (RITE), which is mainly financed by MPT, carries out research projects and studies about future trends in telecommunication and their impact on the society (see also Chapter 2.1.3.4). RITE co-operates with the Institute of Future Technology (IFTECH) which is supervised by the Science and Technology Agency (STA).

The Research Committee on 5th Generation Computers is a study group which is elaborating a concept for a future computer system. Financed by MITI and organised by JIPDEC it brings together members from the computer manufacturers, important general companies, software houses, universities, public and private organisations. It is remarkable that the basis for the considerations are not only technical problems but mainly application problems, user behaviours and social impacts (see [JIPDEC18]).

MITI's promotion measures concentrate mainly on future technologies (see Chapters 2.2.2.3 and 2.2.2.1), for example:

- The Pattern Information Processing System (PIPS) is concerned with character, picture, 3-D object and speech recognition.

- The Optical Measurement and Control System is concerned with light transmission and sensors.

- The Comprehensive Automobile Control Technology System is concerned with advanced methods of traffic control.

- The Computer Basic Technology Research Association is concerned with the development of modern software technologies and peripheral devices.

The laboratories of AIST (i.e. MITI) and of NTT are also concerned with the development of future technologies (see Chapters 2.2.3 and 2.3.3).

Because of government promotion and their own research, Japanese industry is very advanced in technologies which have great importance for the future. As is described in Chapter 6.3, many Japanese and foreign companies have developed Japanese word processing systems. The character recognition technology is already so advanced that no further promotion by MITI is needed. Speech recognition technology is also being developed by many Japanese companies, among others NEC, Hitachi, Fujitsu, Toshiba and NTT. All these companies offer marketable voice input systems which can distinguish a limited vocabulary in a continuous or articulated speech (see EJR Vol.7, page 7 and JCN No. 60, 1981).

In order to raise industrial productivity the Japanese industry puts emphasis on the development of Computer Aided Design (CAD) and Computer Aided Manufacturing (CAM) technologies. At present CAD and CAM systems are particularly used by the electronics industries (especially for the design of integrated circuits and printed circuit boards), and also by the automobile, shipbuilding, aircraft and construction industries (see JCN, June 1981; EJR Vol. 8, page 26; and VDI-Berichte Nr.413, 1981).

Several industrial organisations are also concerned with the future of the Japanese economy. SIA, JEIDA, JECC, and others, periodically publish surveys on the future trends of their branch of industry. Especially worth mentioning is JEIDA's study about the future of the Japanese electronic industry (see [JEIDA4]).

Furthermore the development trends of future technologies are being discussed openly. For example, the NIKKEI SANGYO SHIMBUN, a major economic journal, had in Spring 1980 a series of more than 30 articles concerned with future technological developments. In one of these issues was published the following list of important products from the field of information processing. The list contains 5 columns:

1: sales in 1979
2: estimated sales in 1989
3: applied technology
4: participating companies in 1979
5: expected participating companies in 1989.

CAPTAIN SYSTEM
   1: –
   2: 36 million terminals, 1000-3000 billion Yen
   3: semi-conductor, computer, communication
   4: NTT, FUJITSU, NEC, OKI, HITACHI, MATSUSHITA
   5: all electronics or communication makers

HOME FACSIMILE
   1: –
   2: 50-150 million Yen
   3: semi-conductor, communication
   4: MATSUSHITA, HITACHI, TOSHIBA, NEC, OKI and TAMURA make Telephone Facsimile and MINI FAX for NTT
   5: RICOH, MITSUBISHI, SHARP, SANYO

AUTO-PROGRAMMING SYSTEM
   1: –
   2: 20-30% of software market in 1989
   3: auto-programming technique
   4: –
   5: IBM, FUJITSU, HITACHI, MATSUSHITA, SHARP

PATTERN RECOGNITION (including character recognition)
   1: 25 billion Yen
   2: 300 billion Yen
   3: pattern recognition technique
   4: ITOCHU-DATA SYSTEM, OKI, SHARP, TOSHIBA, TOYO-OFFICE AUTOMATION, NEC, HITACHI, FUJITSU, MITSUBISHI, MITSUBISHI-JIMUKI
   5: –

COMPOUND FACSIMILE
   1: 3 billion Yen
   2: 200-250 billion Yen
   3: computer technology
   4: MATSUSHITA-DENSO, HITACHI, NEC, MITSUBISHI
   5: big electronics or computer makers, e.g. IBM

ELECTRIC MAIL
   1: –
   2: unit cost of high-performance facsimile times number of post offices
   3: facsimile, communication
   4: facsimile and computer manufacturers
   5: –

STANDING IMAGE BROADCASTING
      1: –
      2: –
      3: developed by NHK
      4: all electrical manufacturers, tests in abeyance until broadcasting
         satellites have been prepared
      5: –

MULTI CHARACTER BROADCASTING
      1: –
      2: 90 billion Yen
      3: micro-computer, IC, TV
      4: TV manufacturers
      5: private broadcasting companies

OPTICAL COMPUTER
      1: –
      2: –
      3: optical-IC, optical communication, optical technology
      4: –
      5: IBM, FUJITSU

OFFICE COMPUTER
      1: 100 billion Yen
      2: 500 billion Yen
      3: software, especially application software, and LSI
      4: MITSUBISHI, NEC, FUJITSU, IBM, CASIO, UCHIDAYOKO, RICOH, CANON,
         MATSUSHITA, and 40 other companies
      5: –

WORD PROCESSOR (including alphabet)
      1: 1 billion Yen
      2: 200 billion Yen
      3: Kanji I/O
      4: TOSHIBA, CANON, OKI, SHARP, IBM, ITOCHU-DATA SYSTEM, VIDEOTRON
         JAPAN, ALPS-COMPUTER-ENGINEERING, TOYO-OFFICEMATION
      5: computer, business machines and precision instrument manufacturers

ELECTRIC FILE
      1: –
      2: 10 billion Yen
      3: LSI, optical IC
      4: –
      5: HITACHI, TOSHIBA, NEC, business machine manufacturers

POCKET TELEPHONE
      1: –
      2: 5 billion Yen
      3: VLSI, communication and telephone
      4: –
      5: NEC, FUJITSU, HITACHI, OKI, MATSUSHITA

CABLE TV

    1: -
    2: 10 billion Yen
    3: Computer-software-technique, digital communication, TV technique
    4: MATSUSHITA, PIONEER, TOSHIBA, HITACHI
    5: -

SATELLITE COMMUNICATION

    1: 20 billion Yen
    2: 100 billion Yen
    3: high radio communication technique, rocket technique
    4: MITSUBISHI, NEC, FUJITSU, TOSHIBA, NIHON-MUSEN, ANRITSU-DENKI
    5: OKI

CAR TELEPHONE

    1: 2 billion Yen
    2: 10 billion Yen
    3: radio communication, telephone switching equipment, LSI technique
    4: NEC, MATSUSHITA, KOKUSAI-DENKI
    5: TOSHIBA, MITSUBISHI, FUJITSU, HITACHI, OKI, NIHON-MUSEN, ANRITSU-DENKI

OPTICAL COMMUNICATION

    1: 4 billion Yen
    2: 200 billion Yen
    3: LSI, optical fibre, device technique (magnetic-bubble etc.), digital translation technique
    4: NEC, HITACHI, MITSUBISHI, TOSHIBA, OKI, SUMITOMO-DENKI, FURUKAWA-DENKI-KOGYO, FUJI-KURADENSEN
    5: -

TV TELEPHONE

    1: -
    2: 5 billion Yen
    3: TV, communication
    4: NEC, TOSHIBA, HITACHI, FUJITSU, OKI, SONY, IWASAKI-TSUSHIN
    5: -

DATA BANK

    1: 0,5 - 1 billion Yen
    2: 10 billion Yen
    3: database technique
    4: JICST, MARUZEN, KINOKUNIYA, NIHON-SDC, NIHON-KEIZAI-SHINBUN, SHIKYO-JOHO-CENTRE
    5: publication companies, computer manufacturers, computing centres

HOME DATA BANK

    1: -
    2: 300-400 billion Yen and additional advertising income
    3: organising data and updating them
    4: test system: ASAHI, MAINICHI, YOMIURI, NIHON-KEIZAI-newspaper,

NHK, GAKKEN, DENTSU, HAKUHODO, MITSUKOSHI, PIA, Japanese Travel Bureau
5: leisure   industry,   publication   companies,   communication manufacturers

VOICE TYPEWRITER
   1: -
   2: 10 billion Yen
   3: voice recognition
   4: TOSHIBA, NEC, HITACHI, FUJITSU, IBM
   5: -

VOICE RECOGNITION EQUIPMENT
   1: 2 billion Yen
   2: 40 billion Yen
   3: voice analysis technique,   linguistics,   software techniques, electronic techniques
   4: NEC, HITACHI, TOSHIBA, MARUBENI Electronics, KYOSAN-SEISAKUJI, TAKACHIHO-KOEKI
   5: all electric manufacturers

HOME COMPUTER
   1: 7 billion Yen
   2: 150 billion Yen
   3: software technique, electronics technique, household electronics, house equipment technique
   4: MATSUSHITA, HITACHI, MISAWA-HOME, YAMAGIWA
   5: all   household   electronics   manufacturers,   house   equipment manufacturers, pre-fab manufacturers

OFFICE AUTOMATION
   1: 400 billion Yen
   2: 2000 billion Yen
   3: communications technique, computer system design technique, Kanji processing technique
   4: CANON, SHARP, TOSHIBA, NEC, FUJI-XEROX, PENTEL, RICOH, KONISHI, FUJITSU
   5: communication,   computer,   business machines,   copy and   furniture manufacturers

REMOTE SENSING
   1: 0.5 billion Yen
   2: 10 billion Yen
   3: image processing, analysing, infra-red ray sensor technique
   4: TOSHIBA, SEKIYU-SHIGEN-KAIHATSU, MITSUBISHI, NAK, ASIA-KOSOKU, PACIFIC-KOGYO
   5: FUJITSU, NEC, other computer manufacturers, system houses, etc.

APPENDIX 1(a)

MINISTRY OF INTERNATIONAL TRADE AND INDUSTRY

(MITI)

Provisional Translation

March 17, 1980
NR-226 (80-7)

THE VISION OF MITI POLICIES IN THE 1980s

- SUMMARY -

1. Introduction

2. The 1980s - The World's Turning Point

3. New National Goals

4. Milestones in Economic Management

5. External Policies in the Age of Interdependence

6. Overcoming Energy Problems and Preparing for the New Age

7. Towards a Technology-based Nation

8. Improving the Quality of Life

9. New Development in Regional Societies

10. Development of a Creative Industrial Structure

11. The Age of Vitalised Human Potential

1. Introduction

In the 1980's Japan will be increasingly called upon to contribute to the harmonious development of the international community as positively as is comparable to its international status. Japan will also have to cope with the problem of the growing scarcity of energy resources. Appropriate policy is needed to deal with these tasks and problems. It will be more difficult for Japan to fix its course in the '80s, yet it will be essential to select the right course.

The essential task for the Ministry of International Trade and Industry is to set up guidelines which the people, business sector and government can follow in their concerted efforts to overcome the difficulties of the present decade and to open the way for a new age.

MITI has directed its policies in conformity with two reports submitted by the Industrial Structure Council: [1] "The Industrial Structure in Japan" in 1963, and "The Vision of MITI's Policies in the 1970s" in 1971. Currently, the council has submitted its report, entitled "The Vision of MITI Policies in the 1980s", whose outline is given below.

2. The 1980s -- The World's Turning Point

The 1980s will mark a historic turning point in the energy situation, and the political and economic environment. The manner in which we handle worldwide problems in the coming decade will be the key in determining whether we can engineer a promising future.

Energy

The major sources of energy supporting our economic activities have shifted from firewood to coal, and then to oil. In the 21st century the world economy may be able to derive its energy mainly from the sun and the atom. However, during the long period for transition from conventional energy sources to new ones, we must face an unstable oil supply situation. During these decades in the transition starting from the 1980s various energy sources, conventional, alternative and new, must be sought simultaniously to the utmost extent possible.

Political and Economic Multipolarisation

The political and economic stability of the world throughout the most part of this century has been rhetorically called Pax Americana in an analogy to Pax Britannica referring to the Peace of Europe in the 19th century. Although the U.S. remains the pre-eminent world power, its relative status is declining. Militarily, the bi-polarisation of the two superpower blocs - the U.S. and Soviet Union - will continue, while politically and economically the world will experience further transition toward a multipolar and multifaceted structure, causing an intensification of political and economic instability.

----

[1]   The Industrial Structure Council, an advisory organ which discusses and deliberates on the direction of MITI policies, is composed of the representatives of academic and industrial circles, consumers and labour unions.

The 1980s should be a period of co-operation among developed nations, while developing nations will have a stronger voice in the operation of international politics and economics. In addition, the oil producing countries of the Middle East are expected to be more influential, controlling the supply and price of oil. The politics and economics of China, now appearing to gradually liberalise its society, and the East-West relationship may also contribute to the further multi-polarisation and complication depending upon their evolutions.

On the other hand, interdependence among nations is expected to deepen further in the coming decade. Politics and economics will become more closely related with each other, making the world even more complex.

Current State of the Japanese Economy

After successfully rebuilding its war-torn economy in the '50s, Japan developed heavy and chemical industries in the '60s and added new dimensions and leverage to its economy by developing knowledge-intensive industries in the '70s. Today, Japan accounts for 10% of GNP of the world, even though Japan has only 3% of the world's population and 0.3% of the world's land. Though on a stock basis Japan is still behind industrialised countries, on a flow basis, its per capita national income has reached 90% of that of the United States, exceeding the average of the EC countries. On the other hand, in view of an unstable world energy situation, the heavy dependence on foreign supplies of energy – 89% of its total energy requirements – now casts serious problems upon the future Japanese economy.

Since the Meiji Era, Japan has struggled to achieve a level comparable to that of Western countries by modernising and developing an industrial society. Japan today has achieved the goal it set for itself. Yet immediately after the fulfillment of that goal comes the turning point. Japan in the 1980s will have to seek new directions and face new challenges.

3. New National Goals

The Japanese economy has attained the national goal of the past hundred years, reaching the level of Western industrial nations. It is time for Japan to establish new national long-term goals and to envisage the course to reach them. We propose the following three national long-term policy goals.

    (1) Contributing positively to the international community

    (2) Overcoming the limitations of natural resources and energy

    (3) Attaining co-existence of dynamism of the society and the improved quality and comfort of life

Building a Reputation for Trustworthiness

Japan has now a strong influence in the international economy. In the 1980s and beyond, Japan must contribute as much as possible to laying the foundations for the maintenance of world peace and the development of the world economy. Japan should, for example, play its part in the maintenance of the free trade system, play a larger role in the concerted efforts by developed nations in the technological research and development, and continue steadily the economic co-operation for developing countries. The general populace must be willing to accept these responsibilities.

Economic Security through Technological Innovation

In order to secure the welfare and economic security of the nation, Japan must endeavor to overcome its vulnerability as a nation with scarce natural resources. To this end, the following measures will be implemented to prevent the development of crises, as well as to formulate a system for crises management.

    (1) The degree of mutual dependence with both advanced and developing nations will be heightened.

    (2) Japan must seek to diversify sources of oil supply as well as to develop alternative and new energy sources, to increase stockpiling and to step up energy conservation efforts.

    (3) The development of innovative and original technology will be promoted to help Japan stabilise its economic foundation.

Maintaining the Vitality of Society along with an Improved Quality and Comfort of Life

(1) The nation's vitality must be sufficient for the sustenance of its economy in order to fulfill its international responsibilities and overcome its lack of natural resources.

(2) Japan must improve the quality of life through a better living environment and increased leisure time.

(3) Strengthened wisdom cannot be found in a society lacking vitality, and a new vitality cannot be attained by a society without flexible thought and action. In the 1980s, vitality and flexibility must co-exist to achieve our goals.

Japan's unique problem-solving capability is supported by the industriousness of its people, the high standard of education, the narrow income differentials, and relatively stable labour-management relationships. Therefore we believe that these long-term national goals, encompassing the 1980s and beyond, are attainable with the people's efforts.

4. Economic Management

Economic Growth Policy

(1) An objective of economic growth is an improved standard of living to be maintained for a long period. Coping with possible constraints of economic growth, such as the energy problem, trade friction, future uncertainties, and diminishing social vitality, we should seek an appropriate rate of growth. Without an appropriate rate of growth it would be difficult to realise various structural changes and avoid friction among interest groups.

(2) Growth constraints in the 1980s will become more complex than in previous years and policital alternatives will be more limited.

(3) Since the establishment of economic security is one of the most important

priorities for the 1980s, Japan's economic growth must be sufficient to meet the following requirements.
i) Japan must emphasise investment in energy measures and technological development.
ii) Japan must stimulate investment by the private sector in equipment for energy conservation, improved productivity, and international division of labour.

(4) To improve living environments, investments in private housing and related social overhead capital must be emphasised and increased.

Improving Employment Opportunities

(1) Increased employment of elderly workers, female workers and college graduates will change Japanese-style employment practices.

(2) The share of people over 65 years old in Japan's total population was 9% in 1978, and will be 11% in 1990, 14% in 2000, and in 2020 19%; the highest in the world. We should provide appropriate social security and form a new national consensus to share the additional burden. Proper handling of the ageing population problem will be vital in the decades ahead.

Price Policy

Price stabilisation measures must aim at improving supply conditions in such areas as productivity and energy, in addition to managing effective demand.

Vitality of the Private Sector and the Role of Government

(1) Japan's economic system is based on free market mechanisms, and the vitality of the private sector is essential to its maintenance. Realising the increased public needs, we should avoid excessive reliance on government administration by the private sector and should encourage their competitive activities.

(2) Government action will be required mainly in the following areas: technological development demanding large amounts of funds, incurring high-risks, and needing long lead times; protection of public safety; realisation of social justice; and government-level negotiations.

(3) In the 1980s, as a stronger inclination towards trade protectionism and the advancement of developing countries is anticipated, efforts must be made to maintain open markets. As a result of these efforts, reduced employment and other impacts may cause social frictions. Accordingly administrative action will be required more often than in the past to alleviate such frictions.

(4) Better understanding must be promoted between the Japanese government and foreign governments, the government and the people, and central and local governments.

5. External Policies in the Age of Interdependence

Trend of the World Economy

(1) The overall economic growth of the world is anticipated to be slightly below

4% recorded in the 1970s. While the average growth rate of the industrialised nations will be only 3% (Japan anticipates growth of a little more than 5%), that of developing nations will be comparatively high, in particular the Newly Industrialising Countries (NIC's) and ASIAN nations. The growth rates of the Soviet Union and Eastern European nations are expected to be almost equal to the overall world growth rate.

(2) As industrialised nations are expected to increasingly focus their efforts on their own domestic problems, future international co-operation may encounter difficulties.

(3) Among the developing nations the disparity between oil-producing nations, NIC's, and less-developed nations will expand, thus intensifying the trend toward polarisation.

(4) To soundly sustain the world's economic system during the 1980s, we need to effectively cope with energy problems, to continue to promote international trade, to endeavour to narrow North-South disparity in income and to stabilise international monetary situations.

(5) Every nation must strive to attain progress and security for itself with a spirit of international co-operation. Endeavouring to maintain the principle of freedom and equality, Japan must formulate a respectable national image in the international community and strengthen its relationships of mutual dependence with foreign countries.

(6) As the Pacific Basin has a great potential for progress, that potential needs to be realised. In the Basin there are many countries with different historical, cultural and economic backgrounds. Japan must promote international exchanges of human resources, culture and information in this Basin. In addition, in the context of global considerations we need to promote economic co-operation and international division of labour, as well as joint development of resources, energy, and the ocean.

Maintenance of the Free Trade System

(1) In dealing with industrialised nations, Japan needs to increase imports of manufactured goods and the production of goods with larger added value, specialising in sectors with a comparative advantage. Furthermore, "industrial co-operation" among industrialised nations will become prevalent.

(2) In dealing with the newly industrialising countries, Japan needs to encourage domestic industries to switch into new lines of upgraded products.

(3) In dealing with developing countries, Japan needs to increase imports of labour-intensive products, processed primary products and raw materials.

Promotion of Comprehensive Economic Co-operation

Concerning economic co-operation with developing countries, emphasis will be placed on "comprehensive economic co-operation" combining official development assistance, direct investment and trade. In this context we propose the adoption of a comprehensive economic co-operation index consisting of the imports of manufactured goods, official development assistance, export credits and direct overseas investment. We aim at increasing the overall amount of comprehensive economic co-operation to a level of about six times the current value in nominal terms by the end of the '80s. When achieved, the ratio of comprehensive economic co-operation to GNP will increase from 1.6% in 1978 to 3% at the end of the 1980s. (At present this ratio of the European countries stands at 2.0% to 2.5%, while that of the U.S. is 1.3%.)

Promotion of Direct Investment in Overseas Markets

Direct overseas investment, which is expected to expand further in the coming decade, is valuable for the following requirements:

(1) to sophisticate the domestic industrial structure and to promote international division of labour,

(2) to promote international communication through exchanges of people and transfer of particular corporate activities to foreign countries,

(3) to promote the transfer of management resources and job opportunities,

(4) to secure a stable supply of energy and resources, and

(5) to consolidate the management of Japanese firms.

Increased International Use of the Yen

We need to make positive efforts to enlarge the role of the Yen in international transactions, and to promote liberalisation and flexibility in financial markets in order to establish a Tokyo International Financial Market. These efforts will help to stabilise the international monetary system and encourage international activities of industries.

Deepening International Communication

Given the increasing tendency toward interdependence among the countries of the world, the problems requiring international adjustments, bilateral or multi- lateral, are expected to increase in the coming years. To avoid such problems resulting in international emotional frictions, the Japanese people and societies need to become more internationally-oriented, taking into account more fully the international consequences and implications on every occasion, making its institutions and their procedures more accessible to foreigners, and developing better channels for international communications.

6. Overcoming Energy Problems and Preparing for the New Age

Energy Problem

The oil crisis of 1973 brought to an end the age of abundant cheap oil. Worse yet, the revolution in Iran starting toward the end of 1978 and OPEC's oil strategy have made the oil supply outlook increasingly pessimistic.

Until we can prepare other energy sources, the instability of the world's oil supply will cast dark clouds over the world economy. Our energy supply structure is far more fragile than those of Western industrial nations for the following reasons:

(a) Japan depends on foreign countries for about 90% of its primary energy requirements,

(b) 75% of Japan's primary energy comes from imported oil, and

(c) the oil producing areas supplying Japan are concentrated in a few
countries with limited transportation routes.

For these reasons, our greatest national priority is to establish long-term
energy security. For that purpose, diversification of energy sources and the
conservation of energy are essential.

Importance of Worldwide Perspectives

Energy measures need to be formulated on the basis of worldwide perspectives
covering the political aspects of the energy problem, co-operation among the
advanced nations, co-operation with the oil-producing countries, and
stabilisation of international financial situations. In addition, a system for
collection, compilation, analysis, and distribution of information must be consolidated.

Energy Supply and Demand in Japan

Assuming that Japan's economy will grow at an average rate of more than 5%
annually in the '80s, and that the structure of energy consumption will remain
unchanged, we will need in 1990 twice as much as the amount of energy consumed
in 1977. The most important need in the coming decade is to conserve energy. As
a result of our efforts to save the energy consumption by 15%, the energy consumption in 1990 will remain 1.7 times that of 1977. Our second objective is to
reduce the nation's dependence on oil from the current 75% to 50% of total
energy requirements by 1990. We will have to vigorously promote the development
and introduction of alternative sources to a level of more than triple the
current level in order to raise them from 25% at present to 50% in 1990 of the
total energy mix.

Development of Alternative Energy Sources

The best method to achieve more stability in the face of the energy crisis is to
diversify energy sources. The government will vigorously accelerate the development of the following various energy sources.

(1) Nuclear Power
Nuclear power stations must be sited with greater attention to their
safety and reliability. Efforts should also be made for the establishment
of our own nuclear fuel cycle and for the development and introduction of
new types of reactors.

(2) Coal
Because of the abundance of its reserves and the relative variety of its
deposits locations, coal has great expectations as a source of energy. We
will promote coal-fired power stations and switch from oil to coal for
fuel in other industries. The coal technologies to be developed are
liquefaction and gasification, and we must spread the results of their
technological developments for commercial uses.

(3) Liquefied natural gas and liquefied petroleum gas.

(4) Solar energy, hydraulic power, geothermal energy and other types of syn-
thetic fuel.

Local Energy Systems

We need to develop and introduce local energy sources including solar energy, geothermal energy, small- and medium-scale hydro-electric power plants, factory waste heat, methane produced by fermenting waste, wave power, wind power, tidal power, and biomass.

Securing Stable Supply of Oil

Despite efforts for the conservation of energy and the development of alternative energy sources, Japan will have to depend on oil from foreign countries for more than 50% of its energy requirements. Therefore we must continue our efforts to secure the stable supply of oil through the following activities:

(1) Vigorous expansion of economic and technological co-operation with producing countries;

(2) promotion of better mutual understanding with oil producing countries;

(3) active participation in oil exploration;

(4) diversification of sources of oil supply by increasing the imports of oil from Asia, Mexico and other countries; and

(5) the development of cracking facilities for heavy oil.

Energy Prices

(1) The oil producing countries are likely to make efforts to use their limited natural resources more sparingly, curtailing oil production to a level adequate to steadily develop their domestic economy. We must realise that such moves spell an age of high energy prices.

(2) The cost of a stable energy supply must be shouldered by the national economy as a whole. Specifically, this would mean a shifting of the cost to consumers in terms of prices through the market mechanism, and entrepreneurs' efforts for rationalisation. However, for some energy-related investments full transfer of cost to price is difficult, and policy measures are therefore required.

Crisis Management

Should the supply of oil be reduced to a level that may threaten economic security, we would need to establish a system of crisis management to minimise any possible damage and ensure swift recovery.

7. Towards a Technology-based Nation

Philosophy

(1) Technological innovation is a source of progress for Japan as well as the world. Great expectations are therefore placed on technological innovation providing the key to the solution of various problems in the 1980s. Japan must strive to develop its creative capacity and contribute, as an innovator, to world progress.

(2) As technological development is a means of attaining economic security by
strengthening a country's bargaining power, Japan must stand on the ground of
technology.

(3) The now prevalent apprehension is that technical progress is about to stag-
nate. In the 1980s, however, the following types of technological efforts
will be made:

    (a) new application and combination of existing technologies,

    (b) flowering of new technology resulting from a new application of science
    and technology, and

    (c) the preparation for the next generation's epoch-making technological in-
    novations expected in the years after 1990.

If these efforts are successful, the economy and society are expected to move
into a new, prosperous stage.

Objectives of Technological Development in the '80s

The principal tasks for technological development to be stimulated by economic
and social necessities in the '80s are the following:

(1) Energy
    (a) Energy-saving technologies such as magneto-hydrodynamics (MHD) power
    generation, highly efficient gas turbines, fuel cells and a waste heat
    recovery system.
    (b) Alternative energy technologies such as nuclear power, coal, solar energy
    and geothermal energy.
    (c) New energy technologies such as nuclear fusion for commercial application
    in the 21st century.

(2) Improving the Quality of Life and Community Facilities
    (a) Social systems related to personal and community life including a medical
    information system.
    (b) New energy-saving housing systems and artificial ground for intensive use
    of land.

(3) Knowledge-Intensive and Innovative Technologies
    (a) Knowledge-intensive production systems equipped with micro-computers, and
    upgraded resource-saving and energy-saving technologies.
    (b) Innovative technologies such as new materials, optical communication,
    VLSI (very large scale integrated circuit) and laser beam technology.

(4) The Next Generation Technologies
    (a) In the field of life sciences:
    treatment of cancer, genetic manipulation, investigation into a photo-
    synthesis process and its application for food production.
    (b) In the field of energy:
    nuclear fusion and MHD power generation.
    (c) In the field of data processing:
    applying newly discovered principles such as the Josephson effect.

(5) Among the above themes, particular emphasis must be placed on three areas:
    (a) Development of technologies inventing new materials,
    (b) Development of technologies, applying a large-scale system including

those for alternative energy sources.
(c) Development of technologies related to a social system, including that in the field of personal and community activities.

New Phase in Policy on Technology

The principal role of the government policy for the development of technology is to encourage development efforts in the private sector. In the past, Japanese industry achieved brilliant results in improving and applying imported technologies. In the '80s, however, it will be essential for Japan to develop technologies of its own. For this purpose, it is necessary to systematically pursue policies with an emphasis on the following three points.

(1) Development of Creative Technologies
   (a) Switchover to "forward engineering":
      Now that it has become increasingly difficult to find specific goals of development of imported technologies, Japan needs to press ahead with projects for the research and development of original technologies through trial and error and the accumulation of basic data.
   (b) Training of personnel capable of achieving technological breakthroughs.
   (c) Establishment of a system to encourage taking risks and squarely facing new challenges.

(2) Systematic Promotion of Technology
   (a) Technological developments must be promoted by presenting a "Long-term Vision for Technological Development", which identifies the priority goals for technological developments, as well as systems for development and funding.
   (b) In the area of energy-related technologies and in other pressing areas requiring a large amount of development funds, the government must launch national projects on its own initiatives.

(3) Increased Allocation of Research and Development Funds
   (a) Efforts must be made to increase the budget available for research and development of technologies.
   (b) The share of government expenditures for R & D in total R & D expenditures is in the order of one-third in Japan, compared with around a half in Western industrialised countries. This share should be raised in spite of the expected deficit in the national budget.
   (c) Recognising that research and development of technologies are the nation's best interest, the government must make every effort to find a new source of funds for financing such projects.

International Co-operation in Technological Development

In the 1980s, co-operation among industrialised nations in research and development will be vital to the progress of the world's economy.

Joint research projects, in which all participating countries contribute their achievements, will be most effective for technological development to solve universal problems (e.g., energy and food problems) and for the development of large-scale technologies (e.g, aircraft and marine exploitation); Japan is willing to participate in such joint projects. Moreover, Japan will contribute by opening its facilities for research and development to foreign nations, including the establishment of a research institute inviting world-renowned researchers in the fields of life science and energy.

The transfer of technology to developing countries is one of the most important fields for Japan to contribute for the purpose of international co-operation.

8. Improving the Quality of Life

(1) Efforts must be made to improve residential conditions, particularly to increase comfort and spaciousness, on the basis of a comprehensive and systematic plan covering improvements in housing, housing lots, and social overhead capital related to personal and community life.

(2) Efforts must be made to study the possibilities of establishing a system of bonds whose value is designed to slide with a land price as a means of marketing financial assets rather than land in order to promote its transactions. In addition, efforts must be made to create new housing lots through the use of artificial grounds.

(3) Among industrialised nations, Japan is the only country yet to establish a five-day working week system. At the early stage of the 1980s, the five-day working week should be fully established and a long vacation system should be introduced gradually and set in full practice by the mid '80s.

(4) Efforts will be made to provide diverse educational opportunities, and sports and cultural facilities, in order to elevate the quality of lengthening leisure-time.

(5) Consolidation of the consumer credit industry and the establishment of a method of providing information on consumption will be effected to allow for more individuality in consumers' life styles. In order to meet more individual and sophisticated consumer needs, automation in the production of a larger variety of goods in smaller quantities will be promoted.

9. New Development in Local Societies

Interdependence Between Region and Industry

(1) In recent years, the narrowing of the income gaps between major cities and local communities as well as other factors has begun to attract more and more people to local areas. As a result, the increased local population is enlarging the possibility of progress in these regions. However, since Japan anticipates a population growth of 20 million by the year 2000, the problems to be caused by over-concentration in large cities cannot be ignored.

(2) For this reason, each local area must construct an attractive economic society for the promotion of appropriate re-location of industries. In order for each region to provide diverse employment opportunities and a stable economy, efforts are needed for the following purposes:
   (a) A multi-layered local industrial structure and systematic inter-regional co-operation.
   (b) Cultivation and promotion of local industries based on characteristics of each local community.

(3) Appropriate re-location of industries must be promoted, based on the following viewpoints:

(a) Incentives must be provided for the construction of industries in local areas and burdens must be given to industries situated in large urban areas.
(b) Comprehensive development of industries, including tertiary industries, must be carried out.
(c) Industries utilising local resources must be developed and promoted.
(d) The potential for regional development will be increased by securing industrial sites and water resources, and improving traffic conditions and transportation facilities.
(e) Re-development programmes in big cities will be encouraged.
(f) Investment for social overhead facilities must be promoted preceding industrial development in local cities.

Formulating Local Visions

(1) For the promotion of local economies, each area needs to implement its own original measures. It must formulate a vision for the promotion of its local economy in harmony with the industrial economy of the nation, and must implement appropriate measures in conformity with this vision.

(2) The vision for the promotion of local economies needs to cover improvement of traffic conditions and transportation facilities taking into account a long-term plan on the country's main transportation network. Moreover, each region must seek progress presupposing the internationalisation of Japan's economy. Local areas need to promote exchanges of information with urban centres or international communication on its own.

(3) A specific example is a scheme for an international trade city focusing on improvement of its international airport, and a scheme for a techno-polis aiming at the achievement of creative knowledge-intensive local industries and a new local culture.

(4) Attractive local communities must also maintain harmony with the environment.

(5) A manual needed at the time of natural desasters such as earthquakes must be compiled after identifying all possible events that may occur during a disaster. Moreover, disaster prevention and saftey measures must be further strengthened through an improvement of refuge roads and parks, and the construction of fire-proof or inflammable houses.

10. Development of a Creative Industrial Structure

Objectives and Criteria of Industrial Structure

(1) The following needs must be considered concerning the ideal industrial structure in the 1980s.
(a) Contribution to the harmony and development of the world economy — criteria for dynamic comparative advantage.
(b) Satisfaction of people's needs to improve quality of life — criteria for satisfaction of the people's needs.
(c) Surmounting of the unstable energy situation: criteria for energy and resource conservation.
(d) Construction of a foundation for long-term economic development and economic security: security criteria.

Knowledge Intensification Emphasising Creativity

The knowledge-intensive industrial structure aimed at in the 1970s must be promoted further in the 1980s with an emphasis on creativity.

(1) A creative, more knowledge-intensive industrial structure needs to be promoted, based on the capability for original technological development.

(2) Specifically, production of higher value added products will be encouraged through an enhancement of technology focusing on software and knowledge intensification.

Application of Three S's and Three F's, Industry by Industry

For many-pronged knowledge intensification, the following areas must be emphasised. (Three S,s and three F,s)

    (1) In addition to the development of selected knowledge-intensive industries as major industries in Japan, knowledge-intensive products and production processes must be promoted even within other industries.

    (2) The following efforts are needed for each industry:
        (a) Basic material industry
            i) With the application of computer control systems in the production processes, energy saving efforts will be pursued; quality, performance and reliability be improved; and comprehensive technological ability be enhanced. (Large-scale Systematisation)
            ii) New materials with better performance and sophisticated functions will be developed. (Speciality)
        (b) Processing and assembly industries
            i) Application of electronics and information systems in various fields such as industrial production, clerical work, social systems and private households will be advanced greatly.
               New types of products will be developed by incorporating software information processing functions. (Software Application)
            ii) Production methods enabling flexible and automated assembly and processing of various types of products will be developed. (Indroduction of Flexibility)
        (c) Industries related to personal and community life
            i) Products must meet the increased sophistication of people's tastes and the changes in their life style. (Fashion)
            ii) Products that emphasise such functions as durability, safety, and energy conservation will be developed to meet steady consumer demand.
            iii) Systematic linkage of the upstream, intermediate and down stream sectors must be promoted in planning a new product or developing new technology. (Feedback)
        (d) Energy industries
            i) An industrial structure that will promote development and introduction of alternative and new energy sources must be established and strengthened.
            ii) Regarding petroleum, Japan must secure its own sources of supply, develop and introduce heavy decomposition facilities, and accumulate stockpiles.
            iii) Equipment industries related to alternative or new sources of energy and conservation of energy are anticipated to make

    progress.
(e) Social system industries
   i) Social service demand, among other things, for medical, educational, waste processing, and traffic services are expected to be efficiently met through systematisation. (Systematisation)
   ii) It is preferable to rely on technology, funds, and efficiency of the private sector for the development, programming, building and management of social systems. For this purpose, consolidation of government financial assistance and an improvement of a legislative framework are required.
(f) Technology-leading industries
   i) Extremely large-scale technologies -- new energy, development of sources, aviation and space, and information processing -- form the basis for long-term economic progress.
   ii) The ability to develop original technology must be fostered through the co-operative efforts of the government and the private sector, and international joint projects.

Realisation of an Ideal Structure

In order to achieve an ideal industrial structure, the following measures will be implemented as a measure complementary to the efforts to be primarily made by the private sector.

(1) Proposing the Vision
By disseminating the vision of the industrial structure and sufficient information to the people, the formulation of concensus and smoother distribution of resources need to be achieved. Concurrently, vigorous progress in the private sector must be maintained and promoted.

(2) Promotion of Technological Development
The government must take the initiative in development and basic experimental research in high-risk fields. It must also provide strong assistance to large-scale private research and development projects that may contribute to social progress.

(3) Promotion of Industrial Labour Policy
In promoting the potential, creativity, and flexibility of human resources, the employment structure must be converted smoothly to facilitate knowledge intensification of the industrial structure.

Smooth Implementation of Industrial Adjustment

(1) Industrial adjustment measures based on active responses of the private sector must be promoted. Such adjustments must have the following properties:
(a) Economical efficiency from a medium and long-term point of view,
(b) Complimentary to changes in the market structure,
(c) Temporary nature,
(d) Limited scope with clear-cut objectives.

(2) Adequate growth must be sustained, and the following measures must be taken in order to promote smooth industrial adjustment:
(a) The economic outlook of each industry must be clarified,
(b) Assistance must be rendered for a location and re-employment of workers,
(c) Excess equipment must be promptly scrapped,
(d) Switch to more advantageous business must be facilitated,
(e) Measures must be taken to achieve a more efficient industrial

organisation,
(f) Steps must be taken to moderate the impact on local economy.

Progress in the Service Sector

(1) In the service sector, progress is particularly expected in the following areas:
  (a) Service industries supplementing the secondary industries,
  (b) Service industries progressing in conjunction with the secondary industries,
  (c) Service industries improving the quality of life,
  (d) Service industries facilitating social activity.

(2) The following steps will be taken to achieve progress in the service sector:
  (a) Productivity (supply of services) and quality will be improved,
  (b) Technological development will be promoted,
  (c) Some public services will be carried out by the private sector applying its efficient, industrialised methods.

Rationalisation of Distribution Systems

The distribution industry will experience vigorous competition within the industry, in particular in competition among different channels, firms with different degrees of integration and firms with different size. Maintenance of this competitive nature, on the basis of the private sector's originality, will bring about a more desirable distribution industry that can meet diverse consumer demand.

As a result, measures must be implemented in such a way that modernisation and advancement of distribution is induced and re-inforced. Specifically, this refers to guiding measures complementary to the private initiatives embracing various industries. These include the following measures:

  diffusion of the POS (Point of sales) system, which controls information at the point of sales;
  increasing efficiency in intra-city transport;
  measures that promote modernisation of the distribution system of each industry in accordance with its characteristics;
  a policy-mix of promotional measures and adjustment measures that will promote medium and small-scale distribution industries enabling them to take advantage of their smallness and flexibility.

Industrial Vitality and Market Functions

In order to maintain the market functions and enable a fulfillment of its role, efforts must be made to strengthen the activities for comprehensively monitoring the major industries, for grasping and evaluating the actual situations, for improving the competitive environments, and for properly guiding enterprises' behavior.

In those fields where the market mechanism does not function effectively, the government will attempt to make positive adjustments. In so doing, however, care must be taken not to hinder the long-term vitality of the economy or industry.

Enlivening Small and Medium Enterprises

(1) The scope of activity for medium and small enterprises will further expand

due to a progressing shift of economic activities to local areas and expansion of the service sector.

(2) However, the environment surrounding these enterprises will become more severe with the progress of internationalisation and changes in the distribution channels.

(3) Under these circumstances, measures need to be implemented so that medium and small enterprises can maintain vitality and spirit of enterpreneurship with originality and individuality. At the same time, in order to cope with newly arising tasks, measures for small and medium enterprises are desired to be strengthened to enable more effective utilisation.

11. The Age of Vitalised Human Potential

Progress is hindered by external and internal constraints: external constraints concern energy, the environment and international relations; internal ones, human wisdom and attitudes, and social systems. Although we need considerable efforts to overcome the difficulties anticipated in the 1980s and to achieve the promise of the future, we are convinced that the nature of the Japanese people will bring success.

Education has played a vital part in the process of Japan's modernisation. In order to foster the qualities needed in the 1980s and beyond -- creativity, individuality, and internationalism -- education is expected to play an even more important role. The period when we made progress by applying and improving existing ideas has already come to an end, and a period of creativity and initiative will begin. Japan must formulate an industrial civilisation based on its own culture and the creative knowledge to be applied for industrial uses. It must protect the security of the nation's welfare, improve the quality of life, and provide a respectable image in the world community.

Japan overcame many difficulties in the 1970s through an intensified use of knowledge. While this will continue to be important, penetrating insight and good judgement are essential to cope with the problems of the 1980s crowded with uncertainty. The 1980s must become an "Age of Vitalised Human Potential", that is, the age when obstacles and problems are to be overcome through full utilisation of creative knowledge.

APPENDIX 1(b)

MINISTRY OF INTERNATIONAL TRADE AND INDUSTRY

(MITI)

September 9, 1981
NR-262 (81-11)

REPORT OF THE INFORMATION INDUSTRY COMMITTEE

INDUSTRIAL STRUCTURE COUNCIL

(SUMMARY)

Introduction

The Information Industry Committee of the Industrial Structure Council has recently released its report which outlines the direction for "informatisation" and the information industries to pursue in the 1980s. In addition, it emphasises the need to establish an information oriented society, and identifies the role of the computer industry as well as the information processing industry in guiding the Japanese economy toward promoting a creative, knowledge-intensive industrial structure in the 1980s.

The report discusses the following topics:

1) Significance and Effectiveness of Informatisation
2) Present State and Problems of Informatisation in Japan
3) A View of an Information-Oriented Society in the 1980s
4) Prospects and Problems of the Information Industry in the 1980s
5) Basic Direction of Measures for Informatisation and the Information Industry
6) Improvement of Foundations for Informatisation and the Information Industry
7) Development of Social Systems
8) Promotion of Development of Information Related Technology
9) Trend of International Development

PART 1.   PRESENT STATE AND PROSPECTS

Chapter 1. Significance and Effectiveness of Information

Section 1. Significance of Informatisation

1. Concept and Significance of Informatisation

A considerable change has been brought about in the past ten-odd years regarding the concept of information. Today, computers are widely used in various fields of economic and social life, and a large variety and quantity of information is available to us. Based on this general trend, there is a common desire to acquire information from an independent standpoint and use it effectively; this is generally known as "informatisation".

The result of informatisation is not only a contribution to higher productivity and conservation of energy and resources, but it also plays an important role in solving social problems, expanding the overall scope of human activities. Eventually through its influence on the life of each individual, it may affect the people's sense of cultural values. The effects of informatisation on society as a whole will be both broad and deep, and could, in a sense, be compared to the 18th Century's Industrial Revolution. It may safely be said that the future of human society depends on the issue of informatisation.

2. Informatisation in the 1970s

Full-scale development of informatisation in Japan started in the late 1960s with the introduction of computers, and showed a remarkable upward trend throughout the 1970s. It cannot be denied, however, that problems still remained, such as gaps between primary and secondary industries or between large, medium and small industries, and insufficient legislative measures to deal with the rapid expansion of informatisation despite its variegated develop-ment. A characteristic trend that can be seen from then on is that although there is a large quantity and variety of information available, this flood of information often is not used satisfactorily.

3. New Aspects of Informatisation and the Second Information Revolution

Informatisation in Japan has entered a new phase with changing needs: remarkable technological progress in the use of semiconductors, spread of micro-computers, and a closer relationship between information processing and communications; characterised by the establishment of well-balanced informatisation to remove various restrictions, enlarge the sphere of human activities, and thus create a lively economic environment and comfortable daily life.

The penetration of informatisation into society and individual households will accelerate, providing numerous conveniences and creating a new frontier for human activities. Information may be put in an advanced systematic order through further developments in processing technology and the data base, so that ready access to information can be secured at any time to suit the needs of each user. If the informatisation spread to industrial circles only from the late 1960s through the early 1970s can be called the "first information revolution", the informatisation now infiltrating every field of our daily life can be called the "second information revolution".

4. Establishment of a Dynamic Information-Oriented Society

In view of the ever-changing situation in this country and abroad, the promotion and improvement of informatisation is essential to the establishment of a vibrant, affluent society. From a nationwide viewpoint, the result of informatisation can be said to be a basic factor in determining what Japan will be like in the 21st Century.

The expansion of informatisation may create complex problems. It is hoped that efforts will be made to solve such complex problems from a long-term, global standpoint by concentrating the wisdom of the private and public sectors so that a subjective information-oriented society can be constructed as soon as possible.

Section 2. National Obligations and Effectiveness of Informatisation

According to a "Report on MITI's Policies in the 1980s" drawn up by the Industrial Structure Council (March 17, 1980), the following three items are presented as national goals:
    (1) international contribution as a "major economic power",
    (2) conquest of resource and energy constraints, and
    (3) co-existence of "vitality" and "affluence or comfort".
The attainment of these three goals largely depends on the promotion of informatisation and the progress of the information industry.

1. International Contribution as a "Major Economic Power" and Informatisation

Japan is expected to make its contribution in the world by promoting international co-operation in the field of information-related technology, establishing a data base system, diffusing information through an international information network, giving aid in informatisation to developing countries as a part of economic co-operation, and facilitating the progress of the international information industry.

2. Conquest of Resource and Energy Constraints and Informatisation

The information industry, a typical knowledge-intensive industry, is considered extremely helpful in conserving resources and energy in various fields of a highly developed society through the use of information-related technology.

A policy aimed at establishing a state based on technology will contribute greatly to overcoming resource and energy constraints, while the evolution of information-related technology will play an important role in pursuing this policy.

3. Co-existance of "Vitality" and "Affluence or Comfort" and Informatisation

The progress of informatisation is expected to increase productivity in industry, rationalise distribution, and improve management. The progress of informatisation is considered helpful in meeting the future requirements of our society, in which the aged will account for a greater percentage of the total population, e.g., aids in offering better medical services and promoting lifetime education programmes. The introduction of new media, including image information systems and home-computers, into households will promote a more comfortable living style and preserve a favourable living environment.

Chapter 2. Present State and Problems of Informatisation in Japan

Section 1. Outline of Informatisation in the 1970s

With the introduction of computers, informatisation in the 1970s made great
progress, especially in the industrial sector (private enterprises) and the social sector (administrative organs). The growth of demand for computers was
encouraged by both the diverse needs of the users and the rapid progress of computer technology.

Section 2. Progress in Informatisation in Industrial Sectors

1. Production Sector

Throughout the 1970s, informatisation made great progress in manufacturing companies. This was because automation and unattended operation were promoted and
efficient production control and product development were attained in the
production stage with the aid of progress in computer technology, the spread of
micro-computers, and the establishment of data base systems. Both the design and
development sectors, where there has been a delay in informatisation, started a
late introduction of the computer aided design system (CAD) during this period;
but the spread of this system has not necessarily been sufficient in these
sectors.

2. Office Work and Management Sectors

In the 1970s, computers came into common use for handling quantitative work.
With an increase in the amount of work handled by computers, the computer systems reached the limits of their capacity. Attempts were made to make maximum
use of computers in a more efficient manner. On-line real time processing
replaced off-line batch processing on a large scale. After the oil crisis,
office computers were introduced to aid in the rationalisation of management.

3. Distribution and Sales Sectors

Wholesale and retail business in the 1970s tried to introduce large-scale
management by establishing more branch stores. Computers were first applied to
accounting in particular, then to quantity control of products, and then to the
automatic re-ordering system. Wholesale and retail business usually deals with a
large assortment of goods and, accordingly, it is always necessary to determine
good selling items quantitatively at the point of sales. It is also necessary at
the point of sales to feed information concerning good selling items to computers, but this is not necessarily a common practice.

4. Others
   (Medium and Small Enterprises)

Medium and small enterprises in the 1970s lagged relatively behind other industries in informatisation. To meet the emphasised need in recent years for
rationalisation, labour-saving, or deliberate management in the office and
production sectors, the introduction of micro-computers and office computers was
promoted.

   (Primary Industry)

Primary industries, such as agriculture, forestry and fisheries in the 1970s

also lagged behind other industries in informatisation. In the case of agriculture in particular, informatisation was applied only to office work, such as
deposits and savings service, mainly at agricultural co-operatives. The use of
computers for technically sophisticated work, such as production control, has
been carried over until today as a subject for further study.

Section 3. Progress in Informatisation in Social Sectors

1. Administrative Sector

The use of computers by administrative organs in the 1970s steadily increased to
facilitate "desk work", improve the quality of administrative services, and thus
stabilise national life. At national administrative organs, computers were
mainly applied to data processing of large quantities, such as statistical control and administrative work. The introduction of on-line real time systems was
promoted in order to meet the people's diversified needs. By local administrative organs, computers were applied approximately for the same purposes as by
national administrative organs. By 1978 every prefectural government had been
provided with a computer.

2. Medical Sector

Informatisation in the medical sector in the 1970s was promoted mainly with
regard to desk work, such as patient registration, accounting at the window, and
in-hospital medical work, such as inventory control of chemicals and pre-
engagement of diagnostic services or beds. The number of computers used in the
field of local emergency medical care gradually increased. In the field of medical information equipment and service, however, informatisation was still in an
experimental stage.

3. Educational Sector

Extended consideration was given to the practical application of electronic
technology, which made great progress in the 1970s, to the field of education;
but the spread of informatisation in the educational sector during this period
was not necessarily satisfactory. For example, the introduction of computer
aided instruction systems was discussed, but had not been popularised, because
both soft- and hardware for this system were very expensive and because development of programs for this system was insufficient.

4. Traffic and Other Social Sectors

Informatisation in traffic and other social sectors in the 1970s varied with the
individual sector; in some sectors it made some progress, while in others it was
still in an experimental stage.

Section 4. Progress in Informatisation in Living Conditions

The effects of informatisation, including the use of computers, in living conditions (in the field of daily living or in the living sector) first appeared as a
secondary effect originating as side effects of informatisation in various
enterprises and administrative organs. In the 1970s, however, the effects of informatisation were felt directly by the "living sector" through the development
and popularisation of various on-line real time systems.

Section 5. Appraisal and Problems of Informatisation in the 1970s

1. Factors in the Promotion of Informatisation

The factors in promoting informatisation in Japan can be listed as follows:

(1) the significant advance of semi-conductor technology and the progress of information-related technology especially by computers,

(2) ideal social environment unique to Japan, including the high intellectual level of the people as a whole, high quality manpower, first-rate education system producing high quality manpower, the people's enterprising spirit and the will to increase productivity, and favourable labour management relationships,

(3) Japanese traits, such as a positive, constructive mentality of a homogeneous people, and

(4) appropriate government measures to promote technological development and management re-organisation related to informatisation.

2. Problems of Informatisation in the 1970s

(1) MIS Boom and Subsequent Review

The purpose of MIS (management information system), which once rode the crest of a boom, has not necessarily been implemented in each industry. In the 1970s computers were largely used for processing standardised data but seldom for determining business strategies. In any case, it can be favourably regarded that the trial and error process repeated by each enterprise in establishing MIS has been useful for improving the common practical usage of computers in Japan.

(2) Actualised Informatisation Differentials

Japan's informatisation in the 1970s, which mainly extended into the larger enterprises in manufacturing, financial and insurance industries, resulted in producing a gap between industries and areas classified as urban and those classified as rural. Such informatisation differentials may foster the growth of economic activity differentials and finally impair social equity.

(3) Delay in Forming New Social Systems

It has become evident that conventional social systems cannot deal with the rapid progress of informatisation. Consequently, complex problems have been created, e.g., delay in providing adequate protection for software and for privacy, delay in devising proper crime prevention measures, and the need for conducting a re-examination of the use of communication channels.

Chapter 3. A View of an Information-Oriented Society in the 1980s

Section 1. A View of Desirable Information-Oriented Society

1. Desirable Information-Oriented Society

In the 1980s, it is necessary to make more effective the material foundation of economic affluence achieved by informatisation in the 1970s and make information-oriented society sufficiently humanistic and comfortable to allow people to develop their individuality and solidify a new foundation for Japan in the 21st Century by directing these achievements toward the true qualitative improvement of people's lives and making use of information.

A desirable information-oriented society in the 1980s may be defined as "a unique humanistic information-oriented society supported by vital economic activities while fulfilling the duties as an important member of international society".

2. Information-Oriented Society Contributing to International Society

As a tendency toward internationalisation progresses, Japan, as an important member of international society in the 1980s, must make an enthusiastic contribution to its development.

Japan must promote the development of information-related technology, as a pioneer type of technology, from a long-term and worldwide point of view and must co-operate in promoting worldwide informatisation including arrangement and furnishing of Japan's unique information, and technological and manpower communications.

3. Information-Oriented Society Permitting Maintenance and Improvement of Industrial Power

In order to actualise an information-oriented society which permits the maintenance and strengthening of industrial power in the 1980s, it is necessary to build up creative and independent technological development, while promoting the informatisation of industry, achieving breakthroughs in knowledge, and attaining high added value.

In the 1980s, further informatisation is expected to penetrate every corner of industry, promoting automation of production, and higher productivity resulting from unmanned operation and automation of multi-line small-lot production required by ever differentiating needs, and permitting breakthroughs in knowledge and the achievement of higher added value, while resulting in a wide increase in production due to the promotion of informatisation in fields which have previously been barely productive.

4. Information-Oriented Society which Helps Personality Develop and Gives Importance to Humanity

The 1980s must aim at an information-oriented humanity-based society which promotes the independence of individuals and enables people to lead a worthwhile life based on material affluence.

In an information-oriented society in the 1980s it is desirable to establish an information system which enables individuals to select independently information useful in enriching individual life, e.g. adult education, general culture, hobbies and amusements, which are desired as people have more leisure. Also, developing informatisation is expected to enrich social life by producing local communities and building up medical information systems, while securing the safety of people's lives by improving security measures aided by crime and disaster prevention information systems.

Section 2. <u>Prospects in Industrial Fields</u>

Usually, industry is divided into three fields:

> 1) manufacturing sector which carries out direct production including the designing, machining and assembling of products;
>
> 2) the managerial sector as an indirect function of companies in service businesses and the manufacturing industry;
>
> 3) the distributing and sales sector including distributing businesses and distributing departments of companies;

but here we add a fourth characteristic sector, medium and small enterprises and primary industries, to aid in reviewing industrial activities.

1. Manufacturing Sector

After the anticipated intelligent industrial robots with advanced productive functions are developed, promoting re-arrangement and consolidation of production processes, multi-line small-lot production is expected to be automated resulting in higher productivity and better quality control.

In the designing field, in which a vast amount of labour is invested over long periods, the development of advanced CAD (Computer Aided Design) systems will enable productivity to be widely increased with further potential for larger results being achieved by the combination of CAD systems with CAM (Computer Aided Manufacturing) systems through the use of data bases.

In addition engineering technology, which enables technology to be accumulated and utilised, will become important.

2. Managerial Sector

In the managerial sector, heavily burdened with conferences and office work, processing involving word and numerical data in plans, surveys, paper work, and counter work, office automation is progressing to make present manual office work more efficient.

It is desirable to create intelligence-intensified, functional office information systems together with comfortable office environments suited to Japanese offices, while adopting techniques for Japanese language processing, sound-character-image recognition and electronic filing.

3. Distribution and Sales Sector

In order to meet the differentiated needs of consumers, it is necessary to further advance the functions of the distribution industry by recognising consumers' needs accurately by promoting the informatisation of the distribution industry, and using this recognition as an important channel of consumer information flow in an opposite direction to that of the material flow, i.e., feeding it back to the production department.

Future important problems will be to establish distribution information systems which link such industries as manufacturing, transportation, finance, wholesaling and retailing effectively, and propagate POS systems on a broad basis, enabling the user to obtain data on sales, inventory management, sales programmes, orders received or issued for goods, etc., promptly, accurately and in detail.

Also, it will be necessary to provide for changes in social situations by introducing systems such as EFTS (electronic funds transfer system) in response to a growing cashless shopping.

4. Other Characteristic Fields
(Advance of Informatisation in Medium and Small Enterprises)

The growth of medium and small enterprises is essential to the future development of Japan's economic society. In order for medium and small enterprises to maintain and improve their power in the 1980s, it is necessary to develop management tactics making strong use of information.

The use of highly functional, low-cost, light-weight, compact office computers and micro-computers will permit sensitive management, using the flexible nature of medium and small enterprises.

Raising the quality and added value of products, energy-saving production, multi-line small-lot production, etc. can be expected by acquiring advanced techniques.

Also, it will be another future important problem to accumulate and elevate the level of technology by adopting technique training systems through the use of computers.

(Advancing Informatisation in Primary Industry)

It is expected in primary industries, such as agriculture and fisheries, in Japan that informatisation will advance and computer equipment will widely prevail.

Vegetable producing plants placed under consistent environmental control from sowing to harvest, automatic livestock breeding systems, hatching and breeding control systems in farming etc. are anticipated, which together with new comprehensive systems such as storage and shipping controls linked with markets, will achieve energy saving, higher efficiency and wide increases in productivity.

Section 3. Prospects in Social Fields

People's needs for a higher quality of life tend to be multifarious resulting from advances in income levels, ages, and changing awarenesses. Thus it will be possible to meet social needs and render extensive, high quality services related to administration, medicine, traffic, education, cities, housing, etc.

Also, new information media will penetrate social and individual lives, helping to create a "live society" and "comfortable life", which will allow human individuality to develop, resulting in a qualitative improvement of people's lives.

1. Administrative Fields

In order to promote high efficiency, high quality and energy saving in administrative work in proper response to differentiated administrative needs, it is necessary to adopt office automation including Japanese language data processing systems; and it is desirable to establish comprehensive administrative information systems, including information network systems between ministries and between central and local governments.

Also, in local governments in particular, administrative services are expected to improve by promoting the informatisation in "window work", including the issue of resident certificates and certificates with seals, through the use of advanced systems such as Japanese character data processing systems. As informatisation progresses in administrative fields, there will arise problems about disclosure of information and the protection of privacy. These problems must be dealt with carefully.

2. Medical Fields

In order to cope with problems in the medical field such as rising expenses for medical treatment and congestion in hospitals, it is necessary to improve the quality of medical services. This requires the development of advanced computer information equipment systems for input and output of images and sounds, and the establishment of advanced medical data bases for disease history control and medical records.

Again, in order to eliminate local differences in medical services and improve medical services in remote areas, it is desirable to develop and promote health care and network systems. Furthermore, computers are coming into use in card control, monitoring of symptoms of in-patients, and the handling of out-patients. If these trends are promoted, it is expected that more time will be devoted to examinations and care which are proper medical functions, resulting in overall improvement of medical services.

3. Traffic Fields

The recent rapid progress in motorisation has brought about various problems such as atmospheric pollution, traffic accidents and traffic congestion due to heavy automobile traffic. To solve these problems, trends are emerging to adopt a medium-load track transit system called "full-automatic operation system" which makes use of information-related and communication technology.

It is desirable in the future to adopt a personal rapid transit (PRT) system as a transit means to meet demands for traffic services arising from expansion of local cities and construction of new towns. In addition, traffic control systems which make use of computers and communications will be operated to eliminate traffic congestion.

4. Educational Fields

Since information-related technology has made computers compact and more cheap, it has become practicable to adopt CAI (computer aided instruction). Although there is criticism that the introduction of educational equipment including CAI systems will lead to commercialism in education, CAI is expected to prevail because it will permit education by personal instructions in accordance with students' abilities and provide education which is not restricted in time or place. Also, in education, computer processing will be promoted as a means of increasing the efficiency of school administration, including office work in general and control of the students' records.

In addition, it is expected that there will be an increasing need for life-long education, and it will be necessary to improve the educational environment through informatisation, including the building of continuing education and hobby instruction which will help to enrich daily life.

Section 4. Prospects of Life Fields

(Rationalisation of Life)

If computers become compact and cheap enough to be widely adopted in individual homes, it is possible that home appliances and housing devices will be arranged into systems to be placed under central control, resulting in advanced informatisation in home automation and increased rationalisation of life.

(Enrichment of Life)

The rationalisation of life, resulting from the adoption of the 5-day working week system and informatisation, will increase leisure time, providing opportunities to enjoy sports, culture, hobbies, etc. Also, home computers will permit life-long education while supplying various kinds of information, such as information on hobbies and shopping, helping to "enrich life".

(Improvement of Amenities)

Furthermore, if information networks covering local communities are formed, they will permit new services such as image information services, contributing to the creation of amicable and stable communities, which will possibly lead to the improvement of amenities.

Chapter 4. Prospects and Problems of the Information Industry in the 1980s

Section 1. Prospects and Problems of the Computer Industry

1. Significance and Role of the Computer Industry

The computer industry is technologically highly intense and provides high added value, having an extensive effect on other industries. Also, it is itself by nature energy-saving and resources-saving while contributing to saving energy and resources and informatisation in the rest of society. Furthermore, it will have a strong impact on surrounding industries, helping them to develop. Thus it is expected to be a core industry in Japan which will lead surrounding industries in evolving potentialities into the 21st Century.

2. Current Trends in and Prospects for the Computer Industry
   (Current Trends)

Production of the computer industry in 1980 in Japan amounted to 1.3 trillion Yen. Though this is not so high a level, the industry has shown high growth, consistently exceeding the growth of GNP.

(Prospects)

In the 1980s the adoption of computers will dominate every field, inviting differentiated needs in computer systems. Under these circumstances, the computer industry will have to supply various systems from ultra-large to personal computers and from general-purpose to special-purpose computers such as micro-computers. As for the makers, various industries in addition to computer makers, will come to participate in this industry. Thus the computer industry is expected, in the 1980s, to establish itself as a central industry with a broad ring of related activities surrounding the hub of general-purpose computers.

3. Tasks for the Computer Industry

The first task imposed on the computer industry is the challenge to create and pioneer technological progress, concentrating on the development of technology combining the needs of pioneer technology with the needs of data processing. The second task is to take appropriate measures to differentiate needs. The third task is to promote effective competition through market mechanisms and achieve efficient informatisation. The fourth task is smooth international development and contribution to global informatisation.

Section 2. Prospects and Tasks for the Information Processing Industry

1. Significance and Role of the Information Processing Industry

The information processing industry is, so to speak, the nervous system of economic society which controls a growing economy and a society which is becoming increasingly complicated while making them more efficient, smoothing their functionings, and helping them develop harmoniously. The information processing industry, which is significant in bringing about the information society in 1980s, is required to play the roles of "specialist" in information processing services, "promoter" in reducing information processing costs to users through the use of advanced techniques and improvements in productivity, and "co-ordinator" of information processing systems between different types of industries and businesses.

2. Current Trends in and Prospects for the Information Processing Industry

(Current Trends)

In 1979 the entire information processing industry had total sales of 596.6 billion Yen and was composed of 1761 establishments and 1390 companies. In the most recent 5 years it has shown a mean growth of about 20%. However, it is still in an immature phase, operating under unfavourable environmental conditions.

(Prospects)

Although it is difficult, because of the diversity of the information processing industry, to find a consistent way to advance, it is desirable for companies to strive for the following, depending on their characteristics:

first, the use of specialisation which tries to accumulate information processing technology in the specialised fields concerned, in order to meet the needs of users immediately and accurately;

second, the promotion of on-line network systems to satisfy extensive technological innovations in communications fields and new demands for information systems in industrial and social sectors;

third, the development of data base services which select appropriate pieces from the inundation of information;

fourth, the development of market-goods-type software products to meet demands for reduction of software costs;

fifth, the establishment of system supply functions capable of producing and selling software and hardware as a unit;

sixth, international development including competition with foreign companies in markets in Japan and advances into foreign markets.

3. Tasks for the Information Processing Industry

To achieve the above goals, a lot of difficulties must be overcome:

first, the improvement of management foundations to allow the elimination of subcontract work;

second, the improvement of productivity, making pioneer information processing technology practical and the build-up of technological development power to facilitate strategic penetration of specialised technological fields;

third, the establishment of responsibility control required by increasing social effects such as safety measures for electronic computer systems.

In addition, the improvement of external environmental conditions, such as gaining more favourable treatment by tax laws, standardising software, and utilising largely restricted communication circuits is another task in the development of the information processing industry.

PART II.   MEASURES TO BE TAKEN IN THE 1980s

Chapter 1   Basic Direction of Measures for Informatisation and the Information
            Industry

Section 1   Necessity of Measures

In order to promote informatisation effectively, it is necessary for the government to declare policies for informatisation and develop necessary measures based on industrial creativity and power, while seeking people's understanding and co-operation.

In order to develop new policies, it is essential to take measures enthusiastically and resolutely, strategically confining them to important fields.

Measures for informatisation and the information industry are a kind of investment in social foundations, which will yield large profits directly or indirectly throughout industry, society and people's lives. Thus they must be carried out after elaborate planning from a long-term point of view. It must definitely be emphasised here that any hesitation in performing this, because of short-term financial circumstancs, is likely to create a calamity sometime in

the future. In addition, when carrying out these measures, it is also necessary
to give consideration to the way to secure stable sources of revenue.

Section 2. Basic Direction of Policies

The basic direction of future policies for informatisation and the information
industry are the improvement of foundations, the promotion of technological development, and international development.

    (Improvement of Foundations)

The Improvement of foundations must include the removal of restrictions on systems, such as restrictions in using communication circuits; the promotion of
distribution of software; and appropriate remedies for informatisation problems
such as computer security.

    (Promotion of Technological Development)

In promoting technological development, it is necessary to give sufficient consideration to the roles of government, industry and academic circles from a
long-term point of view, and carry out pioneer and creative technological development based on comprehensive technological development.

    (International Development)

In order to promote international development, it is necessary to carry out
technological communications and international co-operation among advanced
countries, and make a willing contribution to the advance of worldwide informatisation including the promotion of co-operation with developing countries
in informatisation.

Chapter 2. Improvement of Foundations for Informatisation and the Information
           Industry

Section 1. Review of Systems for Utilising Communication Circuits

1. Background

    (Importance of On-Line Information Processing)

In the 1980s on-line data processing is expected to grow increasingly diverse.
Information-related technology, in particular, has made such progress that terminal units have become intelligent, functioning as independent computers. This
suggests that network systems will develop further in data processing.

On-line data processing will not only promote network systems between the same
or different lines of business, but will also permit information network systems
to be used in local society. Thus it will be an essential means of promoting
smooth informatisation in industry and society in Japan.

    (Problems in Systems for Utilising Communication Circuits)

Communication circuits used for on-line data processing in Japan, however, have
strict restrictions imposed on their usage under the Public Telecommunications

Law, etc. This has invited criticism from wide circles pointing out that these restrictions serve as an obstacle to the free development of on-line data processing.

Problems in systems for utilising communication circuits in Japan consist of:

1) restrictions on the use of communication circuits;

2) tariff systems for the use of communication circuits, and

3) competition in data communication services between Nippon Telegraph and Telephone Public Corporation and other industries.

2. Key Points in Reviewing Systems

(1) Restrictions on the Use of Communication Circuits

On-line data processing is a type of advanced use of computers which consists of data processing using communication circuits and differs by nature from the telegraph and telephone. The use of circuits for on-line data processing must, in principle, be free and it is a questionable practice to impose various restrictions on it from the same point of view as the telegraph and telephone.

Therefore, the use of communication circuits must be liberated from restrictions inappropriate to the current situation, so that the public can exercise their creativity and designs to the utmost. Minimum requisite restrictions, such as those concerned with the removal of technological obstacles, must be clearly defined and must be of a "negative list" type which allows free use except when restricted.

(2) Tariff Systems for Use of Communication Circuits

The communication circuits which are used for on-line data processing are used to transmit data and thus are different from telephone circuits which are intended to transmit sound.

Thus tariff systems for the use of communication circuits must be separate from the telephone tariff system and must be rational with differences due to distance corrected on the basis of technological advances.

(3) NTT's Data Communication Equipment Services

On-line data processing services must by their nature be offered based on the principle of free and fair competition promoted by the creativity and design of industrial circles. Regarding NTT's data communication services, relevant conditions must promptly be improved to ensure fairness to industry.

First, restrictions on the use of communication circuits must be removed, to correct unfairness in the use of circuits by NTT's equipment services and industry's on-line data processing services, and to avoid competition between NTT and industry by confining NTT's equipment services primarily to those based on the three principles: technological vanguard, public spirit, and national scale. Furthermore, if industry's services advance enough to equal NTT's equipment services, a transfer of NTT's services to industry should be considered.

Section 2. <u>Measures for a Combination of Information Processing with Communi-
            cations</u>

Technological innovations have gradually obscured boundaries between data
processing and communications, resulting in the emergence of a new field composed of both. This indicates the possibility of new data services developing.
In the communication field, non-speech services which transmit sound, symbols
and images, such as videotex, teletex, broadband picture data systems and
facsimile are expected to dominate. Also, data processing and ISDN via satellite
communication will be realised.

In order to promote smooth informatisation in response to these trends, it is
necessary to promote technological development, improve digital communication
circuit   networks,   and   revise   laws   relating   to   telecommunications,
electromagnetic waves, and broadcasting which form obstacles to new data
services.

Section 3. <u>Measures to Deal with Problems Arising from Informatisation</u>

1. Computer Security

As informatisation progresses, taking measures to ensure computer security has
become a pressing problem. Thus it is necessary to provide for new developments
by:

      1) establishing standards for safety measures for electronic computer sys-
      tems,

      2) surveying and reviewing cases of system breakdowns and determining
      guidelines for remedial measures in specific industries, and

      3) carrying out technological development and reviewing existing laws for
      the prevention of crimes.

2. Protection of Privacy and Disclosure of Information

There has been increasing apprehension of infringement on privacy by computers.
In order to promote informatisation in Japan, and in response to requests,
domestic and foreign, for the protection of privacy, it is necessary to take
prompt measures including the improvement of laws concerning information owned
by public agencies, and reviewing carefully the information owned by industry.
In addition, careful measures are required relating to the disclosure of
administrative information, because it involves troublesome problems, such as
privacy, and the handling of exceptions, in the case of national security.

3. Effects of Micro-Computers on Employment

There is apprehension about the effects of micro-computers on employment.

Effects of micro-computers on employment are both positive and negative and
cannot be evaluated in a simple manner. At any rate, the emergence of micro-
computers must be viewed as part of a large flow of technological innovation,
and is expected in the long run to contribute favourably to labour conditions by
creating new industries and employment.

However, it is necessary to consistently conduct thorough surveys and improve
systems for re-education and re-training in view of such trends as the transition of Japan's economy to stable growth and the increasing average age of the
population.

4. Formation of Public Acceptance of Informatisation

Because of rapid progress in informatisation,   negative opinions of informatisation, including "a view of information pollution" and the evils of "a
way to a controlled society", are presented. In taking appropriate measures
dealing with these problems, it is necessary to form public acceptance of informatisation. Thus it is necessary to:

    1) engage in public relations,

    2) improve the educational environment,

    3) take appropriate measures for the protection of privacy and proper dis-
    closure of information, and

    4) present Japan's policies for informatisation clearly.

5. Promotion of Standardisation

The information industry lags far behind other industries in efforts at
standardisation. Thus it is necessary for the government to uniformly promote
measures for standardisation while observing trends in international standards
of data processing elements, such as computers, software, peripheral and terminal equipment. Also, Japan must take earnest measures so as to play a leading
role in international movements towards standardisation.

Section 4. Promotion of Distribution and Establishment of Value of Software

Because of increasing demand for the development and distribution of general-
purpose software products, in order to avoid any duplicate development of software and reduce development costs, the government must establish the value of
software, improve the foundations of distribution, such as the legal protection
of unbundling and software, and create incentive policies for technological development and tax systems.

Section 5. Improvement and Promotion of Data Base Services

In a phenomenon called "the inundation of information" there is anticipation of
an increasing requirement for data base services to meet the need for appropriate selection of information. Under these circumstances, the information
processing industry is required to be willing to tackle data bases through
overcoming initial difficulties of the construction of data bases, and using on-
line networks as the most effective weapons. The government must assist the industry in this endeavour through financing and technological development.

Section 6. Improvement of Foundations of Information Industry

1. Computer Industry

    (Promotion of Effective Competition)

In the computer industry, since its emergence, gigantic foreign companies have monopolised the world market. Japanese computer makers are still behind foreign companies in the areas of technological development and marketing. Under these circumstances, the alteration of computer generations is starting and Japanese computer makers have undertaken a large financial burden in the field of marketing. Because of these circumstances, it is also important to take measures to maintain competitiveness through effective marketing.

(Measures for Users)

In response to the expansion of the supporting business base of the computer industry, it is necessary for the government to give appropriate guidance in establishing sales responsibility systems for office automation equipment and personal computers, and also to establish a customer complaint system.

(Training of Specialised Technicians in Information)

The computer industry is growing faster than the supply of information technicians. Thus it becomes necessary to provide systematic education on information through general information education agencies, computer education at high schools and universities, and improving and utilising "miscellaneous" schools.

2. Data Processing Industry

In order for the data processing industry to play its anticipated role in the future development of Japan, it is imperative to fortify its fragile managerial foundation. For this purpose the government must:

1) facilitate the supply of money to raise the level of the data processing industry,

2) invest administrative money to improve systems in the data processing industry through joint ventures, and

3) improve the proficiency of data processing technicians and security personnel.

Chapter 3. Development of Social Systems

Section 1. Needs of the Social System

Social systems make use of computer technology and systems technology to respond to the social problems of cities, transportation, medicine and the environment. They offer extensive services to meet social needs while contributing to the improvement of the foundation of an information-oriented society.

No new social systems can be conceived that do not include information technology. The utilisation of a medical information system will lead to a solution of local disparities, and the utilisation of an educational information system will permit educational activities to be free from the restrictions of time and place, and ultimately even more convenient systems will be created.

Section 2. <u>Development and Prevalence of Information-Oriented Social Systems</u>

One of the features of information-oriented social systems is the potential for forming a nationwide system by connecting local systems with communication networks, which will allow Japan's present vulnerability to earthquakes to be overcome.

A life picture information system and a medical information system have already been developed. In order to achieve energy saving at the city level in the future, it is desirable to promote both the development of alternative energy utilising community energy systems, which comprehensively makes use of energy and information, and underground market hazard prevention systems.

However, providing broad social systems will require enormous investment over long periods. Additionally, high profitability is hardly expected because of their public nature. Thus subsidisation with public funds will be necessary so that the initial capital can be easily procured.

Chapter 4. <u>Promotion of Development of Information Related Technology</u>

Section 1. <u>Improvement of Research and Development Systems</u>

It is necessary to establish comprehensive technology development programmes and tactics from a long-term point of view for the effective use of limited research and development resources; make attempts at creative and elaborate technological development and pioneer and lead technology; strengthen ties between government, academic circles, and industry; foster industrial power; and give consideration to plans to establish comprehensive research and development mechanisms for both hardware and software. Also, it is necessary to review the optimal way to achieve international co-operation in research and development.

Section 2. <u>Selective Development of Software Related Technology</u>

1. Necessity of Development

With recent trends towards higher performance and lower costs of hardware, software costs as a part of total information processing costs are rising and the necessity for technological development of software is increasing. Software's history, however, is short and production systems have not yet been established. Japan is far behind Europe and the U.S. in technology for developing large-scale software and pioneer data processing technology, and this constitutes a large constraint on Japan's advance in informatisation.

2. Measures to be Taken

Thus the government must willingly promote software development, concentrating on:

   1) basic software technology for computers of the ensuing generation, which have various high order functions and are easy to operate;

   2) technology for producing and maintaining software that aids in developing and maintaining highly reliable software to make effective use of computers;

3) pioneer data processing technology in the application of pioneer data processing technology including pattern data processing in practical fields;

4) large-scale software technology for developing new energy sources, space research, and oceanic studies;

5) development of general-purpose and highly operable software to promote the distribution of software.

Section 3. Development of Guiding and Innovative Technologies

1. Research and Development of High Speed Computer Systems for Science and Technology

In the field of science and technology, enormous calculation work is required in forecasting weather, research on nuclear fusion, and space development; and there is a strong demand for a high-speed computer system for science and technology. To create such a system, it is necessary to develop new elements, such as the Josephson joint element, and a super-parallel processing system. As these projects entail huge expenditures and risks, smooth development cannot be expected by entrusting the work to the private sector, and the government finds it necessary to expedite development work.

2. Research and Development of a 5th Generation Computer

With the progress of an information society there is a strong demand for high-performance computers which are easy to use and do not require expert knowledge. With regard to increasing utilisation of conventional computers, various problems, such as the large-scale increase in the size and the complexity of software, have been pointed out. It is necessary to solve these problems and also to pursue research and development of 5th generation computers which can meet the high-level performance requirements of the 1980s.

Section 4. Expansion of Basic Research and Development

1. Development of Technology for the Next Generation Industrial Base

In order to establish a high technology industry, research and development of basic high technology, which will form its foundation, must be promoted. As big risks are involved in developing high technology, adequate results cannot be expected by relying on the private sector alone. Therefore the government initiated a research and development system for the next generation industrial base, but it is also necessary to further promote the development of basic technology which is deeply related to the information industry, such as new functional elements (e.g. super-grid elements and three-dimensional circuit elements).

2. Optical Information Technology

The optical industry is a high technology industry which will be the foundation of and driving force for the electronics industry in the future.

It is one of the few industries in which Japan opened up top-level technology in the world. However, the optical industry has a wide base which must be developed, and efforts made to push comprehensive development forward to practical use. The government has started developing a measurement control system using optical control and hopes for its further expansion.

3. Development of Sensor Technology

The field of application of sensors is limited and, moreover, research and development of sensors has not been sufficiently undertaken. Reasons for this are:

1) there are many different kinds of sensors produced in small quantities,

2) sensor technology is lagging, and

3) informatisation in the field of application has not progressed.

Sensors are an input means of information processing and are indispensable to informatisation. However, as there are many kinds of sensors, huge amounts of funds are needed to develop all of them. Therefore, it is necessary to promote the development of the sensors which have wide fields of application. The government should take a leading part in this project.

Section 5. <u>Research and Development of Applied Technology</u>

1. Development of Intelligent Robots

In order to liberate labourers from working in unfavourable environments and from performing monotonous work, intelligent robots which move about freely are needed. To develop such intelligent robots, comprehensive high technology, such as information-related technology, machine technology and sensor technology, must be developed. As the objects of development cover a wide range, efficient development cannot be expected by relying on the private sector alone. Consequently it is necessary for the government to play a most active part in the development project.

2. Development of Automatic Translation Systems

With the progress of internationalisation of society, there is an increasing need for speedily transmitting large quantities of information, e.g. Japanese opinions, materials and data, to foreign countries, and to promptly process information received from abroad. Translating Japanese requires much labour and time, and in order to overcome this, it is necessary to develop an automatic translation system using information-related technology. If the position in which Japan finds itself in the international community is taken into consideration, creating an automatic translation system should be undertaken as a national project.

3. Development of Medical Electronics (ME)

Since the debut of medical electronics utilising computers, treatment of some diseases which had been difficult in the past has become possible. Development of higher performance ME devices is hoped for, but there are many cases where such devices become large-scale systems. Moreover, as research and development work entails huge expenditures, it is difficult for the private sector to undertake the project by itself. Thus it is desirable that the government actively promotes research and development.

Chapter 5. Trend of International Development

Section 1. Positive Contribution to the World's Informatisation

It is believed that, in the 1980s, the international information network will be
in an age of full-scale formation. In order that the Japanese response to this
will not be inappropriate, it is necessary to grasp the trend and situation in
each country, to fully study problems of international difference in circuit
rates and the outflow and inflow of data across national boundaries, and to complete necessary preparations.

1. Improvement of International Data Base

The international data base, which has been improved, can be regarded as Japan's
own information resource, which is used internationally, and it is necessary to
make positive efforts to build up this base.

2. Positive Contribution to International Co-operation among Many Countries

It is necessary for Japan to actively make proposals for regulating international policies concerning information measures by fully utilising OECD/ICCP
meetings, etc.

Section 2. Promotion of Co-operative Set-up with Advanced Countries

It is basically important for Japan itself to take up the initiative in tackling
high, innovative technological subjects. It is necessary to arrange for the exchange of international information and talent. Japan's information industry
should promote industrial assistance in diverse fields, and consider financing
from a policy standpoint. Among developments in information-related technology,
emergence of large-scale, complicated technologies, which exceed the capability
of one country, is anticipated, and it is necessary to study what should be done
to promote development through international co-operation.

Section 3. Promotion of Information Co-operation to Developing Countries

As a part of economic and technical co-operation to the informatisation efforts
of developing countries, it is necessary to positively co-operate in building a
social system to improve the medical and educational fields, and to train technicians, engineers and specialists. Also, it is worth studying co-operation in
developing special language information processing technology, which conforms to
the actual conditions of developing countries.

It is therefore necessary to promote informatisation co-operation at the government level. Informatisation co-operation on a private basis is also important,
therefore it is necessary to promote informatisation co-operation making the
most of the ingenuity and ideas of the private sector.

APPENDIX 2

"Grey Literature" on Information Processing in Japan

Because of the language problem it is difficult for Westerners to have access to the lastest news about information processing in Japan. However, since the Japanese are very interested in an information flow between Japan and the Western industrialised countries, many publications have been and will be trans-lated into English. For example, almost every Japanese institution concerned with information processing has an introduction to its activities written in English.

Books, journals, magazines and newspapers are available in bookshops and libraries, but other publications are difficult to obtain and can therefore be called "grey literature". They include publications from government offices, companies and organisations about their activities, descriptions of hardware and software systems, trends in information technology, etc. The difference between this "grey" literature and "normal" literature, however, cannot be clearly defined. In the following an attempt is made to give an indication of the kind of literature in this categorie and how to obtain it. Publications of computer manufacturers and software houses about their products, however, have been ommitted.

- Ministry of International Trade and Industry (MITI)
  3-1 Kasumigaseki 1-Chome, Chiyoda-ku, Tokyo 100, Japan

    The MITI Information Office publishes "News from MITI" which is mainly concerned with MITI's industry policy. In this series, among others, reports of MITI's advisory boards and committees have been published, e.g. summaries of the reports of the Industrial Structure Council and of the Information Industry Sub-Committee (see [AIST2] and [AIST11], as well as Chapter 2.1.2.1 and appendix).

    MITI's Electronics Policy Division compiles, from time to time, overviews about the current state of the information industry in Japan, and MITI's Data Processing Administration Division publishes reports about the data processing activities of MITI (e.g. see [MITI1] and [MITI3], also Chapters 2.1.2.1 and 5.2.1).

- Agency of Industrial Science and Technology (AIST)
  1-3 Kasumigaseki 1-Chome, Chiyoda-ku, Tokyo 100, Japan

    MITI's Agency of International Science and Technology (AIST) publishes, among others, publications about the R & D projects carried out or super-vised by its laboratories. These include projects of the "National R & D Project System", for example, the "Pattern Information Processing System" (see [AIST1], [AIST4], and Chapter 2.2.3).

- Ministry of Posts and Telecommunications (MPT)
  1-1 Kasumigaseki 1-Chome, Chiyoda-ku, Tokyo 100, Japan

MPT publishes annually in English the "Report on Present State of Communications", which is a summary of the "White Paper on Communications" written in Japanese.

- Nippon Telegraph and Telephone Public Corporation (NTT)
  International Affairs Bureau
  1-6 Uchisaiwaicho 1-Chome, Chiyoda-ku, Tokyo 100, Japan

  In the series "NTT Publications" various laws and regulations concerning communication have been published, e.g. the Nippon Telegraph and Telephone Public Corporation Law (see [MPT7]).

  The series "NTT Technical Report" contains publications about new technical developments, e.g. about the DIPS computer system (see [NTT12]).

  NTT's Electrical Communication Laboratories (ECL) publish the "E.C.L Technical Publications" which contain articles about new technical developments of ECL, e.g. about its Program Development System for Microprocessors (PMP), see [NTT8].

  Furthermore, NTT and ECL publish booklets about their business and about special subjects, e.g. about NTT's dc circuit services (see [NTT5]).

- Science and Technology Agency (STA)
  2-2-1 Kasumigaseki, Chiyoda-ku, Tokyo 100, Japan

  The Science and Technology Agency (STA) of the Prime Minister's Office annually publishes the "Outline of the White Paper on Science and Technology" which is a summary of the "White Paper on Science and Technology" written in Japanese. Furthermore, STA publishes studies and surveys about the state and future trends of science and technology in Japan.

- Administrative Management Agency (AMA)
  1-1 Kasumigaseki 3-Chome, Chiyoda-ku, Tokyo 100, Japan

  The Administrative Management Agency of the Prime Minister's Office occasionally publishes reports about data processing in the Japanese government, e.g. [AMA1], [AMA16] and [AMA17] (see also Chapter 2.1.2.3).

- Local Authorities Systems Development Centre (LASDEC)
  25 Ichiban-cho, Chiyoda-ku, Tokyo 100, Japan

  LASDEC publishes reports about data processing in local governments, e.g. [LASDEC1] and [LASDEC3] (see also Chapter 5.2.3).

- Japan Information Processing Development Centre (JIPDEC)
  Kikai Shinko Kaikan Bldg.
  5-8 Shibakoen 3-Chome, Minato-ku, Tokyo 105, Japan

  JIPDEC's "Computer White Paper" is a summary of the "Computer White Book", written in Japanese and published annually. It contains information about trends in computer technology, the information industry policy of the Japanese government and the state of computer usage in Japan.

  "JIPDEC Report" is a summary of the Japanese "JIPDEC Journal" published quarterly. It contains articles about current topics in the field of information processing, and news in brief.

Furthermore, JIPDEC issues English summaries of some of its studies on special subjects which it carries out for the Japanese information in- dustry, e.g. the Interim Report on Study and Research on 5th-Generation Computers (see [JIPDEC18]). From time to time JIPDEC also compiles overviews of the present situation of information processing in Japan (see [JIPDEC17]; see also Chapter 2.1.3.4).

- Joint System Development Corporation (JSD)
  No. 15 Mori Bldg. F6
  2-8-10 Toranomon, Minato-ku, Tokyo 105, Japan

  JSD publishes reports about its research projects, e.g. about its software engineering project, see [JSD6] (see also Chapter 2.1.3.3).

- Software Industry Association (SIA)
  5-8 Shibakoen 3-chome, Minato-ku, Tokyo 105, Japan

  Because the Japanese software industry does not yet have many interna- tional activities SIA has only a few booklets in English. However, from time to time it publishes the booklet "Present Situation of Information Processing in Japan", including an overview of SIA's activities and a list of SIA's member companies (see [SIA4] and Chapter 4.2.1).

- Japan Electronic Computer Company (JECC)
  New Kokusai Bldg.
  4-1 Marunouchi 3-Chome, Chiyoda-ku, Tokyo 100, Japan

  The periodical "Japan Computer News" of the joint rental and sales firm of the Japanese computer manufacturers issues news about the Japanese compu- ter industry, mainly about new technological developments and market con- ditions (see Chapter 2.1.3.1).

- Japan Electronic Industry Development Association (JEIDA)
  Kikai Shinko Kaikan
  5-8 Shibakoen 3-Chome, Minato-ku, Tokyo 105, Japan

  Besides overviews about its own activities and about the Japanese electronic industry (see [JEIDA1] and [JEIDA2]), JEIDA issues English summaries of important studies which have been carried out by joint research committees of its member companies, e.g. about the future of the electronic industry in Japan [JEIDA4], and software engineering in Japan [JEIDA3], (see also Chapter 3.3.2).

- Centre of the International Co-operative for Computerisation (CICC)
  Kikai Shinko Kaikan Blgd., Room No. 313
  5-8 Shibakoen 3-Chome, Minato-ku, Tokyo 105, Japan

  The CICC News is published monthly and gives information about CICC's activities and about current technological developments in the Japanese information industry.

  CICC's annual or biennual booklet "Continuing Progress of Computerisation in Japan" (see [CICC2]) gives an overview of the current state of the Japanese information industry and information processing technology.

  Both periopdicals are mainly intended for potential customers in developing countries (see Chapter 3.3.3).

- The Japan Iron and Steel Federation (JISF, TETSUREN)
  Keidanren Kaikan
  1-9-4 Ote-machi, Chiyoda-ku, Tokyo 100, Japan

  JISF publishes, among others, booklets about its own information
  processing activities and those of its member companies (see [TETSU4] and
  [TETSU5] as well as Chapter 5.1).

- International Data Corporation Japan (IDC Japan)
  4-7 Kudankita 1-Chome, 3179 Chiyoda-ku, Tokyo 102, Japan

  IDC Japan's "EDP Japan Report" corresponds to IDC's "EDP Industry Report"
  and IDC Germany's "EDP Deutschland Report". It contains information about
  new technological developments and market conditions in the field of information processing.

- Dempa Publications, Inc.
  11-15 Higashi Gotanda 1-Chome, Shinagawa-ku, Tokyo 141, Japan

  Dempa Publ. publishes the "Journal of the Asia Electronics Union" which
  contains articles about current technological developments in electronics,
  as well as the market conditions in Asian electronic industries including
  Japan.

APPENDIX 3

Institutions visited by the Author during his stay in Japan

1. Administrative Management Agency (AMA)

2. Labour Market Centre

3. Local Authorities Systems Development Centre (LASDEC)

4. Tokyo Metropolitan Government

5. Information-technology Promotion Agency (IPA)

6. Joint System Development Corporation (JSD)

7. Kaihatsu Computing Service Centre Ltd. (KCC)

8. Fujitsu Limited

9. Japan Iron and Steel Federation (TETSUREN)

10. Nippon Hoso Kyokai (NHK)

11. Asahi Chemical Computing Centre

12. Computer Centre, University of Tokyo

13. Software AG of Far East

14. Mitsubishi Oil Co. Ltd.

15. Information Service International Dentsu Ltd.

16. Nippon Telegraph and Telephone Public Corporation (NTT)

17. Medical Information System Development Centre (MEDIS-DC)

18. Japan Information Centre of Science and Technology (JICST)

19. Keio University, Laboratory of Computer Engineering

20. MITI, Electronics Policy Division

21. MITI, Data Processing Administrative Division

22. Japan Information Processing Development Centre (JIPDEC)

23. Tool Software Company

24.   Toshiba, Computer Division

25.   Nippon Yusen Kaisha (NYK)

26.   Nippon Electric Co. Ltd., EPD Planning Office

27.   Computer Basic Technology Research Association

28.   Ministry of Posts and Telecommunications (MPT)

29.   Agency of Industrial Science and Technology (AIST)

30.   Software Industry Association (SIA)

31.   Hitachi Ltd.

GLOSSARY OF ABBREVIATIONS

ACOS-Series	General purpose computer series (of NEC)
ADP	Automatic Data Processing
AEU	Asia Electronics Union
AIQ	Automatic Import Quota
AIST	Agency of Industrial Science and Technology
AMA	Administrative Management Agency
APGB	Application Program Generator for Business (of NTT)
BSC	Binary Synchronous Communications
CAD	Computer Aided Design
CAM	Computer Aided Manufacturing
CAPTAINS	Character and Pattern Telephone Access Information Network System (of NTT)
CBTRA	Computer Basic Technology Research Association
CCITT	Comite Consultatif International Telegraphique et Telephonique
CDL	Computer Development Laboratory (members: Fujitsu, Hitachi, Mitsubishi Electric)
CICC	Centre of the International Co-operation for Computerisation
COSMO-Series	General purpose computer series (of Mitsubishi Electric)
CWP	Computer White Paper, published annually by JIPDEC
DBMS	Data Base Management System
DC (dc)	Data Communication
DCNA	Data Communication Network Architecture (the network architecture of NTT)
DDX	Digital Data Exchange Circuit Service (of NTT)
DEC	Digital Equipment Company
DEMOS	Dendenkosha Multi-access On-line System (of NTT)
DIALS	Dendenkosha Arithmetic and Library Service (of NTT)
DIPS	Dendenkosha Information Processing System (of NTT)
DP (dp)	Data Processing
DRESS	Dendenkosha Realtime Sales Management System (of NTT)

189

ECL	Electrical Communications Laboratory (of NTT)
EDP	Electronic data processing
EJR	EDP-Japan Report, published by International Data Corp. of Japan (IDC Japan)
EPA	Economic Planning Agency (of the Prime Minister's Office)
ETL	Electro-Technical Laboratory (of AIST)
FY	Fiscal Year
GE	General Electric Co.
GNP	Gross National Product
HDLC	High Level Data Link Control
HIPO	Hierarchy plus input-process-output (a program development technique of IBM)
IBM	International Business Machines
ICAS	Integrated Computer Aided Software Engineering System (of Hitachi)
IDC	International Data Corporation
IPA	Information-technology Promotion Agency
IQ	Import Quota
ISDOS	Information System Development Optimising System (of Michigan University)
ISID	Information Services International Dentsu
ISO	International Standardisation Organisation
JAPATIC	Japan Patent Information Centre
JCL	Job Control Language
JCN	Japan Computer News, published by JECC
JDB	Japan Development Bank
JECC	Japan Electric Computer Co.
JEF	Japanese Processing Extended Facility (by Fujitsu)
JEIDA	Japan Electronic Industry Development Association
JETRO	Japan External Trade Organisation

JICST	Japan Information Centre of Science and Technology (of STA)
JIP	Journal of Information Processing, issued by the Information Processing Society of Japan
JIPCA	Japan Information Processing Centre Association
JIPDEC	Japan Information Processing Development Centre
JIPNET	JIPDEC-Network System
JIS	Japanese Industrial Standard
JISF	Japan Iron and Steel Federation (Japanese = TETSUREN)
JITA	Japan Industrial Technology Association (of AIST)
JNR	Japan National Railways
JR	JIPDEC-Report, published quarterly by JIPDEC
JSD	Joint System Development Corporation
JSMI	Japan Society for the Promotion of Machine Industry
KDD	Kokusai Denshin Denwa Co. Ltd., Japan's International Telephone and Telegraph Company
KIJOHO	Machinery and Information Industry Law (Japanese abbreviation)
LASDEC	Local Authorities Systems Development Centre
LSI	Large-scale integration
M-Series	General purpose computer series of Fujitsu (FACOM M-Series) and Hitachi (HITAC M-Series)
MoF	Ministry of Finance
MEDIS-DC	Medical Information System Development Centre
MHW	Ministry of Health and Welfare
MITI	Ministry of International Trade and Industry
MOC	Mitsubishi Oil Company
MPT	Ministry of Posts and Telecommunications
MRI	Mitsubishi Research Institute
NCR	National Cash Register Co. Ltd.
NEC	Nippon Electric Company
NECIS	NEC Information Systems Inc.

NECSYL	NEC Systems Laboratory Inc.
NEEDS	NIKKEI Economic Electronic Databank Service
NHK	Nippon Hoso Kyokai, Japan Broadcasting Corporation
NSC	Nippon Software Co.
NTIS	NEC-Toshiba Information Systems
NTT	Nippon Telegraph and Telephone Public Corporation
OS	Operating System
PATOLIS	Patent On-line Information System (of JAPATIC)
PIPS	Pattern Information Processing System
PMP	Program Development System for Mikroprocessors (of NTT)
R & D	Research & Development
RAM	Random Access Memory
RCA	Radio Corporation of America
RITE	Research Institute of Telecommunications and Economics
RIYOKEN	Technical Research Council on Computer Utilisation (Japanese abbreviation)
RSS	Resource Sharing System
SBC	Small business computer
SDEM	Software Development Engineer's Methodology (of Fujitsu)
SDSS	Software Development Support System (of Fujitsu)
SIA	Software Industry Association
SIS	Steel Information System
SPC	Software Product Centre
SPS	Software Production System
STA	Science and Technology Agency (of the Prime Minister's Office)
STEPS	Standard Technology and Engineering for Programming Support (of NEC)
SWB	Software Work Bench (of Toshiba)
TAMA CCIS	Tama New Town Coaxial Cable Information System

TSS   Time Sharing System

TUA   Telecommunications Users Association

US   United States

VLSI   Very large-scale integration

YEN   Japanese currency: In 1977 the average exchange rate of 1 US
                       Dollar was 268 Yen, and 1 Deutsche Mark (DM) was 115 Yen. The
                       exchange rate, however, so fluctuates that it cannot be quoted
                       exactly. As a rough approximation 1 US Dollar can be estimated
                       as 200 Yen and 1 DM as 100 Yen.

REFERENCES

AEU   Journal of Asia Electronics Union, published by Dempa
Publications Inc., Tokyo

AIST1   AIST, Agency of Industrial Science and Technology, 1979,
published by MITI

AIST2   The Vision of MITI Policies in the 1980's, published in "News
from MITI", 17th March, 1980, NR-226(80-7)

AIST4   Pattern Information Processing System, National Research and
Development Program, 1978, published by ETL of AIST of MITI

AIST6   Outline of the Electro-technical Laboratory, June 1980,
published by AIST of MITI

AIST11   Report of the Information Industry Committee, Industrial
Structure Council (Summary), published in "News from MITI", 9th
September 1981, NR-262(81-11)

AMA1   The Status of Computer Utilisation in the Japanese Government,
published by the Administrative Management Agency, February
1979

AMA16   Organisation of the Government of Japan, January 1978,
published by the Administrative Management Agency, Prime
Minister's Office

AMA17   An Interim Report on the Measures to be Taken to Protect
Privacy in Relation to the Utilisation of Computers in
Government Agencies (summary), April 9th 1975, The Commission
for Administrative Management and Inspection, Administrative
Management Agency

CICC1   Guide to CICC, published by the Centre of the International
Co-operative for Computerisation

CICC2   Continuing Progress of Computerisation in Japan '77-'78,
published by CICC

CWP   Computer White Paper, published annually by JIPDEC

DENTSU2   NSS, Network Software Services Program Index, 6104.03D Mark III
Service Index, January 1979, General Electric Information
Services Company

EJR   EDP-Japan Report, published by International Data Corporation
(IDC) Japan

FUJI13   Nakamura et al, Complementary Approach to the Effective
Software Development Environment, COMPSAC '78, page 235

FUJI15   Fujitsu Limited, Annual Report, March 1979

GID1   Information and Documentation in Japan, 1978/79, published by
the Tokyo branch of GID (German Association of Information and
Documentation)

HITACHI4   Systems Development Laboratory, Hitachi Ltd., October 1980

HOWARD1   N. Howard / Y. Teramoto; The Really Important Difference
                between Japanese and Western Management, in Management
                International Review, 3/1981, page 19

IPA3   IPA Software packages catalogue 1979.3 (in Japanese)

JCN   Japan Computer News, the periodical of JECC

JEIDA1   Guide to JEIDA, 1979-1980, published by Japan Electronic
                Industry Development Association (JEIDA)

JEIDA2   Electronic Industries in Japan '79-'80, published by JEIDA

JEIDA3   Software Engineering in Japan, published by JEIDA (partly
                translated into English)

JEIDA4   Future of the Japanese Electronics Industry, 1980, compiled by
                JEIDA, published by Fuji Corporation

JICST1   JICST 1979, The Japan Information Centre of Science and
                Technology, a booklet

JIP   Journal of Information Processing, published by the Information
                Processing Society of Japan

JIPDEC17   Present Situation of Information Processing in Japan, 1980,
                published by JIPDEC

JIPDEC18   Interim Report on Study and Research on Fifth-Generation
                Computers (Outline), JIPDEC, August 1980

JR   JIPDEC Report, published quarterly by JIPDEC

JSD1   Outline of Joint System Development Corporation, July 1979

JSD6   Overview of the "Software Engineering Project", JSD, August
                1979

LASDEC1   Local Authorities Systems Development Cerntre (LASDEC), May
                1977

LASDEC3   Computer Utilisation in Local Public Entities, 1979, published
                by LASDEC

LASDEC9   HYOJUNTEKI KIHON system NO CHOSA KENKYU HOKOKUSHO (report about
                standard basis systems, dealing with Kanji On-line inhabitants
                information systems), LASDEC, March 1980

NAKAMURA1   The Future of Payment Systems in Asia, Conference Proceeding of
                the American Express International Banking Corporation, April
                1979, Manila

MEDIS1   Outline of the Medical Information System Development Centre,
                Sept. 1979, published by MEDIC-DC

MITIO   MITI-Handbook, 1977/8, English Edition, published by Japan
Trade and Industry Publicity Inc.

MITI1   Promotion of Administrative Information Processing, June 1980,
published by the Data Processing Administration Division,
Minister's Secretariat, MITI

MITI3   Approach to the Supply Restrictions Problem (summary), February
1976, Policy Planning Information System Development Office,
MITI

MITI14   SHOWA 54 NENDO JOHO SHORI KANREN SHISAKU NO JUTEN (important
points of the information processing policy for 1979),
published by MITI

MPT2   Public Telecommunication Law, NTT publication G-No.38-2

MPT3   Wire Communication Law, NTT Publication G-67

MPT7   Nippon Telegraph and Telephone Public Corporation Law, NTT
Publication G-No.56-2

MPT9   Demand catalogue of the Telecommunications User Association (in
Japanese)

MPT10   Demand catalogue of JIPCA (in Japanese)

NEC8   This is NEC, 80th Anniversary 1979

NEC10   Mikami et al., Comprehensive Automobile Control System — A new
urban traffic control trial —, NEC Research & Development,
No.52, Jan. 1979, pages 1-10

NEC17   ACOS Series 77, STEPS-2/4 General Description, by NEC

NHK2   Introduction to NHK-TOPICS, 1978, published by NHK

NTT1   Report on Present State of Communications in Japan, Fiscal
1979, published by MPT (based on the "White Paper on
Communications" in Japanese)

NTT2   NTT Data Communication Service, 1977, published by NTT

NTT5   Domestic Leased Circuit Service and Data Communication Circuit
Service in Japan, published by NTT

NTT8   Program Development System for Microprocessors — PMP —, E.C.L.
Technical Publication No.206

NTT12   An Enhanced Large Scale Data Processing System: DIPS-11, NTT
Technical Report T-No.67

NTT16   SYSL — System Description Language, E.C.L. Technical
Publication No.114

NYK3   Outline of the Information System of Nippon Yusen Kaisha (NYK),
                  1980 edition, published by NYK

REPORTS   Reports about Japanese establishments concerned with data
                  processing, reports in manuscript form about the author's
                  visits to various institutions (see Appendix)

RITE1   Research Institute of Telecommunications and Economics, 1981 (a
                  booklet)

SIA2   Business plan of SIA for 1980 (in Japanese)

SIA3   KAIIN KAISHA GAIYO (outline of the members of SIA), SIA, Oct.
                  1979

SIA4   Present situation of Information Processing in Japan, June
                  1978, published by SIA

SIA5   Report on the Trend and Future of the Software Industry,
                  published by SIA, March 1979, No.53-2033 (in Japanese)

SIA6   JOHOSHORI SANGYO KEIEI JITTAI CHOSA HOKOKUSHO (report about the
                  condition and construction of the information industry), IPA,
                  February 1980, No. 54CHO-001

SIA7   Software KAKAKU MONDAI NI KANSURU CHOSA KENKYU HOKOKU (report
                  about the problem of software prices), SIA, Dec. 1979

SIA17   Software RYUTSU NI KANSURU CHOSA KENKYU HOKOKUSHO (report about
                  the distribution of software), SPC, March 1980, No. 54-SC001

TETSU1   The Steel Industry of Japan, 1979, published by the Japan Iron
                  and Steel Federation

TETSU4   Outlines of Planning Process and Information System in the
                  Japanese Steel Industries, 1974, published by the Japan Iron
                  and Steel Federation

TETSU5   Outline of the Steel Information System (SIS), 1977, published
                  by the Japan Iron and Steel Federation

TOSHIBA2   Toshiba, Annual Report 1979

VOGEL1   Ezra F. Vogel, Modern Japanese Organisation and Decision
                  Making, Tuttle, 1979